# ELEMENTS FOR A SOCIAL ETHIC

*Also by Gibson Winter*

LOVE AND CONFLICT

THE SUBURBAN CAPTIVITY OF THE CHURCHES

NEW CREATION AS METROPOLIS

THE IDENTITY OF THE MAJOR FAITHS

# ELEMENTS FOR A SOCIAL ETHIC

*Scientific Perspectives on Social Process*

*Gibson Winter*

*The Macmillan Company, New York, New York*

*Collier-Macmillan Ltd., London*

Library of Congress Catalog Card Number: 66-24054

The Macmillan Company
866 Third Avenue
New York, N.Y. 10022
Collier-Macmillan Canada Ltd., Toronto, Ontario

FIRST MACMILLAN PAPERBACK EDITION 1968
Second Printing 1971

Originally published in a hardcover edition in 1966
by The Macmillan Company

Printed in the United States of America

Grateful acknowledgment is hereby made for permission to quote from the following copyrighted material:

*The Structure of Behavior*, by Maurice Merleau-Ponty, reprinted by permission of Methuen & Company, Ltd., Publishers, and Beacon Press, copyright © 1963 by Beacon Press; originally published in French under the title *La Structure du comportement*, copyright © 1942 by Presses Universitaires de France; *The Collected Papers*, Vols. I and II, by Alfred Schutz, and *The Problem of Embodiment*, by Richard Zaner, reprinted by permission of Martinus Nijhoff, The Hague.

*To* MARCUS, SARA, ANNE, *and* JACQUELINE,
*whose patience permitted preoccupation with a less authentic social world*

*contents*

# *list of charts*

# *acknowledgments*

This work depends upon the contributions of a number of disciplines and individual scholars. Footnotes, however copious, are only a gesture toward such indebtedness. Furthermore, two figures have made a central contribution to this work. George Herbert Mead's conception of the social self was a turning point in American social science, according to the interpretation of this text; despite reservations put forth here about that conception, its immense significance to the present work is evident throughout. In a different though equally significant way, Alfred Schutz has made a fundamental contribution to this inquiry; without his grasp of the bearing of phenomenology on the social sciences, the state of these disciplines would have presented insuperable difficulties.

A personal debt is owed to Dean Jerald Brauer of the Divinity School of the University of Chicago for his support and encouragement in this task. The American Association of Theological Schools made possible the initial research when the project was little more than an uneasiness over the state of the disciplines and their problems. Carl Michalson, whose untimely death has been such a loss to theological scholarship, played a vital role in opening new lines of inquiry during the year which we shared in Strasbourg. In addition, my students offered significant criticisms, especially Wesley Robbins and Robert Terry; my friend Marianne Beth guided me in the difficult German texts of Schutz and Husserl; my friends and colleagues Charles Long, Alvin Pitcher, and Widick Schroeder took precious time to criticize the text and furnished important clues to revision. Mrs. Rehova Arthur worked carefully on the manuscript. These notes are an all too inadequate indication of my gratitude.

G. W.

# Preface to the paperback edition

Phenomenology is almost fashionable in the United States today. Translations of French and German literature in this mode of thought are becoming available. It is no longer as necessary to apologize for the special terminology of this text. As familiarity with the corpus of phenomenological investigation grows, the import of the argument in this volume should become more evident. In this pious hope, the paperback edition is published with only minor revisions. To be sure, more substantial revisions are anticipated, but they concern omissions rather than substantive changes in the argument, so they can be delayed until the argument has been extended into the field of normative ethics.

This inquiry was provoked by two concerns: First, the human sciences were increasingly plagued by ideological divisions in the 1950s; and, second, these various schools were proposing different solutions to the same social problems, and apparently doing so from the same data. These ideological conflicts and differences of interpretation could not be resolved by pitting one style against another nor simply by dogmatizing from one approach. What was needed was to go back to the common subject matter and general insights of these sciences and clarify the conditions of experience which they presupposed.

For a century the sciences of man have elaborated two fundamental insights. These insights were not completely present from the first, of course, but they have become increasingly prominent over a century of inquiry. These two insights of social science—(1) man's social nature and (2) man's continuity with biological evolution—constitute generalizations about human experience which this inquiry seeks to clarify and ground in an understanding of human nature.

The social conditioning of man's nature was brought home to the social sciences by the study of various cultures and their different social patterns. Studies of child development and processes of socialization have only extended and deepended these earlier ideas of cultural conditioning. However, the grounding of this cultural formation of man in his social nature has remained ambiguous. Man's world is shaped by the language which gives it meaning and the shared understandings in which he participates, but the conditions for the possibility of such a common world remain obscure. George Herbert Mead struggled with this problem and contributed directly and indirectly to the understanding of the problem in contemporary social science. This was the occasion, therefore, for reconsidering his solution to the problem of mind and communication.

Mead's theory proposed to describe the emergence of mind and communication as coming from the social interaction of externally related but discrete entities. In the effort to clarify the possibility of communication which he had formulated, we were pressed to the recognition that social interaction emerges from internally related but discrete entities who come to consciousness in communicative acts. The insight into the social conditioning of man's nature was thus grounded in the social nature of man; the possibility of mind, symbol and communication became intelligible.

The insight into man's continuity with biological evolution posed a related but somewhat different kind of problem within the sciences of man. From an evolutionary perspective, social science viewed consciousness as an adaptive mechanism reflecting a higher order of animal response. However, this view of consciousness posed radical questions about the nature of consciousness and the meaning of truth. If consciousness is a product of external forces in evolutionary adaptation, then it is a product of physical forces and sensations which are other than consciousness. If, on the other hand, consciousness is itself independent of this evolutionary process, we are in the idealists' camp and consciousness floats above the embodied nature which embarrasses it.

We sought the answer to this second problem in Maurice Merleau-Ponty's work on the structure of embodied intentionality. Consciousness is the Totality of Being's coming to awareness in the perceptions, expressions, thoughts, symbols and actions of man. Man shares in the generality of this Totality as embodied subjectivity; as body-subject he shares in the structure of the process in which he emerges as self-surpassing freedom. He gains distance from his fixed place within Totality as an initiative opened by Being in reflection. Thus, the self is a finite freedom, having access to generality of structure from a limited perspective within it. Consciousness gains validity as access to the prephenomenal generality in which the body-subject participates. Consciousness is relative to the historical sedimentation of cultural experience in which it takes its initiative. Consciousness also manifests the relativity of its perspective on generality in the particular formulation which it proposes.

Man's social nature, his continuity with biological evolution, and his peculiar status as self-conscious being-in-the-world were thus grounded in the schema of the body-subject which Merleau-Ponty had proposed. (See Chart 2, revised, p. 114.) The freedom and sociality of man could be stated together, and the possibility of a science of the social world could be stated in terms of the access of consciousness to the generality in which all experience is grounded. Various styles of social science could be understood as theories of communication which developed from an interpretation of the schema of the body-subject. A theory may take the lawfulness in the schema of the body-subject, or the self-surpassing freedom of the subject as an organizing principle, or some combination of the two elements. In considering some of these possibilities, we proposed a typology of some of the dominant styles in contemporary social science.

Chart 2, revised (p. 114), has been reformulated to bring out more sharply the grounding of each scientific style in the prephenomenal or implicit level of experiencing of embodied intentionality or what we referred to as the schema of the body-subject. Each style, as can be seen from Chart 2, takes an aspect or element of the total communicative act as a basic principle of continuity and treats other aspects as relatively invariant around this principle. The intentionalist style (the term used for the interpretive sociology of Alfred Schutz which guided much of this analysis) is a style in which the struggle to make sense of the world is the decisive principle. Behaviorists and functionalists have a great deal in common as styles of science, for they work from the lawfulness of the schema of body-subject—pressing toward a conception of a closed, determinate universe. The voluntarist and intentionalist styles are more open, taking the "subject" aspect of the schema more seriously—moving toward an open, creative universe. For different scientific purposes different styles can be appropriate and useful, and the same is true of different aspects of social organization. However, we have removed the ontological presuppositions of the various styles and relativized all of them to the ontology of embodied intentionality.

Relativizing these scientific styles as perspectives on prephenomenal, embodied intentionality does not impugn the significance and validity of the sciences of man. Science becomes perspectival but is not radically relativized in this argument. The ideologial struggle among various styles of science had already indicated the relative character of the perspectives. When these perspectives or principles of order (as Harold Garfinkel characterizes them in his Harvard Ph.D. thesis, "Perception of the Other," 1952) are brought to bear on social policy—shaping the future according to a particular perspective on the order of experience in the past—the evaluative implications of these scientific styles become evident. The various perspectives have implications for value which were bound to come into conflict in an ideological struggle between the scientific styles in which conflicting proposals were made for social policy. By grounding these styles in an ontology of communication, we were able to comprehend their common ground and the difference in their evaluative perspectives. The relevance of the different styles could thus be determined in terms of the problems and values which they considered crucial to particular policies.

Social science gains validity from its access to the generality of prephenomenal experiencing which it formulates and systematizes. Thus, social scientific insights into man's sociality, his continuity with biological evolution and the cultural conditioning of consciousness find common ground in embodied intentionality. In this framework, social science has the creative task of bringing man to fuller freedom through awareness of the general structure of his social experience. Man increases his self-surpassing freedom as initiative in the world through the reflective work of the human sciences. At the same time, the pretentions of some scientific styles to a completely objective knowledge of human behavior are undercut.

Chapter 7 interpreted three moral values of the Western tradition—freedom, equality, and community—within the ontology of embodied intentionality. However, this use of what R. M. Hare would call hypothetical imperatives collapsed the normative problem into the ontological grounding. That moral argument has to be explicated, as Robert Terry has made clear in subsequent discussions. There is no fundamental obstacle to extending the reflections to the moral horizon, and, indeed, these reflections will deepen and complicate the problem of social policy. Until these moral reflections are elaborated, the consideration of science and ethics in relationship to social policy in Chapter 8 remains indeterminate.

The theological question remains implicit throughout these reflections on the nature and role of the sciences of man.

However, a pretheological question becomes explicit in the critique of sociologism. Social science is constantly tempted to convert its insight into man's continuity with biological evolution into a view of man as a complicated animal and society as a rather complicated biological process. Man's continuity in evolution can be stated without obscuring the new order within Being which erupts with subjectivity, self-consciousness, and symbol. This is the immanent form of the theological question in this text—the recognition of man's being-in-the-world as finite freedom and the problem of the meaning of Being which appears with his existence.

*The Divinity School*
*University of Chicago*
*March 1, 1968*

GIBSON WINTER

part one

# *the problem of the social sciences*

# 1 *emergence of the human sciences*

A brief historical look at the development of social science · The focus is George Herbert Mead and the problem of social determination of man

THE CONTRIBUTIONS of social science and social ethics to the creation of social policy require more dialogue between the disciplines than now exists. The radical opposition of these disciplines has, to be sure, been tempered by changes on both sides. Social science emerged in an era of dogmatic positivism and set itself in opposition to a religious ethic which took for granted its traditional tenets.[1] The struggle between natural science and religion in the latter half of the nineteenth century had its counterpart in the struggle between the social sciences and theological social ethics. If one were to contrast the present possibilities of dialogue with that situation a century ago, there would be some reason for optimism about the collaboration of these disciplines. Nevertheless, serious difficulties still confront these disciplines in their collaborative tasks.

Theological ethics undoubtedly occasions many of its own problems with the social sciences by its anxious struggle to maintain its integrity against the inroads of science. Furthermore, the theological disciplines labored after World War I to reestablish the integrity of theology as a discipline—effecting this new lease on life by cutting relationships with philosophical and humanistic disciplines. The hegemony of

[1] This opposition of perspectives was often on a taken-for-granted basis in the theological tradition; even the so-called liberal theology assumed a moral order, even if this was assumed in the general terms of the "Kingdom of God in America." See the discussion of this theme in H. Richard Niebuhr, *The Kingdom of God in America* (New York: Harper Torchbooks, 1959).

this neo-orthodox revival is waning rapidly, although its essential fruits in a redefinition of theological discourse will continue to be significant. Thus, the time is ripe for a new openness to anthropological concerns within the field of social ethics. However much the theologians may have contributed to the barriers which separate social science and social ethics, they are now disenchanted with their biblical theologies and antiphilosophical orthodoxies. The doors are open, although not much traffic is moving through at the present time.

The social sciences, on their part, continue to throw up serious blocks to collaboration with social ethics, largely because they have failed to clarify the significance of their abstract models for concrete, social process.[2] The controversies within the human sciences, as well as between social science and social ethics, are rooted in lack of clarity about the nature of the social reality which forms the backdrop of any science or ethic of the social world. If this interpretation should prove to be correct, and the present inquiry attempts to verify it, then the obstacles to collaboration between these disciplines are largely a consequence of dogmatism on both sides.

The nature of the difficulties besetting the collaboration of social science with social ethics can be grasped from a brief retrospect on the emergence of the human sciences. A detailed history of these sciences would certainly not be appropriate in this context.[3] Our task is to identify the sources of the present distance between the disciplines. This retrospective view is directed by the hypothesis that an adequate understanding of the social world can resolve

[2] This problem is discussed in detail in Chapter 2.

[3] There are several histories of the social sciences which furnish an account of most of the problems and figures. Don Martindale, *The Nature and Types of Sociological Theory* (Boston: Houghton Mifflin Co., 1960), develops the historical material within a formal schematization; Georges Gusdorf's *Introduction aux sciences humaines* (Strasbourg, France: Publication de la Faculté, 1960) is exhaustive but limited to the European traditions.

many of the problems obstructing the cooperation of an ethic and a science of man. The testing of this hypothesis is the task of the total inquiry, but the hypothesis guides the selection of issues and figures for this historical perspective. The historical data are being used, in other words, to illuminate our present situation rather than as an explanatory account of our condition; only on this basis is it appropriate to select a few pivotal figures and issues.

### *A POSITIVE VIEW OF SOCIETY*

Although social science intended to look at man through the eyes of "science," its concern with being scientific obscured its vision of man and his social experience. Social science was actually a quasi-physical science in its earlier phases. After the collapse of the religious world view in the Enlightenment, nineteenth-century Europe confronted social change without guiding principles to shape a new morality and social order. The science of man was an attempt to build a new social order; indeed, Karl Marx's project as "social science" occurs against this backdrop. A social order would be credible for the nineteenth century only if it could call upon scientific principles for its ground; even history became credible only as science.[4] Thus, the first preoccupation of the science of man was with the scientific character of its

[4] This is a generally acknowledged dimension of the emergence of the social sciences. In the English tradition, its leading exponent was Herbert Spencer. See his *The Data of Ethics* (London: Williams and Norgate, Ltd., 1907), Part 1, esp. the Preface, where he notes the moral crisis and the need for a science of society. Auguste Comte was preoccupied with this problem throughout his long career. See *The Positive Philosophy of Auguste Comte*, 3rd ed. (London: Kegan, Paul, Trench, Trübner & Co., Ltd., 1893, translated by Harriet Martineau, esp. Vol. 2, Book 5, Ch. 1, and the problem of the interregnum after the collapse of theology and metaphysics. A similar concern runs through the work of Émile Durkheim. See his monograph *Moral Education* (New York: The Free Press, 1961), p. 101, where he speaks of the moral crisis through which Europe has been passing for more than a century. (When one considers the catastrophic wars of the twentieth century in Europe, these concerns take on a prophetic quality.)

method. The dominance of positivism in early phases of human science originated in this concern for scientific credentials in laying new foundations for society.[5] Somewhat later it became apparent that the preoccupation with being scientific had caused the human sciences to lose sight of their subject matter; not man, but a caricature of man as the pseudoscientist, dominated the scene. For example, religious life was reduced to man's errors in developing technology or his mistakes in the interpretation of dreams.[6] Hence, a science of man emerged which substituted science for human experience. The basic problem of human science thus appeared early in his history—the problem of maintaining a scientific method without destroying the human subject matter. Instead of understanding man as a scientist, science had to be understood as a human activity.

The American experience highlighted these problems, for the human sciences have enjoyed a status in the United States which they never achieved in Europe; in addition, their interchange with other disciplines created a more suitable atmosphere for clarifying many of the issues. However, even in the United States, the protracted struggle by social science to achieve professional status made it very difficult to raise questions about the positivistic views of science which were dominant at the turn of the century.

Social science started, at least on the American scene, with a mechanistic, evolutionary model of man. This perspective is typified in the work of William Graham Sumner. He was influenced by Herbert Spencer's evolutionary understanding. Richard Hofstadter, when he discusses social Darwinism in America, links Sumner's thought intimately with Spencer's

[5] One of the most thorough analyses of the role of positivism in the emergence of social science was made by Talcott Parsons, *The Structure of Social Action*, 2nd ed. (New York: The Free Press, 1949), esp. Part 1.

[6] The work of Lucien Lévy-Bruhl is a remarkable example of the struggle to overcome this dogmatism in ethnological interpretation. For a discussion of this problem, see the author's essay "Society and Morality in the French Tradition," *Review of Religious Research*, Vol. I, No. 5, 1963.

ideas.[7] This point of view dominated the early development of social science in the United States and set the terms for the long struggle over evolutionary development and its social extension. Actually, Spencer was not very popular in England. He found his real vogue in the United States. Thomas Huxley, the English biologist, thought little of Spencer's understanding of the implication of evolution for society, but somehow the inadequacy of this interpretation did not trouble the American audience.[8] Perhaps the American atmosphere was more congenial to Spencer's stress on the competitive struggle—industrialization in a frontier world gave credibility to the idea of an individualistic struggle to survive. At any rate, Herbert Spencer found and maintained an attentive public in the United States, and his views were articulated as social science by men like Sumner.

When William Graham Sumner wrote his famous work *Folkways*, he made an indelible mark on the initial stage of American social science.[9] He examined social customs and interpreted their emergence as the environmental adaptation of highly developed organisms. The work of science was to formulate the laws of this adaptive process—division of labor, cooperation, competition, etc. (laws strangely resembling principles of laissez-faire economics)—recognizing that these were laws of nature which prescribed the only course of successful adaptation.[10] The calculus of forces at work in evolution was formulated in these laws and accounted for a successful species; thus, the laws furnished a scientific calculus of the social process comparable to the laws of

[7] Richard Hofstadter, *Social Darwinism in American Thought*, rev. ed. (Boston: Beacon Press, 1955), *passim*, esp. p. 55.

[8] Thomas H. Huxley, *Evolution and Ethics and Other Essays* (New York: D. Appleton & Co., 1901), esp. pp. 50, 81ff.

[9] William Graham Sumner, *Folkways*, repub. of 1906 ed. (New York: Dover Publications, Inc., 1959).

[10] One of the clearest expressions of this position is to be found in Sumner's essay "Sociology," in *Social Darwinism: Selected Essays of William Graham Sumner* (Englewood Cliffs, N.J.: Prentice-Hall, Inc., 1963), pp. 9–29.

mechanics in physical process. A mechanistic model of evolutionary process thus furnished the model for the human sciences—defining human social evolution through laws of social adaptation.

Having discovered the social laws, man's task was to conform to them and avoid legislative action which might disrupt them.[11] Since these laws determined the successful course of human adaptation, they provided the guidelines for society's progress. Sumner's famous dictum "Stateways cannot change Folkways" was formulated against this theoretical background; it referred to the long-range opposition of adaptive laws to legislative activity. Man may try to disrupt the social laws, causing society untold damage, but the natural processes will win out in the end. Society is not made by man; society develops like any other organic process —evolving according to laws of nature. Society's problem is to recognize the course which nature is taking and to conform to it.

The mechanistic model postulates a set of instinctive forces which are playing upon one another in an environment; these forces move against one another within the limitations set by the environment; various resolutions of force furnish modes of adaptation, and the most suitable modes lead to survival; hence, the construction of laws which express these suitable modes of adaptation enables the scientist to discern the order inscribed in the process. The laws of classical economics were understood in this way and obeyed with a devotion which would have done honor to the medieval church. The devotion to a free market by the English Exchequer during the Irish famine of 1846–1848 is a grim

[11] *Ibid.*, Ch. 6, "State Interference." This point of view has close analogies in contemporary arguments for automaticity by economists such as Milton Friedman, *Capitalism and Freedom* (Chicago: University of Chicago Press, Phoenix Books, 1963), for example, pp. 23f. For a carefully documented treatment of the development of this type of economic theory, see Overton H. Taylor, *A History of Economic Thought* (New York: McGraw-Hill Book Co., 1960), esp. Chs. 12 and 15.

example of the misery which was engendered by men who believed that economic laws were laws of nature; food was shipped out of Ireland all through the famine while people were dying in the streets; the impetus behind this inhuman behavior was the attempt to maintain a free market for what was believed to be the long-range good of the economy.[12] Perhaps no other historical example illustrated so well the obliteration of the human subject matter through preoccupation with a "science" of man. Dogmatism about the form of science became a substitute for scientific inquiry into social realities.

William Graham Sumner exemplifies this perspective. He viewed sociology as the science of life in society. Calculation of the laws of social life gave sociology a role in society comparable to that of physics in its dealing with physical nature. Here we encounter a paradox in the human sciences —instead of increasing man's freedom through knowledge, the sciences of man restrict his freedom. This paradox is symptomatic of the ambiguity in the conception of the social sciences; it reflects an inadequate formulation of the sciences of man. The physical sciences increased man's control over nature by making the forces of nature more calculable; to be sure, man had to conform to the laws of nature in his struggle for mastery, but he could manipulate nature through a knowledge of these laws. Physical science expressed man's control over his environment. When the subject matter of social science is handled like the subject matter of physical science, knowledge of social laws becomes a knowledge of laws which control man's activity. Knowledge of society reveals man's enslavement to societal forces. Man ceases to be a "subject" and becomes an "object" of calculable forces external to him. Whereas physical science increases man's control of his situation, social science discloses man's bondage to his situation. Every attempt to exercise choice in

[12] See Cecil B. Woodham Smith, *The Great Hunger: Ireland 1845–1849* (New York: Harper & Row, Inc., 1962).

shaping social life is rejected unless it reproduces the activities of laws alien to that choice. Man the scientist discovers himself to be the victim of science.[13]

The contrast between these scientific perspectives can be expressed in terms of activity and passivity. Man is active in the natural sciences, for he inquires into the operations of nature and shapes his environment according to his interests and values. In the social sciences, man initiates the inquiry into the social world as an active subject, but he reconceives his nature in the course of the investigation and discovers himself to be the passive object of forces playing upon him. Man, whose science is a sign of his active-creative nature, reinterprets himself as passive, conformed, and adapted. He belies his scientific activity in his social-scientific model.

The proper understanding of the activity-passivity dimension has repeatedly eluded the sciences of man. The net effect is that the application of the term "science" to the social field becomes very ambiguous. Social science seems to refute the possibility of the scientific enterprise itself; if man is a product of alien forces, his scientific activity is only an illusion which is created by those forces; in his attempts to reshape his world, he is passively conforming to irresistible processes. Such an interpretation of man's valuing activity overlooks the creative, self-transcending distance which is presupposed in any scientific inquiry. It is precisely man's freedom to transcend any situation in his symbolic activity which is the presupposition of his physical as well as social sciences.

This paradox of using scientific creativity to reduce society to passivity can be interpreted from Chart 1 of Chapter

[13] Hofstadter, *op. cit.*, pp. 11f., expresses this paradox very clearly: "There is a certain touching irony in the thought that, while writers like these preached slow changes and urged men to adapt to the environment, the very millionaires whom they took to be the 'fittest' in the struggle for existence were transforming the environment with incredible rapidity and rendering the values of the Spencers and Sumners of this world constantly less fit for survival."

3, since the form of spontaneity in the scientific process —disinterested observation for the purpose of diagnosis—is treated as an account of the underlying reality of the societal processes; hence, the struggle for mastery is supplanted by a modification of the perspective of common sense. In the light of this substitution of a scientific perspective for the pragmatic attitude of every day, it is interesting to note that pragmatism was the philosophic approach which made the decisive attack on the Spencer-Sumner outlook.

The nature of science and man's creativity is obscured by this mechanistic model of human adaptation. However, the nature of these "scientific" laws is also ambiguous in the Spencer-Sumner outlook. We have already hinted at this in the notion that the mores ultimately resist man's legislative initiative. However, the ambiguity is much deeper and reflects the inadequacy of the model with which the social process is interpreted. The social scientists—in our examples, Herbert Spencer and William Graham Sumner—oppose legislative action which contravenes the correlation of individual effort and reward; in their views, such legislation subverts the law of social process inscribed in evolution and consequently defeats human progress. Nevertheless, these laws are called "laws of nature," as though they were independent of man—expressing the operation of forces which control man. By contrast, man does not have to worry about the functioning of the law of gravity; he is not going to interfere with it through legislative activity. Social laws and physical laws seem to be incommensurable. A law of nature is not inscribed in process if social scientists must work to protect its operation. One gets the impression that these social laws are man-made—subject to his manipulation and reformulation. Then social laws do not formulate the operation of alien forces; they reflect a social-scientific perspective on man's activity—offering an interpretation of its antecedent forces and proposing one view of its future course.

This ambiguity can be restated as an interpretation of the

task of social science. The human sciences strive to maintain the conditions under which social "laws" can operate, but the "nature" to which they refer is a construction of the social sciences; thus, the "laws" reflect one interpretation of social process. However, man can reconstruct social processes in the light of such a model, so that both the models and the processes which they depict are to be understood as human creations. Karl Polanyi has noted that the opening of a free market in Western Europe was not the expression of a "natural process" but, rather, a remarkable human achievement. It was as much a human creation as the traditional closed market.[14] There is nothing "natural," if one means by "natural" conforming to extrahuman causes, about exposing labor, products, money, and property to the marketplace. Only the most assiduous activity on the part of governments maintained free markets of exchange—actually effecting this transformation at untold cost in human suffering. The manipulative activity of governments was defended in the name of "laws of nature" or economic laws, but the "nature" at work in the process was a humanly constructed theory of exchange. Thus, the mechanistic notion of law is highly ambiguous; it reflects the substitution of an abstract, scientific formulation for societal processes—reading the scientific understanding (law) as a social form inscribed in the evolutionary process. This scientific model also viewed society as recalcitrant to the given laws—thus juxtaposing inexorable laws which *should* be obeyed to human interests which negate them. This is one way of stating the dilemma of positivism in social science; it confuses its own abstractions and formulations with social process (the error of reification of theory), but in turn it sets its formulations of the *real* law of the process over against the interests of the society. The denial of man's freedom to re-create social process placed the social scientist in the anomalous position of persuading

[14] Karl Polanyi, *The Great Transformation* (Boston: Beacon Press, 1957), esp. Part 2.

society to *obey* laws of nature over which it had no control.[15]

These ambiguities were evident in the human sciences wherever the positivistic perspective gained control. Auguste Comte's program of positive philosophy was an outstanding instance; according to Comte's understanding, sociology emerged in the fullness of time—its appropriate evolutionary stage—as an expression of positive science for a rational humanity. This science formulated the laws of social order and was itself the means for dissemination of the truth in the final stage of evolution. The task of science was to formulate the laws which were inscribed in the factual processes and to inform society of its true order. However, society proved recalcitrant. It rejected the revelation of final truth. In the face of such indifference, Comte began to appreciate the need for persuasion and religious motivation in order to adjust man's sentiments to the true social good; this change of heart came also as a consequence of personal tragedy; thus, we find Comte in his latter years developing a religion of positivism. This last phase of Comte's work was embarrassing to his positivistic sympathizers; they dispose of this period as the aberration of an older man. However, Auguste Comte was more logical than his followers; he had come to realize that it was not enough to *invoke* the laws which were inscribed in the processes of evolution—one also had to *persuade* men to obey these laws. Only Comte's dogmatism prevented him from reconsidering the status of the "laws of nature" which men had to be *persuaded to obey;* long after he had plunged into his cultic activities, he clung to the dream of a positive philosophy through which life could be ordered. Whether in positive philosophy or in social Darwinism, the misunderstanding of man by the human sciences produced paradox and self-contradiction.

This self-contradiction occurs also in Émile Durkheim's

[15] We review a contemporary form of this debate in Chapter 2, where it is noted that Winston White purports to *know* what the *real* processes of social development are, whereas those who propose alternative paths for the society are not scientists but "moralizers" or "reformers."

work; it is expressed in the transition from his positivistic starting point to the idealism in the conclusion to his study of religion.[16] Wherever human science obliterated the "human" for the sake of its "science"—and this happened repeatedly in these earlier decades—paradox and ambiguity beset its formulations. In each instance, the cultural task of the human sciences became anomalous; furthermore, ideological perspectives were promulgated as laws of nature. No field of human science demonstrates this more dramatically than economics. Human science fell into self-contradiction because it failed to regard seriously the special character of its subject matter.

## *THE INFLUENCE OF PRAGMATISM*

Whatever the weaknesses of American social Darwinism, the practical bent of American thought soon undermined its dogmatism. The pragmatic philosophy made a major contribution to the human sciences by loosening the hold of mechanistic thought.[17] The Spencer-Sumner outlook, as we have suggested, was beset by self-contradictions; these difficulties were rooted in an inadequate grasp of human behavior—the subject matter of human science. The pragmatic spirit of American life made it impatient with the dogmatism of positive social science; the pragmatic philosophy, in turn, opened the door to a reconsideration of the roots of the dogmatism. Unfortunately, the pragmatic model was not fully incorporated into social science, so that its full implications have yet to be realized in the human sciences. However, George Herbert Mead, working within the broad stream of thought represented by Charles Peirce, William James, and John Dewey, made a significant breakthrough

[16] See the conclusion of Émile Durkheim's *The Elementary Forms of Religious Life* (New York: The Free Press, 1947).

[17] Hofstadter, *op. cit.*, Ch. 7. See also Daniel Boorstin, *The Genius of American Politics* (Chicago: University of Chicago Press, Phoenix Books, 1958).

in the conception of social process and freed the human sciences from the mechanistic model of externally related elements. He made the important transition to an internally related notion of social process. Man as active subject was reinstated.

The direct impact of pragmatism on the human sciences is rooted in two aspects of the pragmatic philosophy: (1) man's perceptual judgments involve an organizing activity of consciousness; (2) man's situation is constituted with reference to his interests and understanding. Despite the behavioristic backdrop against which this pragmatic perspective emerged in the human sciences, passivity of consciousness and submission of subjectivity to an externally determined situation were radically challenged and never again gained control of the human sciences.

Pragmatism views man as active and creative. It conceives him in active rather than passive terms. Therefore, man is understood as shaping himself and his world; he is the one who produces effects in response to the demands of the situation. Pragmatism also sees man as the problem-solver. In this respect, pragmatism accepts the basic motifs of evolutionary thought but sees man as a striving being within this process. Thus, science is conceived as an aspect of man's evolutionary struggle to meet the problems which confront him. Man is not dominated by forces external to him, although his situation confronts him with limitations and problems; he is the one who struggles to understand his situation, to master it, and to utilize it for the realization of his interests.[18]

The difficulty with the Spencer-Sumner outlook was that

[18] This emphasis upon man as problem-solver actually gained its outstanding spokesman in John Dewey. William James's focus upon the constitution of dimensions of reality by the subject was later to become an important theme in the social sciences. Charles Peirce set some of the foundations of this approach but was wrestling more specifically with an alternative to an intuitional method of knowing. See *The Pragmatic Philosophy of C. S. Peirce*, edited by Manley Thompson (Chicago: University of Chicago Press, Phoenix Books, 1963), pp. 37–52. Nevertheless,

it took the problems implicit in evolution superficially. One is repeatedly struck by how much these early theorists took for granted—the evolution of language, understanding, and social organization, as though the intersubjective enterprise could simply be taken for granted as a product of external forces. The emergence of mind—the presupposition of all models of evolving social process—was treated as unproblematic; hence, the complexity of evolution was concealed. The pragmatic movement became a creative force in the human sciences because it grappled with the fundamental problem of the emergence of mind in evolution. In a rationalistic perspective, the scientific observer has a neutral, objective ground on which to stand, since he can formulate laws which hold objectively without regard to his own contribution to the process of inquiry. This nonhistorical, nontemporal conception of the laws of social process lifts the scientist beyond time and space into a world of lawful order. We have already observed the paradoxical role of the social scientist who adheres to this rationalistic position and yet urges men to obey these objective laws. It was pragmatism, at least on the American scene, which pricked the bubble of this scientific rationalism.

If evolutionary process is accepted as the milieu of the human, then reason and its formulation of laws participate in the process. Pragmatism, although it tended toward rationalism at times, was inclined to accept this basic condition of an evolutionary understanding of man. The contrast between pragmatism and rationalistic notions in social science may again be illustrated by Auguste Comte, who is interesting as representing a classic theory—one which is recurring today in the structural-functional model. Comte rejected the Darwinian theory of evolution in which human faculties and consciousness must be conceived as elements which evolve

---

the practical character of knowledge is reflected in an essay like "Issues of Pragmaticism," in *The American Pragmatists*, edited by Milton R. Konvitz and Gail Kennedy (New York: Meridian Books, Inc., 1960), pp. 119–126.

in biological process. Comte's rejection of this radical notion of evolution was as embarrassing to his later sympathizers as were his cultic activities. Comte's rejection of evolution, when one juxtaposes it to his own evolutionary notion of the three stages of man, seems self-contradictory; however, Comte was essentially a rationalist, and he perceived that a radical notion of evolution would undermine his whole position. If science, as well as theology and metaphysics, had to be submitted to evolutionary process, then the scientist had no neutral ground from which to dogmatize about the fulfillment of the evolutionary process; even sociology would have to be relativized to history, since one could not stand at the end of history and could make no final judgments of value about the meaning of the historical process. Comte's attitude toward Darwinism, however, embarrassing to his positivistic sympathizers, was no aberration of impending senility but the shrewd perception of a very logical mind. The positive philosophy and a radical notion of evolution were simply incompatible.

We need not explore in detail the course of pragmatic thought and its impact upon various stages of social-scientific theory in order to accomplish the purposes of this inquiry. This historical retrospect is, in this sense, much more concerned with the emergence of models of social process than with the detailed formation of these models. Hence, our attention will focus upon George Herbert Mead, who represents a crucial starting point for this whole perspective and continues to be a creative source for reflection in the social sciences. However, Mead's consideration of the intersubjective process and the emergence of mind represents a crucial transition in the basic theories of social science. He is the principal link between the pragmatic perspective and the contemporary development of the human sciences.[19] Although Mead's behavioristic starting point inhibited his

[19] The reference is to direct influence and explicit reference to his work; the pragmatic movement as a whole was undoubtedly the principal influence.

full utilization of the possibilities within the pragmatic perspective, his inquiring mind repeatedly broke through these behavioristic limits. In sum, we are concerned with George Herbert Mead not because he stands as a significant figure in the history of social theory in the United States but, rather, because his formulation of the problem of social science was decisive for later developments. The way in which later social theories resolved the problems underlying Mead's formulation was significant for their interpretation of man and his valuing process.

One cannot do justice to Mead with such a limited concern, since some of his most important work touched major philosophic issues. Unfortunately, he wrote very little, and even the extant works under his name are collections of writings and lectures. However, the work edited by Anselm Strauss under the title *The Social Psychology of George Herbert Mead* includes the theoretical considerations of most direct influence in the field of social science.[20] Hence, in considering Mead's basic contribution through this work, we are primarily concerned with a transition in the mental climate of social scientific thought—leaving to others the extension of Maurice Natanson's critical reflections on the significance of Mead as a philosopher.

Mead's understanding of man—the implicit or explicit valuation informing any social-scientific theory—comes to focus in his notion of the social self. He says on this subject: "The 'self,' as that which can be an object to itself, is essentially a social structure and it arises in social experience."[21] The crucial consideration is, of course, that the self is a "social structure." This is to say that the self emerges in social

[20] *The Social Psychology of George Herbert Mead*, edited by Anselm Strauss (Chicago: University of Chicago Press, Phoenix Books, 1956). A new edition with a few additional essays has been published under the title *George Herbert Mead on Social Psychology* (Chicago: University of Chicago Press, Phoenix Books, 1964). Unless otherwise noted, reference is to the original edition.

[21] *Ibid.*, p. 217.

process. One becomes a self through participation in the social process. Mead started with a behavioristic notion of stimulus and response, but he moved beyond this in order to account for significant communication. Whereas stimulus-response theory takes for granted the existence of meaning and tries to account for its inculcation through conditioning, Mead raised the question of the emergence of meaning itself. In this sense, as we have already noted, he took the evolutionary question in a radical way. His problem, then, is how one accounts for the emergence of mind and communication in the course of evolution. How is it possible for beings to communicate, symbolize, generate language, and think? At some point in the evolutionary process, a change occurs—whether quantitative or qualitative, the change is radical enough to represent a significant discontinuity in the process. Instead of presupposing selves in communication and a scientific observer who formulates laws of their activities, Mead asks about the emergence of these selves and about the rational process which the scientific observer presupposes in his inquiry.[22]

The key words in Mead's account of the emergence of mind are "gesture" and "significant gesture." How does a gesture become a significant gesture? As Mead interprets this process, the self is given to itself through the interpretation which the other's response offers to one's gesture. For example, if I make a gesture—point to something—the problem is to understand how that gesture gains significance for me or how it becomes meaningful to me. I must be able to see the meaning of that gesture by awareness of it from the point of view of the other's response to it—what it means to him. I must be able to take the role of the other and to see myself as an object making that gesture and evoking that response; the meaning given to the gesture by the other's response makes it a meaningful gesture for me. I might, for example, have made that gesture in an exploratory way

[22] *Ibid.*, esp. the essay "Evolution Becomes a General Idea," pp. 9–11.

or playfully, to draw on one of Mead's hypotheses, but awareness of the meaning given to it by the other makes it meaningful to me as a way of expressing that meaning. I know what I meant because I discover what the other interpreted the gesture to mean. In that sense, meaning is utterly social. The self, which receives its meaning from the response of the other, is likewise a social structure created through the social process. I am who I am through the view of my self which is furnished by others. I have a self only as I am conscious of my self as an object—a gesturing being who receives this particular kind of response; the self is mediated to me reflexively by the awareness of the meaning which my gesture has for the other—I receive my self in this coming to awareness through the other's response to me.[23] Hence, the "significant gesture" comes into being through the self-consciousness mediated to the self by the other. To this extent, self-consciousness and significant gesture presuppose each other.[24] In this social process of significant gestures or communication—the process of intersubjective gesture and response—the self comes to be as a thinking, self-conscious self; hence, thought is the internal language of gestures.[25] The self is given to itself in the interpretation of its acts by the other; the self, as Mead expresses it, is a social structure arising in social experience.

Rationality, in this perspective, rests upon the arousal in the individual of the response which he is calling out in the other—a taking of the role of the other, a tendency to act as the other person expects one to act, to act toward this gesture as the other person views it.[26] Mead worked extensively with this problem and its explication in order to maintain continuity in the evolutionary process from sign-behavior to significant gesture without losing sight of the qualitative change which language and mind reflect. We are

[23] *Ibid.*, p. 199, fn. 32.
[24] *Ibid.*, pp. 209–211.
[25] *Ibid.*, pp. 173f., 217–219.
[26] *Ibid.*, p. 224.

also in the realm of interpersonal notions of identity as they have been discussed in recent years, but these latter theories are generally rooted in Freudian notions of cathectic or affective ties of self and other, whereas Mead was working with a highly rational, cognitive model. The framework for the theory of selfhood is intersubjective in both models. The notion of internal relations of self and other—an intersubjective matrix through which selfhood emerges—can be taken as the presupposition of both traditions. We have moved beyond mechanistic theories of external relations, although such theories will continue to play a significant role in the human sciences. Mead's basic notion is that the conversation of gestures begins as an external phenomenon and becomes significant as it becomes internal through emerging self-consciousness. In this respect, taking the role of the other is "internal" participation in his perspective.

Mead's concept of the generalized other provided a comprehensive social conception of the other through whom the mores and sanctions of a society could become a part of the self—through which the self becomes "socialized," to use a contemporary term.[27] By taking the point of view of the generalized other, the self comes into being as reflection of the attitudes, approvals, and meanings of the community. The "me"—my self as social or seen from the perspective of significant others and the community in general—comes to be. This conception can be expressed in the style of the symbolic interactionists, who have carried this tradition forward, by saying that to participate in a group is to share its symbolization of itself and its situation—to "speak its language," as we say.[28]

This social theory conceives of communication as the arousal in one's self of the response which one has aroused

[27] *Ibid.*, pp. 232f.

[28] For this notion, see Anselm L. Strauss, *Mirrors and Masks* (New York: The Free Press, 1959), esp. pp. 148ff. A general treatment in the tradition of George Herbert Mead is given by Tamotsu Shibutani, *Society and Personality* (Englewood Cliffs, N.J.: Prentice-Hall, Inc., 1961).

in the other; you know what you have said when you know how others respond to what you say. This is the triadic structure of communication which formed the basic model of Mead's conception: (1) the gesture—a cry, a call, pointing, whatever; (2) the adjustive response made by the other; and (3) the taking of the role of the other on the part of the self, through which the meaning of the adjustive response is grasped.[29] It is quite obvious that this structure fits a problem-solving notion of communication.

Within this triadic model, Mead attempted to account for the emergence of mind, symbol, and communication as well as the self who is related to others and participant in a society. Hence, a serious attempt has been made to give an account of the emergence of mind in evolutionary process. Rationality, then, refers to the consistency of the process—the type of response which we call out in others should be called out in ourselves if the process is rational. There is thus a correspondence of the outside and the inside in the rational development of the process. The key elements in the emergence of this rational process are self and sociality. The reflexive self—the self which discovers itself in taking the role of the other in response to its own gestures—becomes the medium of rationality.

One of Mead's most telling examples of the emergence of mind is the experience of Helen Keller. In his interpretation of this event, he sees Helen Keller gaining self and thought when, through the contact experience with water which Mary Sullivan brought about, she achieved symbolization and communication—arousing in herself by symbols the responses which she aroused in others.[30] In other words, she achieves mind, thought, and self in a full sense through *significant* gestures—through learning to respond inwardly as others are responding to the same gestures and sounds.

George Herbert Mead's brilliant achievement, inade-

[29] Mead, *op. cit.*, p. 222.
[30] *Ibid.*, p. 226.

quately summarized here, never escapes the ambiguities of the behavioristic framework. The limitations of this framework are, to be sure, much less serious for such a creative mind—especially in his later work, which unfortunately had much less influence on social science. Social scientists were most attracted by the possibilities of a thorough-going social determinism on the basis of his conception of the social self; unlike Mead, they were quite willing to pass over the ambiguities in his theory of the self.[31] The problem in his account comes down to an inadequate notion of the self as centered being—as an "I." Mead gave a brilliant account of the social self—the "me." He took for granted the role of the "I" in the emergence of the "me," with the consequent risk that the "I" would be dissolved into the "me." This became even more likely, as we shall see, when the theory was amalgamated with Freudian notions. Even in Mead's own account, except in his work which is drawn together in *The Philosophy of the Act,* the "I" tends to be assimilated into the "me," or the social self—the "I" comes to be what society creates, or the social self becomes *the* self.[32]

The "me" is the self seen through the eyes of the other. When I see myself through the other person's interpretation of my gesture, or from the role of the generalized other, I discover what the community understands and expects me to be; hence, taking the role of the generalized other is see-

[31] The deterministic character of this formulation is quite evident in the notion of the "generalized other"—for it is in this form that the social process, or community, enters as a determining factor into the individual's thinking (*ibid.*, p. 232). This understanding is taken as the notion of the unity of the self, which becomes a "reflection" of the social process (*ibid.*, p. 221).

[32] George Herbert Mead, *The Philosophy of the Act* (Chicago: University of Chicago Press, 1938), where an approach is made in terms of subjectivity. For the general problem, see the critical treatment by Paul E. Pfuetze, *The Social Self* (New York: Bookman Associates, Inc., 1954), esp. p. 92f.

ing myself in terms of communal expectations. I become a social self through the community, or the community creates man in its own image—the community as expression of the evolutionary process becomes the "deity" or creator. Man is thus the reflection of the society through which he is created—the internal expression of the process of communication within the society. The "me" is the social process in its internal expression as the social self. The "me" is the product of the mores of the community, albeit shaped through internal relations rather than through an adaptive process of external relations. One need no longer persuade man to obey the rules of the game prevailing in the community, since he is merely a creation of those rules—he is the internal expression of the rules. The self is, as Mead expressed it so well in giving an account of his theory, a social structure arising in social experience.[33]

The social self—the "me"—is situated in a social environment and gains its definition of that situation, its perception of its situation, through the perspective on itself which it gains from the role of the generalized other. Granted an impulse life without any particular form, the form and content of the self are received through the community. This is an aspect of W. I. Thomas's notion of the definition of the situation.[34] The "me" is the self-objectification which comes in social process. It is the objectified self. This "me" structure reflects the world of social habit and social code. The "me" is socially determined. It is social process come to self-expression in mind, self, and society.

The reduction of the self to the social self breaks the triadic structure of the act which formed Mead's model. This reduction negates the basic model from which it is

[33] Pfuetze, *ibid.*, p. 102. The "I" is a phase of novelty in this process, as Paul Pfuetze notes; but the social self became the principal concern of social science.

[34] *Social Behavior and Personality*, edited by E. H. Volkart (New York: Social Science Research Council, 1951), pp. 220f. Note the roots of this conception also in Robert Cooley's notion of the primary group and the "mirror effect."

derived. Of the three elements in the model—gesture, response, and perception of the gesture through the response—only the latter two elements come to expression in the notion of the social self. The "me" cannot be *source* of the gesture, since the "me" comes to be through awareness of response to the gesture. The actor's gesture—the movement in which the triadic structure originates—is presupposed. However, the "I" through whom the gesture originates cannot be presupposed in the account without reducing the "I" to the "me," and this is precisely what has happened among the social scientists, with some notable exceptions, who have gained most from Mead's important breakthrough. The initiation of the gesture presupposes the "I" and the relatedness of the "I" to that toward which it moves; moreover, the understanding of the meaning of the gesture for the other presupposes "meaning" and grasp of "meaning." In general, sociality and meaning are presupposed as the milieu in which the "me" emerges, and the initiating gesture of the "I" is the element in which those presuppositions come to focus. The "I"-who-gestures and the "I"-who-interprets-the-gesture in his response are both presupposed in the account of the emergence of mind, self, and society. Judging from his later work, George Herbert Mead was far more sensitive to this set of problems than those who borrowed his ideas for their development of the socially determined self.[35]

Sociality and meaning are presupposed in any conversation of gestures, as well as on higher levels of symbolic activity. Social existence presupposes communication; in turn, attempts to communicate presuppose concern for the response of the other. This concern, in other words, is a social dimension to selfhood which is presupposed in any account of the emergence of the social self.[36] The fact that we *can* communicate is the unquestioned background of

[35] For a discussion of this problem, see Maurice Natanson, *The Social Dynamics of George Herbert Mead* (Washington, D.C.: Public Affairs Press, 1956), esp. p. 19 and *passim*.

[36] Clifford Geertz's interesting hypothesis on the priority of symbol in the emergence of mind would thus be complemented by the intrinsic

our daily life with children, parents, and others. We realize that our communication breaks down. We do not adequately express what we mean. We do not always listen. We do not always understand or interpret properly. And yet we continue to communicate and to try to understand, and we believe firmly that, given time and attention, we can understand. Mead is asking how this is possible, but his question is not radical enough. He assumes our desire and need to communicate and the relatedness of "I" and "other" which such a desire presupposes. Mead moved away from the external relations of a mechanistic model, but he did not move far enough toward the internal relations of sociality which are presupposed in any evolutionary account of mind. The movement toward the other presupposes a belonging-to-the-other, even as an understanding of the other presupposes an internal relatedness of meanings. The "I"-who-gestures opens a process in consciousness which is already present as the substratum of the relatedness between "I" and "other." An account of the social self which passes over this presupposition simply dissolves the first element of the triadic structure (the gesture) into social objectification. Put another way, the self emerges in social process because it is already social. Symbol is thus the actualization of sociality as mind and the medium of the self's participation in otherness.

---

sociality of existence; symbol actualizes this sociality as mediation but gains its power by participation in relatedness. We shall discuss this under "concern for response" (Chapter 4). We need not fall into the hopeless task of trying to remove the mists which cloud the retrospective horizon of prehistory: Geertz's argument is in terms of symbol as the logical presupposition of mind in understanding the data of prehistory; in turn, the presupposition of symbol is the social nature of reality; the actualization of that social reality as mind (intentional consciousness in a life-world) takes place in the process of symbolization, which is the "how" of organic cultural transformation. See Clifford Geertz, "The Growth of Culture and the Evolution of Mind," in *Theories of Mind*, edited by Jordan Scher (New York: The Free Press, 1962), pp. 713–740. On the concept of reality as social, see Charles Hartshorne, *Reality as a Social Process* (New York: The Free Press, 1953), esp. Chs. 1–3, 5.

Social interrelatedness forms the substratum of the initial gesture in the triadic structure. The movement to take the role of the other enters here as a movement toward the relationship to which we belong—seeing ourselves in relationship to the other.[37] There is more initiated by the "I" and presupposed in the "I" than Mead credits in his account. The "I" not only discovers meaning in the other's response but also gestures to gain this response. This interpretative activity by the other is a creative work—giving meaning to the gesture, shaping it. Conversation is creative, even when we know a language and perhaps the more so as the language becomes familiar. The other listens—gives attention—and even here we speak of creative listening; indeed, a whole school of psychological therapy has been built upon creative listening through which the other comes to be himself. Self and other create, and are created, in their social experience.

The reduction of the "I" to the "me" produced a basic paradox in Mead's formulation—a paradox which occurs again and again in subsequent adaptations of Mead's work. The paradox can be stated thus: selves emerge in social experience through communication, and yet a social process of communication presupposes selves. Selves and social process presuppose each other. Mead certainly opened the broad lines for a conception of the social self. However, his account is deficient in two ways: (1) it bypasses the relatedness—the sociality—which underlies the notions of gesture and response; (2) it passes over the centrality of the "I" in the emergence of the "me."

Our task is not to develop a critique of Mead except as

[37] Alfred Schutz's discussion of the reciprocity of perspectives—our imputation to the other of a similar typification of common objects which have similar relevance for practical purposes—also presupposes the social nature of reality; the pregiven interrelatedness cannot be constructed in external determination without the kind of paradox which George Herbert Mead's analysis discloses. See Alfred Schutz, *The Problem of Social Reality, Collected Papers* (The Hague: Martinus Nijhoff, 1962), Vol. 1, pp. 11f.

this bears on the development of the human sciences. This historical retrospect is intended to clarify the problems in the understanding of man with which social science has wrestled. The human sciences were much less influenced by Mead's rationalism than by his notion of the socially determined self. However, this notion of the social self loses its rational character under the influence of a Freudian model, so that the socially determined self becomes a self which is largely the product of unconscious forces. This transformation of Mead's conception has its foundation in the instability of the triadic structure which we have already noted, since the significance of the "I" can easily be obscured in Mead's model.

Despite these limitations, Mead contributed significantly to social science by breaking with mechanistic notions of externally related forces. He moved social science toward a more organic notion of social process in which self and other—self and society—are internally related. The term "interaction" emerged to express this notion of internally related processes of gesture, response, interpretation, and communication. New forms emerge in social experience. These forms are not produced by social "forces." The mechanistic model is overcome; an internally related process has taken its place, and the way is open for dealing more adequately with man in his life-world. The new form is "mind"; the self is both created by and creator of this emergent form. Hence, self, symbol, and sociality are the parameters of the life-world. The triadic model was too unstable to preserve those dimensions of Mead's contributions. The instability of the relation of the "I" to the "me" in this formulation has continued to plague the human sciences. Hence, the break with mechanistic thought produced its own series of paradoxes, and the possibilities inherent in the pragmatic approach were obscured.

Other theoretical developments in the human sciences were also moving away from mechanistic models. Although

Émile Durkheim originally worked with a mechanistic model, it became clear in his study of suicide that social control presupposed an internal relation of units within the social whole.[38] Max Weber's influence also did much to accentuate the role of internally appropriated values and ideas in social process. Robert Cooley's notion of the primary group and W. I. Thomas's formulation of the "definition of the situation" also contributed to overcoming the mechanistic model. To this extent, Mead's conception of the social self needs to be set within the broader context of social-scientific developments; in fact, this fuller picture helps us to evaluate his positive contributions more adequately. Mead was in harmony with the social-scientific tradition in playing down the creative role of the "I." In terms of our broader concern with man's valuing activity, the human sciences tended to see this valuing as a product of social determination. Man's choosing and valuing were interpreted in terms of the social formation of the self, so that his sense of determining his course was only a reflection of the course expected of him by his society. Simple notions of social determination had been dropped with the dissolution of mechanistic theories, but a much more radical social determination had taken its place—the social self.

### *LIMITATIONS AND POSSIBILITIES*

We opened the question of man in the human sciences by considering the paradox that a science of man subordinates man to his environment, whereas physical sciences have enhanced man's control over his environment. The major step in overcoming this ambiguity was accomplished through George Herbert Mead's notion of the emergence of the self; the self is now seen as internally related to the emergence

[38] See the discussion of this transformation in Parsons, *The Structure of Social Action*, Ch. 10. See also the author's article "Society and Morality in the French Tradition."

of culture; in this view, as the self is conformed to its culture, it realizes its true freedom and possibilities, although novelty emerges from the uniqueness of perspective of each "I" on the process. What had seemed a domination of alien forces —the society and its social process—can now be reinterpreted as domination by the structures appropriate to the self, since the form and content of the self are culturally determined. The culture is now understood through the internal relatedness of self and society, so that the task of social analysis comes down to understanding the direction in which this social determination is moving. When the social scientist discovers the forces shaping the self and its destiny, he is discovering himself, since the self is the product of societal processes.

This resolution of the paradox of social science reflects the behavioristic background of Mead's thought rather than the important contributions of his inquiry. To the extent that this social determination triumphed in the appropriation of his ideas, his behaviorism won out over his basic insights. Mead's triadic model, as we have seen, cannot be understood without maintaining a proper tension between the "I" and the "me." When the "I" is reduced to the socially determined self, this tension dissolves and the model fails to give an adequate account of mind, self, or society.[39]

We also noted the paradox that mechanistic thought *exhorted* men to obey laws of nature which were assumed to be inscribed in the social process. Mead's formulation of the social self could have made a significant contribution

[39] The "me" can be translated as social role in later development of this basic insight. Erving Goffman's insightful treatment of "role distance" indicates the significance of the "I" in role analysis; nevertheless, he seems at times to contradict his own insights with a field notion of the "I" as a point which is determined by a constellation of roles. See his study *Asylums* (Garden City, N.Y.: Anchor Books, 1961) for empirical examples of role distance; and see the theoretical treatment in *Encounters* (Indianapolis, Ind.: Bobbs-Merrill Co., Inc., 1961), esp. pp. 151f. Goffman's work is cited as the most insightful treatment of role; for the handling of this problem in terms of secondary structures, see Chapters 4 and 5 of this text—attempts to do justice to both "I" and "me" in social process.

to clarifying this ambiguity, since the social self is a social structure and reflects the social codes of the community, while at the same time the perspective of the self on those social codes is unique and sets itself against the determination of the community. However, the notion of the self as simply a unique perspective is quite inadequate to express the tension of self and society which the earlier, paradoxical formulation had disclosed. However much selves may be determined by social process, they also reshape that process according to their interests and values. These interests and values are more than unique perspectives; indeed, they reflect the constitutive role of the ego in social process. The significance of ideas and values in Max Weber's theory takes this creative tension of self and society much more seriously than the deterministic notions of the social self; however, even Weber's analysis placed value in an irrational sphere, so that social science simply took it as socially "given."[40] The instability in Mead's triadic structure likewise prevented his resolution of the paradox of social determination and human initiative. Only an adequate polarity between the notions of "I" and "me" can do justice to our social experience: on the one hand, human existence is socially structured; on the other, man's appropriation of those structures constitutes new meaning and possibility. An adequate appreciation of man's valuing and choosing has to take account of the social determination of the social self, but it also has to take account of the active, creative determination of social process by the self. The paradox of the mechanistic formulation is not overcome simply by internalizing social determination, although this was a significant advance.

If George Herbert Mead's basic insights can be formulated

[40] The dualism in Max Weber's understanding of reality is considered in more detail in Chapter 6. The two essays in which it is most strikingly expressed are "Politics as a Vocation" and "Science as a Vocation," in *From Max Weber's Essays in Sociology*, edited by Hans Gerth and C. Wright Mills (Fair Lawn, N.J.: Oxford University Press, 1946), Chs. 4 and 5; the significance of ideas and values, which Weber had documented in his work, was thus relegated to irrational forces.

in such a way as to protect both creativity and determination in social process—overcoming to this extent the limitations of the behavioristic tradition—then these dimensions can be seen in an adequate perspective. The presupposition of an adequate social theory is an adequate notion of the self in its valuing as well as in its social determination. The problem is essentially whether society determines the content of the self or furnishes the cultural and social milieu in which the self actualizes its freedom and fulfillment. If society provides the substance of the self, then freedom is basically to be found through conformity to the possibilities made available by society. If the self is more than an expression of social process, then freedom is the presupposition of culture, even as culture is the actualization and enrichment of human freedom and sociality.

A behavioristic framework prevented Mead from developing the full implications of pragmatism for a notion of the self. In a similar way, this behavioristic model shaped the difficulties and controversies of subsequent work in the human sciences. Despite these limitations, the breakthrough effected by Mead transformed the social sciences and opened the way to a significant advance in the understanding of social process. Unfortunately, the fruits of this breakthrough will not be harvested until the problem of the relationship between *creative self* and *social self* is adequately formulated. The scope and seriousness of this problem becomes quite evident in the ideological controversy which now divides the human sciences. Contemporary controversies are more than a heritage from George Herbert Mead, to be sure, but they revolve around the basic problems of self and sociality with which he struggled. They reflect ambiguities in the presuppositions of the scientific models; these are ambiguities, moreover, which will not yield to empirical refutation: this fact, more than any other, undoubtedly accounts for the bitterness which has characterized these controversies. However, we shall have to trace the course of present controversies before we can return to the relationship between *creative self* and *social self* (Chapter 4); the contemporary discussion raises the issue of the self in terms of conflicting evaluations of society, so the nature of true evaluation is the starting point for our methodological clarification.

## 2 *the debate within the social sciences*

The consequences of this unresolved issue are traced to the struggle between functionalists like Talcott Parsons and voluntarists like the late C. Wright Mills; the behaviorists merely say a pox on both your houses · This is really an ideological controversy—prescribing for society

THREE DOMINANT STYLES of social-scientific work developed during the first century of the human sciences. These styles are at odds over the nature and possibility of an evaluation of contemporary society by the sciences of man. The historical account in the preceding chapter clarified the nature of one of these styles—the physicalist approach, which reduces human processes to a product of external forces. This style persists in the human sciences but remains aloof from the controversy over evaluation of the social process. This physicalist style reduces problems of value to questions of fact; consequently, it treats values as irrelevant to science, as epiphenomenal to social process.

The debate in the human sciences is being conducted by two styles of social science—the functionalist and voluntarist styles.[1] This debate has its roots in differences over the

[1] This broad distinction will be refined and documented in the subsequent discussion. The perspective of the theory of action on contemporary society is stated most explicitly by Winston White in *Beyond Conformity* (New York: The Free Press, 1961). Similar themes are pursued by Talcott Parsons in his essay "Christianity and Modern Industrial Society," in *Religion, Culture and Society* (New York: John Wiley & Sons, Inc., 1964), pp. 273–298; the theoretical generalization of this perspective is given by Talcott Parsons in his essay "Evolutionary Universals in Society," *American Sociological Review*, Vol. XXIX, No. 3, June, 1964, pp. 339–357. Critiques of this functional perspective have been made from a variety of points of views; some of these critiques occur in two volumes of essays published in honor and memory of C. Wright Mills, who was the most

understanding of man and sociality. However, the controversy emerged over somewhat different issues which derive from this common root. The debate has centered on the evaluation of the quality of life which is being produced by a technological society. If this line of controversy is followed, it will lead back to the basic understanding of man which is at stake.

The seriousness of the controversy in the human sciences is aggravated by the growing influence of these sciences in the everyday affairs of the society. The most dramatic example is, of course, the role which the human sciences have played in the civil-rights struggle. The famous study of this issue by Gunnar Myrdal, *An American Dilemma*, the significance of social-scientific findings in the 1954 decision of the Supreme Court, and the present contributions of social science to problems of school integration are merely samples of the widespread use of the human sciences in the formation of public policy. The social impact of human science extends to economic policy on all levels, to general educational development, and to international and military strategies. Whether the actual findings of social science have a large or small influence in particular policies, the place of human science in contemporary culture is rather well established. This cultural significance gives special importance to the controversy over cultural values.

There are, to be sure, many other conflicts in the human sciences and particularly within special disciplines. Moreover, there are perspectives on the sciences of man which are not even represented in this major controversy; these

---

outspoken antagonist of functionalism: *The New Sociology* (Fair Lawn, N.J.: Oxford University Press, 1964), edited by Irving Louis Horowitz; *Sociology on Trial* (Englewood Cliffs, N.J.: Prentice-Hall, Inc., 1963), edited by Maurice Stein and Arthur Vidick. In addition, several essays in *The Social Theories of Talcott Parsons*, edited by Max Black (Englewood Cliffs, N.J.: Prentice-Hall, Inc., 1961), raise fundamental questions about the implicit values of this theoretical approach, especially the essay by Andrew Hacker, "Sociology and Ideology."

other perspectives have not yet won sufficient support to enter the lists; indeed, the present inquiry is informed by such a perspective, as will become evident in the course of this discussion.[2] Within these limits, certain major issues of the human sciences do come to focus in the present controversy over social criticism; hence, this conflict can furnish clues to the problems and possibilities of a science of man.

Controversy is not new to the human sciences. From their inception, they have suffered bitter conflicts on fundamental questions. One of the earliest instances was the break between John Stuart Mill and Auguste Comte—a break with some similarities to the present controversy.[3] Auguste Comte set forth a theory which Don Martindale has helpfully characterized as organic functionalism—the notion of an organic system in which every part could be understood through its function within the whole. Mill's view of science presupposed individual perspectives which could be tested for truth in open discussion—a notion involving individual differences if not radical conflicts. However, this classic schism in perspectives never came to open debate and centered much more upon different notions of science: on the one hand, Mill found Comte's point of view increasingly dogmatic; on the other hand, Comte assumed that a true scientific theory was something to be accepted and acclaimed.

[2] One could identify the perspective which informs this analysis under the broad rubric of phenomenology; for a discussion of this perspective, see Herbert Spiegelberg, *The Phenomenological Movement*, 2 vols. (The Hague: Martinus Nijhoff, 1960); for a discussion of this perspective in psychology, see *Existence* (New York: Basic Books, Inc., 1958), edited by Rollo May, Ernest Angel, and Henri F. Ellenberger. Another, much less common perspective is rooted in the Whiteheadian tradition and may ultimately prove to be one of the most significant ways of approaching a science of human phenomena; for a critical discussion of Talcott Parsons' theory from this perspective, see Widick Schroeder, "Talcott Parsons' Ordering of the Sciences: A Résumé and Critique," *Journal for the Scientific Study of Religion*, Vol. IV, No. 2, Spring, 1965, pp. 162–174.

[3] For J. S. Mill's view on this difference of perspectives, see his volume *Auguste Comte and Positivism* (London: Trubair, 1866); for a summary of the differences, see Lucien Lévy-Bruhl, "Comte et Mill," *Révue Philosophique de la France et L'Étranger*, Vol. XLVI, 1898, pp. 627–644.

John Stuart Mill and Auguste Comte had very different notions of the operation of society and, consequently, different interpretations of the cultural task of the human sciences, since their models for the relation of knowledge to reality were quite different. This controversy turned more upon the nature of science than upon social criticism, but its implications for the organization of society were comparable to the contemporary discussions. The next century was marked by rapid growth in the sciences of man and a growing significance of fundamental debates within the disciplines.

Comte and Mill shared a positivistic interpretation of the nature of science; in fact, it was Mill's positivistic leanings which first attracted him to the works of Auguste Comte. The positivistic perspective has been the source of endless controversy within the human sciences; indeed, the issue is far from settled and may never be settled, since it turns upon a fundamental question in philosophical interpretation. In the field of psychology, that issue has come to new prominence with the resurgence of behavioristic theory; hence, it is premature to consider the issue resolved.[4] Nevertheless, this issue has receded into the background in recent decades. Conflicts between theories are stated now in terms of different models of personal and social process. We shall follow this general trend in the present inquiry, but the positivistic issue underlies some of the basic questions which confront the human sciences. Thus, we bow to fashion in the contemporary discussion without losing sight of the basic issues. Ultimately, the differences in evaluation of the emerging society come back to differences in interpretation of social process; this is, in essence, the positivistic question which seemed to have been carefully interred a few years ago. The

[4] For some discussion of these issues in psychology, see May *et al.* (eds.), *op. cit.* See also *Behaviorism and Phenomenology: Contrasting Bases for Modern Psychology*, edited by T. W. Wann (Chicago: University of Chicago Press, 1964).

most interesting aspect of this situation is that Talcott Parsons, whose work *The Structure of Social Action* dislodged positivistic interpretation in the social sciences, has effected a revival of this perspective through his theory of action.

The description of the perennial character of certain conflicts in the human sciences is not intended to disparage the century of achievements in these disciplines. Many gains have been made in theoretical and empirical work. Certain concepts have achieved widespread acceptance, so that it is possible to speak of this field of inquiry as a "discipline." Nevertheless, there are basic issues which have not been resolved; as happens so often in a discipline, certain unresolved problems are dropped for periods of time, only to reappear in a new guise after many years. The principal issues which have plagued the human sciences during the past century continue beneath the surface, but the focus of the present controversy is upon evaluations of contemporary society. This new focus is quite understandable in the light of the enlarged role of the human sciences in the decision-making processes of the society; at a time when social science was an aspect of social philosophy, its social critiques were quite secondary to the philosophical debates which shaped its contexts and terms. The social sciences are coming of age and now face the task of defining the scope and significance of their cultural responsibility.

The issue among these sciences is not whether they should enter significantly into the decision-making processes of society. That influence is more or less taken for granted now. The problem is, rather, the legitimacy of critiques directed against contemporary society on the basis of social scientific study. The theorists who work with "conflict" models have tended to be rather critical of the trends toward conformity and organizational control which they discern in recent social changes. The "equilibrium" theorists, on the other hand, take a positive view of these social changes, although they recognize the tensions and strains which are being generated through these social transformations.[5] Differences in evaluation of social change are inseparable from the conceptions of man implicit in the contrasting models of social process. This, at least, is a fundamental hypothesis of the present inquiry—a hypothesis which even on this preliminary level points to the seriousness of the present controversy. Radically different views of reality are involved in this struggle within the human sciences; these differences become manifest in the conflicting interpretations which are being made of contemporary society. However, the conflicting interpretations are rooted in perspectives on the social process, and these perspectives are determined by the social models with which the two groups are working.[6]

## *THREE STYLES OF SOCIAL SCIENCE*

Edward Shils has identified three clusters of sociological orientation and procedure: the manipulative, the alienative, and the consensual. These characterizations are drawn from the stance which each sociological approach takes toward public policy. The manipulative stance sees sociology as a resource for the rulers in controlling those who are subject to their power. The oppositional, or alienative, stance understands the role of sociology to be one of criticism of the society from the outside. The consensual stances takes its place within the social process and sees the role of sociology as enhancement of self-understanding and relationships. This is a useful categorization, since it refers to research methods

[5] The significance of these differences was acknowledged by the American Sociological Society in their meeting, September, 1965, where the place of "Conflict versus Equilibrium" was made a principal theme.

[6] These differing conceptions of man and social process are also of crucial importance in the selection of methods of social research and in the role ascribed to mathematical manipulation of social data. C. Wright Mills appreciated the significance of these differences in methodology and was particularly sensitive to their import for the selection of problems for research, although he did not always discuss such issues in an elegant way. See his volume *The Sociological Imagination* (Fair Lawn, N.J.: Oxford University Press, 1959).

and conceptions of sociology as well as to interpretations of the role of social science in the society. Shifting somewhat away from Edward Shils' ideological characterization of the types, we can recognize three styles of sociological orientation which he has apprehended in these clusters: physical sociology, functional sociology, and voluntaristic sociology. It is difficult to identify this third model without introducing ideological terms such as "voluntaristic," since the third type takes for granted an ideological dimension in social-scientific perspectives. We can, perhaps, approach this style most objectively by treating it in the tradition of Max Weber.[7]

Today, the lines of battle are actually drawn between the functionalists and the voluntarists. The functionalists, whom Edward Shils calls consensualists, are primarily represented by the theory of action, although functionalism is too variegated a phenomenon in the social sciences to be represented by a single theory. The voluntarists, whom Edward Shils calls the alienative sociologists, are principally represented by C. Wright Mills, Maurice Stein, and the more humanistic social critics. Our introductory discussion of the debate within the social sciences will center around the issues raised by these contending styles—functionalist and voluntarist. However, the significance of what we have chosen to call physical sociology should not be underestimated; a few

[7] Edward Shils, "The Calling of Sociology," in *Theories of Society* (New York: The Free Press, 1961), Vol. 2, esp. pp. 1435–1441. A programmatic statement of the physicalist perspective can be found in "Cultural, Behavioral and Ecological Perspectives in the Study of Social Organization," by Otis Dudley Duncan and Leo F. Schnore, *The American Journal of Sociology*, Vol. LXV, No. 2, pp. 132–146. A general treatment of methodological issues in functionalism can be found in *Functionalism in the Social Sciences* (Philadelphia: American Academy of Political and Social Science, 1965), Monograph No. 5 in a series sponsored by the American Academy of Political and Social Science, edited by Don Martindale. No particular brief is held for this nomenclature, but it will serve to distinguish Shils' types without the ideological overtones of his formulation; we cannot do more than identify broad styles of scientific investigation of social processes until some systematic framework can be developed within which these perspectives can be located.

additional remarks on this latter style may indicate its significance.

The physical style in the human sciences is represented by behaviorism in psychology, ecology and demography in sociology, and the search for structural determinants of behavior in social psychology and political science; for example, many studies of voting behavior are in this style. The guiding principle of this style is the notion that human action and social process can be understood as a concatenation of external forces which are observable, quantifiable, and calculable. The *model* for this style of social science is the work of the physical sciences. The *credo* of this approach is the dogma that scientific investigation requires understanding, prediction, and control—no matter what its subject matter. If a subject matter resists this kind of science, then there is no science of that subject matter. The notion of exact measurement in this style presupposes "objective," external relations between entities or concentrations of force —relations which can be mathematically formulated; consequently, aspects of social process which are not amenable to such measurement are simply disregarded. We do full justice to the fundamental aim of this sociological style when we categorize it as a physical style, since its intention is to treat the human field as a physical subject matter in no way different from the subject matter of chemistry or nuclear physics; moreover, these physical fields are interpreted according to a Newtonian rather than an Einsteinian model.

We shall not treat this physical style in the immediate consideration of the debate within the human sciences, but we shall attempt to deal with it systematically in subsequent discussion. By and large, the physicalists are not given to theorizing or debating with functionalists and voluntarists in the social sciences. The physicalists are busy carrying on their research, accumulating masses of data, and ordering the data mathematically; they are engaged in extensive demographic and ecological studies in metropolitan areas and, indeed, throughout the world. They tend, when distracted from their accumulation of data and mathematical manipulation of their materials, to disparage any other kind of social-scientific research, not because they are opposed to the activities of humanistic reflection per se, but simply because they do not consider such work scientific. We recognize that the positivistic dogma on scientific method prevents the physicalists from questioning the adequacy of their methods. As we turn to the debate between functionalism and voluntarism in the human sciences, we acknowledge, therefore, that a principal style of social science stands aloof from the debate and says, "A pox on both your houses!"

Edward Shils' rhetoric in discussing these differences already signals his personal stake in the controversy. The same can be said of the proponents of models of conflict. When, for example, one reads C. Wright Mills' *The Sociological Imagination,* even after discounting Mills' rhetoric, one is struck by the deep feelings of antagonism that had been generated. Much of the antagonism in the controversy came to focus in the struggle between Talcott Parsons and C. Wright Mills just before the latter's death; however, it would be superficial and, indeed, would obscure the issues if one were to let that personal aspect of the controversy obscure the fundamental differences.[8] We are dealing here with basic questions in the sciences of man—questions whose seriousness is marked by the increasing passion with which

[8] An extreme example of distortions introduced by the personal stake of the participants is the essay by Edward Shils which we have cited. For example, he states: "It is still a proud boast of some sociologists that sociology is an 'oppositional' science. Some of those who take pride in the oppositional character of sociology are former Marxists or quasi-Marxists—who, without giving their allegiance to Marxism, wish nonetheless to retain its original disposition" (*ibid.*, p. 1422). This statement (the use of "Marxism" as an epithet of opprobrium) and similar remarks throughout the essay disclose the deep ideological roots of the controversy. Talcott Parsons' critique of C. Wright Mills' *The Power Elite* brings out some of the theoretical differences between these perspectives; see "The Distribution of Power in American Society," in *Structure and Process in Modern Societies* (New York: The Free Press, 1960), Ch. 6.

the differences are being discussed, but questions whose resolution will come only by moving away from rhetoric to fundamental clarification.

There is a tendency to dismiss opponents of action theory as disoriented. We have noted Shils' use of the term "alienation." He also calls them quasi-Marxists. Alienation in the human sciences refers to strains which are created by social dislocation. This is the line which Bennett Berger took in his review of two volumes of essays by friends, collaborators, and fellow scientists in honor of C. Wright Mills in 1964. These volumes, *The New Sociology* and *Sociology on Trial,* cover a wide variety of subjects. Many of the essays are critical of the action theorists. In his review in *The New York Times,* Bennett Berger disposes of these writers as representing an antiestablishment mentality—thus attributing opposition to functional theory to a dislocation in social status.[9] He pictures these antagonists as "angry young men" who are opposing the "sell-out" by sociology to bourgeois values. He also notes their tendency to follow Mills' line of seeking relevance for sociology through concern with the "big-range" problems. Berger's attempt to reduce these attacks on functional theory to a struggle for status, thus dissolving the substance of the critiques, fails, since a good many of these essayists are rather well established. When this attempt to dismiss the critics has failed, Berger finally attributes their disaffection to a desire to enlist social science in left-wing, liberal causes—a desire which Berger considers illegitimate.[10]

Bennett Berger's review, although superficial, is very

[9] *The New York Times Book Review*, September 20, 1964, p. 7.

[10] *Ibid.* This is an indication that the line taken by Edward Shils is not idiosyncratic and that we are dealing with a discussion of scientific perspectives which has devolved to the level of ideological accusations. The deeper problem confronting the social sciences when a difference of perspectives arises is created by the antitheoretical, antiphilosophical bias in their development; the net effect is to assume that differences from a dominant theory reflect "inadequate socialization," sheer perverseness, or disloyalty to one's national heritage—intellectual, if not political, treason.

suggestive, since it finally comes to the focus which is most central to this controversy—the legitimate and illegitimate role of the human sciences in evaluating social process; by implication, one can then examine the perspectives on society generated by the models with which these schools are approaching the development of the society. It is noteworthy that Edward Shils comes to a similar focus in his essay on "The Calling of Sociology" and makes very similar charges against those who differ with the functional model. To a large extent, Berger's review and Shils' essay are rhetorical, but there is sufficient rhetoric on the other side to elicit this type of response. At one point, Berger expresses his disappointment that the two volumes do not deal with the epistemological and methodological issues which are at the root of the disputes. The same disappointment can be expressed at Berger's and Shils' contributions, since only such discussion can move the controversy beyond rhetoric.

### *THE DEBATE OVER SOCIAL VALUES*

This controversy will smolder and become more damaging to the development of the disciplines if the root issues are buried. The difficulty with the action theorists, at this point, is that they are simply astonished that anyone fails to see the "truth"; they seem to be waiting for acquiescence on the part of those who are "holding out." This is far from a realistic appraisal of the state of affairs, as can be seen from a brief consideration of the basic issues in the two volumes which were published in honor of C. Wright Mills.

The basic concerns are evident in the two volumes of essays—*Sociology on Trial* and *The New Sociology*[11]—concerns which bear directly on the significance of the human sciences to the decision-making processes of society. The writers in these volumes are rather uniformly concerned with a qualitative evaluation of contemporary society. They

[11] See fn. 1 of this chapter.

are interested in questions of substance, which is to say that they are not only attentive to the technological changes in process and organization—how the society is functioning—but they are also interested in what these changes are doing *for man* and *to man*. This concern with the *what* which is produced in social process also characterizes the writings of C. Wright Mills. It was the source of his major conflicts with Talcott Parsons, and it characterizes the opposition which Daniel Foss and Andrew Hacker express toward Talcott Parsons' interpretation of the political process. This is not to suggest that the action theorists have no concern with *what* the society is producing; for example, Talcott Parsons was very critical of the McCarthy movement as a deviant trend in American life. Talcott Parsons has his own base line of values, integral to the frame of reference within which he carries on his social analysis; his fundamental values are the maximization of individual choice and the relative independence of the scientific enterprise. The McCarthy movement attacked both of these values.[12] By and large, however, *what* a technological society is producing fits the kind of thing which action theorists believe should be occurring—increasing differentiation and growing complexity of organization fit their model; hence, the action theorists are impatient with criticisms of this society from the perspective of another model. We can generalize this first issue by suggesting that both groups are concerned with an evaluation of the social process, but the way in which they make their evaluations differs according to their models of the social process.

The authors of these two volumes are also sensitive to

[12] See Parsons, "Evolutionary Universals in Society," for a theoretical generalization of these values which form his "empirical" criteria of social development; in this sense, the McCarthy movement is a sign of maladjustment in the adaptation of the United States to its postwar responsibilities in the world. For the diagnosis of McCarthyism, see Parsons, "Social Strains in America," in *Structure and Process in Modern Societies*, Ch. 7.

the engagement of the human sciences in the processes of society. This is particularly true of John Seeley and Barrington Moore, but it is generally true of this whole group of thinkers. When they call for social engagement and concern with the big problems confronting society, they are partly calling for consciousness by the sciences of man that they are already implicated in social processes. They are calling attention to the fact that the human sciences are a dimension of the social enterprise. They are challenging the notion of a neutral science of man. They are pointing to the perplexing issue of social responsibility in the human sciences. How, indeed, can one engage in these sciences without altering the social process? What are the criteria which determine the responsible exercise of this cultural role?

In contrast to some of the charges which are leveled against this social criticism—alienative, quasi-Marxist, angry, etc.—one gains the impression that the heart of the controversy is to be found in the different evaluations which are being made of the contemporary social scene. Both groups have concerns for *what* is being produced by the new society; but the functional group trusts the processes of technological transformation, and the voluntarists do not.[13] Both groups seem to be aware of the social impact of the human sciences, but the voluntarists seem much more sensitive to the ambiguity of this impact; one gains the impression that the functionalists trust their "science" much more and feel more confident that their *scientific* judgments are enunciations of "truth." Thus, beneath the rhetoric of the debate, one finds a common concern with the *product* of the society but a sharply divergent evaluation of that product; moreover, despite the acerbity of the controversy, both groups are aware of the increasing impact of the human

[13] One of the most incisive critiques of the effects of American social development was made by Maurice Stein in his *Eclipse of Community* (Princeton, N.J.: Princeton University Press, 1960); note also that a number of the studies upon which his interpretation is based also express a critique of emerging values.

sciences on the society; furthermore, the action theorists seem to have much less concern about the ideological aspects of their own impact and much more concern with the distorted ideological impact of their opponents.[14]

The degeneration of this conflict to ideological controversy came to full expression in Winston White's book *Beyond Conformity*.[15] Although no single author can be taken to speak for action theory, since many lines of development have already branched out from this general approach, Winston White's monograph expresses more adequately than any other statement the attitude of the functionalists toward other models of social process. White discriminates between science and ideology: action theory is scientific understanding of social process, giving an account of the way things are; other theories are more or less ideological, which is to say deformed by partiality, prejudice, or particular value commitments. Our hypothesis that different models of social process are at stake in this controversy would thus be converted into the hypothesis that a *science of man* (action theory) is in conflict with relatively less scientific perspectives (each to some degree tainted by subjective values, strains, and interests).

Winston White actually takes up a great number of social critics, many of whom would not consider themselves to be operating within the discipline of human science. (White's sample of social critics is drawn from intellectual journals and thus includes literary figures and social philosophers.) His evaluation of these critics bears out our preceding identification of two issues: (1) what the society is producing; (2) interested engagement in social process.

[14] With the "objectivity" which characterizes the essay cited above, Edward Shils remarks: "Both the manipulative and alienated forms of sociological research, and theories associated with them, are afflicted by intellectual deformity. . . . Consensual sociology is alone capable of satisfying the requirements of an adequate theory and of a proper relationship with policy" (*op. cit.*, p. 1440).

[15] White, *op. cit.*

Winston White offers an alternative interpretation of what is being produced by the emergence of complex societies. He sets these events within an evolutionary hypothesis which has been developed in the theory of action. The evolutionary process is one of specialization and of reintegration into more complex wholes. The specialization of functions in human society has increased through technological control of the environment, but this differentiation of functions has also required the dissolution of the ascriptive ties which constituted the fabric of simpler societies. This process creates much more flexibility and movement for individuals, and at the same time it generates larger organizations through which their activities can be coordinated. Thus, the arguments for atomization of individual units and increasing conformity to organization have some warrant in the actual state of affairs, but they are partial interpretations of the total process. Despite the inevitable strains which are experienced in such social transformation, the resources of the society are immeasurably increased through functional specialization, and choices are multiplied. Thus, freedom, as White interprets it, increases with social complexity; organization and social integration increase simultaneously with increasing freedom of the individual units. Both the moralizers and the reformers have seen part of the truth of this process, according to White, but they have missed the full scope of developments both because of their prior value commitments and for lack of a comprehensive social theory with which to grasp the total process. Since White has an adequate theory, he knows what is *really* happening in the new society.[16]

Although this summary of White's interpretation of con-

[16] Winston White's imputation of values to the process of social differentiation and increasing organizational complexity is only a particularly clear statement of the social evaluation which is implicit in the theory of action. So far as an understanding of man forms a common term between theological ethical perspectives and social analysis, the affinities in social critiques between these disciplines, however latent, become quite significant. The general significance of these affinities will be traced in Chapters 5 and 6.

temporary society is much too condensed, the main thrust of his views is represented. He proposes a science of society to replace the ideologies of the moralizers and reformers. In this way, the cultural task of human science can be executed responsibly, and unwarranted criticisms of social process will be discouraged. A proper science of society will give us knowledge of what is really happening. We shall then see that the evolution of complex society brings a ". . . greater mobilization of resources, increased capacity to pursue whatever goals are deemed desirable, and greater freedom of choice for more individuals."[17]

Winston White's statement of the issues accentuates the crucial significance of a social model in appraising the course of social process. If one grants the increasing importance of the human sciences in the decision-making of the society—even if indirectly through popularizations, and most social scientists would grant this—it becomes quite clear in White's presentation that the model of the process is decisive for the evaluation of the product of that process.[18] White's principal line of argument is that his view is scientific—thus, that the model which he uses is a scientific model which can deal comprehensively with the actual states of affairs, while the models employed by the moralizers and reformers are distorted by their value commitments. One can see immediately, however, that the principal difference on the level of evaluation is that White's model implicitly trusts the evolutionary process and rationalizes what happens as beneficial to man, whereas the views of the moralizers and reformers, in one way or another, question the beneficence of this process. For example, all groups might agree that the number of choices has increased, but White evaluates this positively, in accordance with his model, and the other

[17] White, *op. cit.*, p. 211.

[18] Maurice Duverger, who takes a dim view of the theoretical confusion in the social sciences, acknowledges their growing importance in the public realm; see his monograph, *An Introduction to the Social Sciences*, translated by Malcolm Anderson (New York: Frederick A. Praeger, Inc., 1964), p. 11.

group questions the quality of the available choices and the capacity of the choosers to make adequate choices in this kind of society. White is even ready to grant, if only momentarily, that his perspective might be considered ideological, but he disposes of this problem by accepting the prevailing values in the American society as valid. Thus, he shrugs off responsibility for evaluation by claiming that what is produced in American society is all that is available to him. This is, of course, in itself a positive evaluation of what is given, since the goodness of this evolutionary process and its expression in American society are far from self-evident.

Winston White's attack on the moralizers and reformers ends, of course, in a cul-de-sac. There is no escape from the vicious circle which is created by disposing of one's opponents as ideologizers. Once a scientific theory is asserted to be adequate and comprehensive—precisely the position taken by Auguste Comte in the nineteenth century—then one's opponents are simply in error, or they are suffering strain and confusing their ideological notions with scientific fact. At this stage, scientific discussion ends. With Edward Shils, one simply awaits the return of the prodigals; any further discussion comes down to rhetoric and counter-rhetoric.[19] The only way out of this cul-de-sac is to take up the basic issue which was noted in passing by Bennett Berger --the task of methodological clarification.

## *SCIENCE OR IDEOLOGY*

The methodological issues are particularly serious in the sciences of man. For example, Winston White makes many assertions about the comprehensiveness of the theory with which he is looking at the social process, but his whole

[19] Edward Shils puts this point incisively in referring to the senseless resistance which is still being offered to the theory of action: "Many sociologists squirm over the *medicina forte* that this theoretical undertaking imposes, and hostile critics find in it a ground for ribaldry. The fact remains, however, that inferiors, however much they scoff, know their betters; and the theory goes on imposing itself, even on those who believe they are rejecting it" (*op. cit.*, p. 1410).

discussion forces one to ask what distinguishes a human science from an ideology. What is it that makes White's position, or Parsons' or Mills', scientific rather than ideological? Here the "deconstruction" effected by the sociology of knowledge undermines any notion of a science of man; this is the death knell for Karl Mannheim's conception of a group of intellectuals who have no special interest in the promotion of a particular cause in society and can thus prescribe objectively for the social good. All sides have interests, because social science is a human enterprise and a part of the total social enterprise—even if only in its hopes of gaining adequate research funds in order to continue its "objective" research. The human sciences are engaged in the social processes which they explore. Their very existence alters that process, and each of their publications, if it gains attention, alters the process further. Moreover, each significant change in that social process will in turn have its effects on the total project of human science. There is no stable ground here; to this extent, White is undoubtedly right in falling back ultimately upon his claim of possessing an adequate social theory. The problem is what gives this warrant of adequacy. How does one assess the adequacy of such a theory? What is the criterion in terms of which one adjudicates between different models of the social process?

There has been a tendency in the human sciences to deal with ideological questions by "unmasking"—finding strains or social dislocations which account for false consciousness.[20] The presupposition of such "unmasking" is that one knows

[20] Paul Ricoeur, in lectures at the University of Chicago, drew the analogy between this "external deconstruction" by which ideas are reduced to biological and social processes and the "internal deconstruction" of myth and symbol in the process of demythologizing; in both cases, false consciousness replaces the depths of symbol and reason is impoverished; as a consequence, the very rationality which initiated the enterprise is annihilated. For Edmund Husserl's critique of this crisis of reason arising from a positivistic science, see *Phenomenology and the Crisis of Philosophy*, translated by Quentin Lauer (New York: Harper Torchbooks, 1965), esp. the final paragraphs, pp. 191–192.

what science is and what comprises a science of man. The implication is that one stands within such a science and unmasks one's opponents. This, as we have seen, is the way in which opponents are handled by Edward Shils and Winston White. This has been the method of Marxists in dealing with their opponents, but the theoretical perspective of Marxism is quite different from the theory of action.[21] According to Marxism, only the Marxist dialectic gives true perspective on history; all other perspectives are ideologies which need to be unmasked. It has become increasingly evident that such a struggle is ultimately a battle of ideologies in which Marxism falls under its own judgment as ideology. In the scientific struggle, a similar phenomenon occurs, and the controversy devolves into a battle of ideologies. The only hope for a human science, in this situation, is to seek the grounds of science—to bring into question the notion of a human science, which had been taken for granted. What is there about the scientific attitude toward the human enterprise which distinguishes it from any other stance? How do we define a science of the total human enterprise? Rather than unmasking the ideological views or even attacking all the human sciences as ideological—a logical consequence of White's line of argument—can we not take the tack of discerning what is scientific about various interpretations of the human enterprise? This search for common elements can guide us reflectively to the essential structure of a science of human activities in society.

Such questions precede any evaluation of the various models of the social process which are proposed by different groups within the human sciences. The prior question of the meaning of a scientific attitude does not resolve the question of adequate models, but it defines the limits of relevance of *any* theoretical reflection in apprehending the nature of man's practical activity.

We could interpret our present situation in rather

[21] The differences are explicated methodologically in Chapter 6.

radical terms: society has come of age in viewing itself "objectively" and taking responsibility for the consequences of its decision-making; by the same token, the sciences of man are coming of age and have to give an account of the limits of their grasp of social process and the scope of their validity for social policy. A mature society will be conscious of these limits. The science of man has matured to the point of entering more significantly into the decision-making processes of society. If this is so, the human sciences should be ready to give an accounting of the sense in which they are "sciences" and of the sense in which they study man and social process. However, it contradicts man's "interest" in his own projects to make such disclosures, so it behooves those who are concerned with the practical issues of the public realm to consider the credentials and scope of relevance of scientific judgments on man's enterprise.[22]

We shall pose the problem of a scientific attitude toward the social process in the most radical sense, but we do this without any claim that this question is raised for the first time. One finds this question appearing repeatedly in the century during which the sciences of man have emerged; indeed, it is posed more often in the humanities and physical sciences than most social scientists realize. These are questions which arise in the very nature of the case—the possibility of taking oneself as an object of scientific study is hardly to be taken for granted. Can a society be objective about its own internal process and the course of its movement? In this respect, much of the methodological discussion in the human sciences has been superficial; it has

[22] We have already noted the wide range of academic disciplines and public activities in which such a critique goes on day by day; the advantage, if any, looking at these problems from the perspective of theological social ethics is the wide scope of interests within which the human sciences can be appraised: the relevance of theoretical perspectives to the practical sphere; the scope and nature of the public realm; the relations between religious and political dimensions of society without an implicit commitment to reduce one dimension to the other or to refer both dimensions to irrational values which are determined by underlying "forces."

taken the possibility of a human science for granted and preoccupied itself with methods for improving precision in objective observation and increased power of mathematical manipulation of data. One begs the real question if one starts with a "human science" and proceeds to settle methodological questions by sharpening instruments of observation—simply refusing to ask what one is actually observing. The issue is the *possibility* of such a science and the kind of orientation which would distinguish a scientific perspective from an ideological formulation.

In attempting to clarify the meaning of a scientific perspective on social process, we are attempting to shift the present c ntroversy to a more constructive level; rather than excluding some of the scientific perspectives by bringing them under a rubric of ideology, we are concerned with identifying the scientific aspects which are common to a variety of "objective" considerations of society. The crucial test for this approach will be its capactiy to elicit the common ground in these perspectives without obliterating the significant differences. The principal contenders in the ideological debate within social science stand within the tradition of human science. They follow, to differing degrees, the procedures of empirical science, and they attempt, so far as possible, to give a reliable interpretation of their findings. So far as these scientists suffer ideological strains, and all to varying degrees undergo such strain, this is perhaps the human condition.

To achieve methodological clarification, one is pressed back to a common ground in experience; this ground, in the present inquiry, is man's "lived" experience of the social world. The criterion of adequacy of any science of man, over and above internal clarity and logical consistency, is man's experience of his social and cultural world; if that experience is illumined by the human sciences, then to that degree science has achieved a level of adequacy. Moreover, social experience furnishes the bench mark for a critique of the adequacy and limits of particular scientific styles. "Lived" experience is a rich, concrete, and manifold reality from which many kinds of theoretical reflection can develop. Methodological clarification requires a return to this concreteness in order to distinguish the nature of various theoretical reflections. Only from some such ground can we clarify the ideological aspects of social science and the nature of a scientific perspective.

Grounding knowledge in "lived" experience is the essential mark of a phenomenological approach to man's life-world.[23] All sciences would, to be sure, claim to ground their knowledge in experience, but the interpretation of experience varies with the understanding of the nature of science and the way in which scientific methods are related to their subject matters. The positivist, for example, asserts that only one method of external observation is scientific and can yield knowledge; he would claim, moreover, that experience of a perceptual kind provides the ultimate grounding of his operations. For the phenomenologist, perceptual experience is understood in a richer sense, although perceptual consciousness is likewise treated as foundational to knowledge. Consequently, the concern with "lived" experience does not automatically solve the problems of different understandings of science. However, the present inquiry turns to "lived" experience as it is *given* in our commonsense living within the everyday world. This grounding of knowledge in commonsense experience has close affinities with the attempt by contemporary linguistic analysts to base their studies in the everyday language from which a variety of technological and other linguistic forms arise. Rather than arguing the merits of this phenomenological understanding of experience, we shall test its adequacy by the degree to which it overcomes the ideological controversy within the human sciences

[23] We shall have occasion to explore this method in detail in the next chapter. For a basic discussion of the phenomenological approach to scientific orientation, see Schutz, *op. cit.*, pp. 207–259.

without obscuring the legitimate claims and authentic contributions of particular styles of social science; moreover, we shall test the adequacy of this understanding of experience by the extent to which it clarifies the differences between social ethics and social science and illumines their contributions to social policy.

# 3 *the everyday world and scientific reflection*

The phenomenological method is used to distinguish science from ideology and to put the discussion on better ground

THE COMMONSENSE world of ordinary language and activity furnishes the background of our social world. Through that ordinary language, we have a world. By ordinary language, we are guided from object to object and task to task. However, ordinary language is imprecise. It is a rough-and-ready affair, like ordinary justice. If science seeks clarity and precision, is it not going to be misled by looking for a common ground in everyday activity?

To raise this question of a common ground for scientific reflection is already to suggest that there are no neutral or value-free determinations of such a common ground. This inquiry assumes that every science of man must ultimately come to terms with the everyday world and, indeed, that every social science makes assumptions which involve some understanding of the ordinary world of everyday affairs. Nevertheless, certain presuppositions underlie this claim. If the commonsense world is the criterion of adequacy for any science, ideology, or ethic of the social world, then the practical world of *doing* is the paramount reality within which truth is to be sought—the reality which thought seeks to clarify.[1] The historical world of doing is thus the human

[1] The undermining of truth by psychologism, sociologism, and historicism set the context for Edmund Husserl's radical inquiry; see Husserl, *op. cit.* See the discussion of this problem in relation to the sciences of man by Maurice Merleau-Ponty, *The Primacy of Perception and Other Essays*, edited by James Edie (Evanston, Ill.: Northwestern University Press,

world with which any human science must come to terms and against which its understanding is to be checked. Thinking is, of course, interwoven in practical affairs, but the theoretical work of reflection detaches itself from doing for the sake of understanding; in this sense, theory follows doing and brings to light the meanings given in the "lived" world. The priority of doing and the primacy of the "lived" world are fundamental assumptions of this inquiry; they can be tested only by their adequacy to deal with the problems under consideration.

There are, to be sure, different ways of approaching the everyday world in the sciences of man. The "lived" world is a rich world of fearing, wishing, hoping, valuing, and doing. The second principal commitment in this approach is bound up with this richness of concrete experience: understanding "lived" experience is inseparable from participating in it. The self and the world are correlated in such a way that one understands the self only in relation to its world and one comprehends the world as a world only by understanding it in relation to the selves through whom it is constituted. This is an obvious proposition on one level, but its neglect is the crux of most of the difficulties now besetting the sciences of man. One cannot take ordinary language as a point of reference for reflection without knowing the language. One does not know a language from a dictionary but only by living it and speaking it. Similarly, the everyday world is accessible to us only by participation; it is the world already there before we are born—the world within which and through which we come to be as selves.[2]

The common ground for clarification of scientific styles, then, is the practical world of common sense—the world

---

1964), Ch. 3, "Phenomenology and the Sciences of Man," where the author states: "It must be shown that science is possible, that the sciences of man are possible, and that philosophy also is possible" (p. 44).

[2] Schutz, *op. cit.*, esp. the essay "On Multiple Realities," pp. 207–259; see also in the same volume the essay "Symbol, Reality and Society."

accessible to us through participation in its meanings. Everyday experience furnishes the final arbiter on questions of understanding, whether in the form of predictions of courses of events or in illumination of the given. Social science, ideology, and social ethics find their common ground and criterion of adequacy in this "lived" world. Our task, then, is to clarify the meaning of the ambiguous term "everyday world." In this task, Alfred Schutz's research furnishes a sound starting point.[3]

## *THE WORLD OF EVERY DAY*

What, then, do we mean by the "everyday world of common sense," and how does it illumine the scientific perspective? In answering these questions, we shall make no attempt to follow Schutz explicitly, although the present reflections are guided by his basic development of this theme. The everyday world is the working world in which we carry on our day-to-day affairs. It is the world of common sense, where ways of understanding and doing are taken for granted. Whether we are at a machine, engaged in writing, or catching a bus, our minds are "turned toward" the management of these affairs. In catching the bus to get home from work, we are not concerned with what makes the bus work, whether the bus is really *there*, or whether the driver is having a hard time paying his bills. Our minds, in principle, are attentive to catching the right bus, getting our fare paid, receiving proper change, and finding a seat. An extremely complex set of mental activities enters into the shaping of these seemingly everyday matters, although such activities do become routinized. To call this the everyday

[3] A second volume of essays by Alfred Schutz has been published under the title *Studies in Social Theory, Collected Papers,* edited by Arvid Brodersen (The Hague: Martinus Nijhoff, 1964), Vol. 2. In addition, Schutz's original work in social theory has been republished, *Der Sinnhafte Aufbau der sozialen Welt,* 2nd ed. (Vienna: Springer-Verlag OHG, 1960); *The Phenomenology of the Social World,* trans. by George Walsh and Frederick Lehnert (Evanston, Ill.: Northwestern University Press, 1967).

world of common sense is not intended to conceal its internal complexity but merely to suggest that our attitude and attention are very practically oriented to "living in" this workaday world. We "live in" this world insofar as we give it our full attention—not withdrawing to reflect on our experience but *engaged* with the world.

We do, of course, move in and out of the workaday world. We seldom give full attention to practicalities for extended periods of time. We turn our attention away in daydreaming, in wondering, in playful fantasy, and in various kinds of wishing or fearing. There are many modifications of our orientation to the world which do not fit the commonsense world in any simple way, yet we are usually able to give sufficient attention to the practicalities so that we manage. The absentminded professor, for example, is a subject of humor, not only because his reflective preoccupation turns his attention away from these practical demands—losing his hat or accepting the wrong change—but also because all of us stand moment by moment in jeopardy of the same distracted preoccupation. We speak of the everyday world as the world of practical interests—the workaday world—because this is the world which dominates our daily lives even though we may turn away from it at any moment.

This everyday world is made up of objects with which we have to "deal" and which we have learned to manage from our earliest days. The notion of "dealing with" this world is suggestive, because it is a term that comes from "distributing" and carries the connotation of allocating our attention and efforts. We are at work trying to control the affairs of this everyday world. We take it for granted that we understand this world sufficiently to cope with it. We feel that we can "deal with" it, and to this extent, we feel adequate to the world in which we have been placed. Our attitude toward this everyday world is pragmatic—concerned with mastery and measuring success by the effects which are produced by our efforts. A pragmatic philosophy, in this sense, is one which takes the stance of the everyday world as a criterion of philosophy.[4] The everyday world, as the pragmatic philosophy has suggested, draws its criteria of validity from the operative effects of our activity. The everyday attitude is a pragmatic perspective in the sense that it judges theory by its practical effectiveness. One understands, according to this attitude, when one knows how a thing operates and can reproduce its operations with similar effects.

One takes the attitude of "suspended doubt" in the everyday world. Alfred Schutz calls this the "natural attitude." We turn from the natural attitude of everyday life occasionally and question whether the bus exists, even wondering whether there is a conspiracy in the terminal to delay buses which we intend to catch. However, these are not usually intended as serious doubts. We do have doubts in the course of each day, but the natural attitude suspends those doubts. Doubt is part of the distance with which man can live in his everyday world; it is integral to the meaning of his freedom, since he is not bound to this pregiven world but can and does, in fact, repeatedly call it into question. Nevertheless, our everyday attitude in the working world is to take for granted that the bus *is there*, that the terminal is dispatching buses regularly, that the driver is trying to keep his job by making reasonable time with the bus, and, in general, that the world is more or less as it purports to be. Though doubt is intrinsic to human freedom, as we shall suggest in more detail in the course of the inquiry, our everyday attitude suspends doubt and takes for granted that things are functioning in the way that they are "supposed to function." Man in the natural attitude lives in the world as given.[5]

[4] From the phenomenological perspective, this is practical philosophy, since it takes its criterion from the everyday world instead of seeking the presuppositions of this situation. See Schutz, *Collected Papers*, Vol. 1, p. 213; this is, of course, pragmatism in the crude sense.

[5] In the "natural attitude" of suspended doubt, we strive *to make sense* of occurrences in the everyday world, fitting these occurrences into the accepted typifications which prevail in the common culture. For experiment with and discussion of this process, see Harold Garfinkel, "Common-Sense Knowledge of Social Structures: The Documentary Method of In-

As the pragmatic philosophy has asserted, our doubts and questions arise in this workaday world when things do not work out; at least, if we confine our attention to the common-sense world of working, it is a fact that we question the taken-for-granted procedure when it fails to meet the exigencies of the situation. We "live in" that working world until such a point as our taken-for-granted ways fail. These failures, problems, difficulties, and obstacles give pause and open reflection; we begin to reconceive our situation.

The pragmatic philosophy generalizes this understanding of the problematic situation. However much one may question this generalization, its stress on the significance of difficulties in stimulating reflection clearly has direct application to the working world. The impatience of the businessman with theory, for example, often conceals theoretical reflection which he exercises on practical problems. When the man of affairs is impatient with theory, he is actually questioning the significance of theorizing at one remove from practical concerns. The emergence of doubt, the raising of questions, the calling into question of the taken-for-granted world—these are the theorizing of the practical world, and they signify the collapse of the "suspended doubt" which characterizes the natural attitude. When the bus does not appear after a half hour, we begin to look for a taxi or some other means of transportation. We no longer assume that the bus will come "as usual." We drop the attitude of taking for granted. We accept the doubt which had been undermining our confidence.[6]

One can extend the analysis of the natural attitude to the whole sphere of reality in which the everyday world is

---

terpretation," in *Theories of the Mind*, edited by Jordan M. Scher (New York: The Free Press, 1962), pp. 689–712.

[6] As Alfred Schutz points out, such theoretical reconsideration does not form a relatively independent province of meaning—a world—but is actually an "enclave" within the paramount reality of the everyday world; in this sense, the theoretical perspective of the disinterested observer is a distinct province of meaning and appears quite alien to the man of affairs. See his essay "On Multiple Realities," in *Collected Papers*, Vol. 1.

experienced. We take for granted that our words designate the objects to which we refer. We take for granted that we are understood when we speak, that our orders or requests are heard, and that the world of persons and nature to which we are accustomed is indeed the way we assume it to be. To use Alfred Schutz's illustration, we assume that the letter which we post will be delivered. Harold Garfinkel refers to this set of assumptions as a "common culture," by which he means the "socially sanctioned grounds of inference and action that people use in their everyday affairs and which they assume that other members of the group use in the same way."[7] This notion of common culture will recur in the course of our inquiry, but here its main reference is to the taken-for-granted grounds of understanding and acting which make the everyday world a common or public world. We use the term "public" to signify the character of the time, space, and sequence in which we experience this everyday world. Objective clock time makes a common schedule possible. Objective extension makes clear your "there" and my "here." The way one thing follows another—as expected—furnishes a public logic for inference.[8] The natural attitude of the everyday world rests upon that common culture.

When difficulties arise or we withdraw confidence from the everyday world, our common culture comes into question. For example, we sense our difficulties in dealing with a mentally disturbed person, even when the disturbance is mild; we recognize that the grounds on which we have guided our exchanges with other people do not work out with this person. We may be completely naïve in detecting mental disturbance, but looking back upon such instances,

[7] Garfinkel, *op. cit.*, p. 689.

[8] For an analysis of standard time as the intersection of inner time and cosmic time in the intersubjective world, see Schutz, *Collected Papers*, Vol. 1, pp. 218–222. Schutz's analysis is based upon Edmund Husserl's phenomenological research into the structure of time, elements of which are available in English; see Husserl's *The Phenomenology of Internal Time-Consciousness*, translated by James S. Churchill (Bloomington, Ind.: Indiana University Press, 1964).

we recognize the uncertainty which suddenly began to undermine the assumed grounds of inference and action. When we jokingly suggest that the matter is being taken *too* seriously—a common technique of the everyday world for reducing the heat on an issue—we suddenly find the other person taking the situation even more seriously and including us among the enemies. At this point, the technique for managing relationships comes into question; we drop the attitude of taking for granted; we begin to question either the common culture or the other person's balance. Such breaks in the accepted world of everyday relationships are often so disturbing that persons begin to doubt their *own* sanity. When others respond in ways which violate the common culture, our confidence in ourselves and in that culture is undermined. We can no longer "suspend" our doubt.

This brief characterization of the everyday world has focused primarily upon practical mastery and the doubt which arises when difficulties appear. We recognize, however, that our consciousness directs itself upon the world in many ways—dreaming, role-playing new possibilities in fantasy, wishing, enjoying, etc. The world appears to us in myriad ways, according to the intentions with which we direct ourselves toward it. For example, the raising of a curtain on a drama thrusts us into a world which the dramatist has fabricated, and yet our attention to this world is a complex "living in" the drama, reliving our own experiences through the drama, etc., etc. The meaning of the world—the world as it appears in all its rich complexity—is the corollary of our intentional orientation to it.[9] Many of these perspectives on the world are relatively private—for example, our dreams. When we speak of the everyday world of common

[9] These "worlds" which are constituted by modifications of our orientation to the everyday world are called "finite provinces of meaning" by Alfred Schutz; thus, the tension of consciousness, form of spontaneity, form of self-relatedness, time-perspective, and accent of reality are distinctive in each such province of meaning, giving rise to a distinct cognitive style. See his essay "On Multiple Realities," in *Collected Papers*, Vol. 1.

sense, we refer to that world which we share with others within the common culture—the public world of working and of the natural attitude. When we speak of a "science of man" or an "ideological perspective" on the social world, we are referring to particular attitudes toward this everyday world. The paramount reality remains that everyday world from which our different modes of orientation take their departure and with which they must come to terms; thus, communication is an operation in the everyday world. Hence, the everyday world gives us the point of departure for considering the scientific attitude.

### *IDEOLOGICAL REFLECTION*

We have already indicated the doubt which enters into the everyday world when things do not work out as expected. This kind of doubt is "interested" in that it arises in connection with the practical concerns of the individual or group and is suspended when the practical problems are resolved. This is the type of theorizing which is congenial to the man of affairs; it raises questions about *means*, or accepted ways of doing things. However impatient he may become with academic theorizing, he is quite ready to reconceive schedules of production in order to cope more adequately with his practical problems. He may even reconceive the nature of his industry if the occasion warrants, but this is a way of viewing the productive activity as a means to profits.

Political parties or local groups are also brought to reflective consideration of means when their interests are in jeopardy or when they seek to achieve certain advantages in the distribution of rewards. "Interested" reflection breaks into the natural attitude and reconceives the everyday course of events along the lines of particular interests. Doubt is no longer suspended. Doubt enters the commonsense world. However, the doubt is directed by practical interests which arise from an individual, group, or even national situation. In this sense, the doubt introduces an enclave within the everyday world. This is the kind of doubt which focuses upon means available for the achievement of the interests of a group or party. However, the accepted values and norms of common culture may be reconceived by such "interested" reflection; then we can speak of an ideological formulation. Here "ideological" refers to the practically interested reconception of the common culture. Ideology moves beyond *means* to reformulate *goals* in terms of basic values. Such ideological formulation may be more or less adequate to the problems of the total society and the particular circumstances; an evaluation of an ideology is extremely difficult because it brings into question aspects of the common culture—introducing more radical doubt than "interested" reflection on means.

Ideological formulation arises in the midst of uncertainties in the everyday world—particularly as these bear upon the beliefs and values which inform the common culture. Whereas the natural attitude suspends doubt about the legitimacy of elites, the general distribution of rewards and punishments, and the allocation of honor, social change and dislocation may bring any or all of these evaluative grounds into question. The conflicts of interest which occasion such ambiguities call for a reformulation of the horizon of meaning within which various elements of the society are ordered. This is a symbolic task of a higher order and bears upon the unification of the society both in terms of its heritage and in the context of its fulfillment. The peculiar character of ideological formulation is that it selects elements of the cultural heritage and lifts them to a new level as expression of the society's future; in this sense, it has a particularly political character, giving symbolic form to the unity and meaning of the social enterprise. The possibility of such symbolic reformulation arises from the doubt which is focused upon the adequacy of current symbols to give form to the dynamic forces that are at work in the society. The values informing the common culture are thus brought into question, but they come into question largely because practical interests in the everyday world are not adequately expressed; this doubt, in short, is not imposed by disinterested reflection on the presuppositions of the society but is a doubt which has been occasioned by historical processes.

Ideological reflection differs from the kind of practical reflection which forms an enclave in the attention of the everyday world; both kinds of reflection arise from practical interests, but reflection in the context of everyday interests bears primarily upon *means* to taken-for-granted goals, or at least to optional goals in the context of taken-for-granted values and meanings in the common culture, whereas ideological reflection bears upon the formulation of the values and meanings of the common culture itself—the horizon of social and cultural meanings. This ideological reflection is not the radical reflection of ethical inquiry, as we shall see much later in the course of the inquiry, since it does not pose questions about the understanding of man's fulfillment in the common culture in the light of an ultimate horizon of meaning which transcends it; on the contrary, *ideological formulation takes the social and cultural heritage for granted as the source of understanding of personal and social fulfillment, but it selects from this heritage the symbols and meanings which can give more adequate expression to that fulfillment in the midst of social change.* Ideological formulation reconstitutes the future of the society in the light of its past. Ethical reflection, particularly theological ethical reflection, poses questions about the future of the society in the light of a more adequate grasp of that future. Our principal concern, for the moment, is to distinguish the ideological perspective from reflection in the context of everyday interests, and the distinction is clearly a matter of degree and scope, since ideological reflection introduces doubt on a much deeper and broader level of social reality—touching the fundamental meaning of fulfillment in the social enterprise. It is this radical reformulation of social meanings which gives ideology such significance in political struggles, but it is also this historically formative power which has made it difficult to give scientific status to the concept.

At least from the time of Karl Marx and Friedrich Engels, the notion of ideology has implied the social conditioning of knowledge by class position, struggles for power, and historical location. In the social sciences, two lines of conceptualization have dominated the use of the term "ideology": one relating ideology to the pursuit of interests, in which ideas are masks and weapons; another treating ideology as a symptom of strain and remedy for unavoidable tensions. In drawing this broad distinction and opposing these formulations with his own, Clifford Geertz has made a significant attempt to give ideology a positive status in social process.[10] The "interest" and "strain" theories treat the meanings and symbols in ideological formulation as epiphenomenal—reducing the meaning of the ideas to the underlying forces. Geertz grants that the particular direction of an ideological formulation is occasioned by the ambiguities to be handled and that the appropriateness of particular symbols is shaped by the social conditions out of which they have arisen; at the same time, he rehabilitates the imaginative strategy which appropriates these elements in a particular situation and gives new shape to the meaning of the social and historical process. Geertz's formulation contributes significantly to the present discussion of the ideological perspective as constituting a distinctive province of meaning. While his analysis illuminates the literary style appropriate to ideological symbolization, our present concern is to distinguish the ideological from the scientific perspective as a cognitive style; in this respect, the two discussions are complementary. By contrast, the "interest" and "strain" theories start from a dogmatic view of empirical science as the only mode of attaining truth—treating other strategies as deviations from

[10] See Clifford Geertz's essay "Ideology as a Cultural System," *Ideology and Discontent*, edited by David E. Apter (New York: The Free Press, 1964).

truth or rationality; in this way, these theories obscure the formative power of ideology and prejudge the truth-values of ideological formulation. The basic distinction between ideology and science is not one between irrational and rational orientations but is, rather, one between two distinct modifications of the commonsense orientation to the everyday world—modifications with specific styles and achieving particular types of illumination of problems arising in that world.

In the everyday world, our proximate goals and the relations between means and ends in the accomplishment of these goals are part of our stock of knowledge at hand. These sequences are part of the taken-for-granted world of common sense. They are given in idealized forms as "I-can-do-it-again."[11] Nevertheless, both means and proximate goals constantly undergo change or at least slight modifications. These pragmatic calculations take place within the context of a more comprehensive horizon of meaning within which our lives are oriented and interpreted. The symbols and values of this more comprehensive horizon undergo modification on a personal level at crises of identity in our lives and on a social level as the cultural meanings and internal processes of a society become incompatible. The ideological task is to overcome those ambiguities by reorganization of the cultural heritage in terms of social fulfillment. On both personal and cultural levels, this reflective reconsideration of symbols and values extends beyond pragmatic calculations —introducing a much more fundamental doubt into the taken-for-granted world. Scientific dogmatism about "rationality" tends to confine rational operations to the less radical sphere of means-ends relations and calculations of the appropriateness of proximate goals. When basic symbols and values are brought into doubt, the scientific dogmatists tend to treat the reformulations as a logical ordering of irrational or nonrational elements; thus, ideological formulation is

[11] See Schutz, *Collected Papers*, Vol. 1, p. 20 and *passim*, where Husserl's treatment of these problems is outlined.

viewed as an instrumental process of reason which is tainted with irrational interests or colored by the irrational forces of alienation. In both cases, a dogmatic restriction of the operations of reason to cognitive mapping and means-end calculation forces the analysis of ideological formulation into the region of nonrational behavior; then the problem of the scientist is to account for the aberration of reason from causes extrinsic to reason itself. Our attempt to contrast ideological and scientific perspectives is based in principle upon a rejection of this dogmatic restriction of reason; we leave the question open as to the degree to which an ideological formulation may yield a cognitively valid reformulation of the horizon of meaning. The fact that ideological formulation is "interested" does not in principle discredit its operations; as we shall see, even the disinterested reflections of empirical science pursue the "interests" which are defined by the problems to be resolved in the inquiry.

### *SCIENTIFIC REFLECTION*

The scientific attitude is "disinterested" with reference to the practical problems of the scientist or even the scientific group. "Interest" and "disinterest," as indicated before, are defined here in terms of the practical interests of the everyday world. To be sure, scientists, like everyone else, have their practical concerns and operate day by day in the everyday world of common sense. However, scientific inquiry, as disciplined inquiry into aspects of the everyday world—whether physical, social, cultural, or logical—defines its "interests" by the problems of the discipline.[12] The relevant issue for doubt and reflection is determined not by the particular location of the scientist within the everyday world—his family problems, trouble with relatives, difficulty commuting, etc.—but by the stage of development of the discipline and by the problems which need to be solved for the advancement of the discipline; moreover, the common cul-

[12] *Ibid.*, pp. 245–259.

ture and even the culture of science are taken for granted. We speak, then, of the "disinterestedness" of the scientist *qua* scientist—engaged in reflective consideration of one or another aspect of the life-world, bringing into doubt one or another taken-for-granted premise upon which the everyday world operates. The scientist may, in fact, be distracted by his practical interests—the need to advance his career or to obtain adequate research grants; nevertheless, his inquiry into the functioning of the liver or the electromagnetic field surrounding the earth or the trends of population growth in underdeveloped areas is not *in principle* determined by those practical interests. (We recognize incidentally the extent to which the competition for research grants both stimulates and corrupts the scientific enterprise.) We shall recognize, as is quite obvious in this discrimination of "interested" and "disinterested" reflection, that a science of man will be far more interwoven with practical interests than an inquiry into the composition of crystals; nevertheless, we obscure the character of the "scientific doubt" if we lose sight of the radical character of its break with the practical interests of the everyday world.

We recognized that ideology preoccupies itself with the orientation of the society to the *future* in the context of its surrounding ambiguities; in this sense, its task of symbolization grapples with the horizon of meaning within which the fulfillment of the society is ordered. Science, by contrast, is a diagnostic attempt to account for the present in terms of the past—to relate the present order of a class of events to antecedent events of that class. The predictive work of science is built upon its grasp of the regular relationships between given states of a system and antecedent states; it is thus, even in its handling of the future, building upon regular determinations of a "hypothetical" future state by an antecedent state.[13] In a general sense, *ideological formulation*

[13] As Ernest Nagel points out, there are various temporal presuppositions in types of scientific laws; the "sequential order of dependence" fits our model of explanatory science as relating an event or state of a

handles ambiguities of meaning in the *present* by reconstituting the meaning of *future* fulfillment from symbols available in the cultural heritage; *social-scientific formulation* gives an account of processes and projects in the *present* on the basis of *antecedent* processes. Thus, both types of formulations seek to bring clarity and illumination to the historical present, but the ideological perspective deals with the problems of meaning in the projection of the society into the future, whereas social science attempts to account for the present state of affairs from the past.

Science builds a subculture within the common culture. This subculture of science develops general rules of procedure for determining the acceptance or rejection of propositions within the corpus of science. These rules of evidence or verification are general to all sciences, at least within the traditions of empirical science.[14] We shall have occasion to enter more specifically into consideration of the applicability of these rules to the human sphere, but for the moment our principal concern is with the character of scientific inquiry and reflection as such. The development of a subculture of the scientific world preserves disinterested doubt against the particular interests of scientists. Within the corpus of propositions which comprise a particular science, every proposition is subject to rejection in the light of further theorizing and

---

system to antecedent states, and this model is partially actualized in other types of explanation. See Nagel's *The Structure of Science* (New York: Harcourt, Brace & World, Inc., 1961), Chs. 2 and 4, and especially pp. 75–78. For a further discussion of the temporal sequence in scientific explanation, see Robert Brown, *Explanation in Social Science* (Chicago: Aldine Publishing Co., 1963), esp. Ch. 11.

[14] For a presentation of this understanding of science, see Felix Kaufmann, *Methodology of the Social Sciences*, (Fair Lawn, N.J.: Oxford University Press, 1944), esp. Chs. 1–5; differences within the subculture of science occur largely with respect to the cognitive status of scientific theories—what, if anything, is asserted in a theory. On the latter point, see Ernest Nagel's discussion, *ibid.*, Ch. 6, esp. pp. 1414–1452; the status of theory rests upon an understanding of reality which also forms the frame of reference within which theory develops—to this extent playing a more significant role than Nagel would allow. See also Chart 2, Chapter 4.

testing. Felix Kaufmann calls this the principle of permanent control, by which he means that the restriction of possibilities which is accomplished by a particular judgment is never absolute but is always open to revision or rejection in the light of further inquiry.[15] This kind of radical doubt at the base of an enterprise requires the most rigorous kind of communal discipline; hence, the social character of the scientific enterprise is concretized in the development of its own culture, where grounds for inference and procedure are elaborated and maintained through publication of findings and criticism from within the disciplines.

The peculiar character of the scientific stance is also disclosed in the problems of communication with which the sciences wrestle. Within any particular science, certain categories by which classes of phenomena are identified give rise to special terminology. In the culture of the everyday world, communication is possible on the basis of common language; similarly, the scientific disciplines develop their own language, but they also require the common language to share their findings. Unlike the everyday world, however, both the terminology and the corpus of accepted propositions within a scientific discipline undergo constant transformation. The enormous amount of publication in a field such as the biological sciences is indicative of the problem of communicating and "keeping up" with the dynamic development of one scientific field. Thus, the scientific attitude generates a subculture which guarantees an objective method—a logic of empirical science common to all scientific enterprise; within each particular scientific field there emerges a set of categories, theoretical formulations, definition of problems according to the state of the discipline, and agreed-upon procedures for testing hypothetical propositions in accordance with theoretical formulations. Thus, the "disinterested" attitude is protected by objective methods, and the radical doubt is fostered by publication and critique.

[15] Kaufmann, *ibid.*, Ch. 4, esp. p. 53.

We can speak of the scientific attitude as "disinterested," therefore, only if we apply the term carefully from within the context of the everyday world of common sense. The "disinterestedness" of science refers to the break with the practical interests of the everyday world in this mode of reflection. The "scientific interests" are defined by the particular scientific discipline; and these scientific problems are pursued and resolved, so far as this is possible, according to the rules applicable within the subculture of the scientific world. Hence, science has "interests," including the search for truth, but they are "scientific interests." We consider the scientific enterprise within the everyday world when we speak of the "practical interests of the scientific community" —its struggle for freedom of inquiry versus political pressures, its scramble for financial and institutional support, etc. However, science as a mode of reflection is an attempt to redefine "interests" by problems within a subject matter and discipline. It is a perspective on the world with its own cognitive style.

## *SCIENCE AND IDEOLOGY*

Chart 1 depicts the cognitive style and relevance of the three perspectives which we have been considering—the commonsense perspective, the ideological, and the scientific. Although most of the dimensions in these characterizations have been considered, a few additional comments will illumine some of the points of distinction.

The cognitive styles in Chart 1 represent rather sharply discriminated types. Alfred Schutz suggests that these finite provinces of meaning are distinct enough to involve a "shock" or "leap" as we move from one to another, even as there is heightened expectation and a sense of "leap" when we see the curtain rise for a dramatic performance—opening the way for us into a fictional world which has its own accent of reality. If we consider briefly the orientational aspects of each style, the significance of these differences of perspective may be etched somewhat more sharply.

The notion of tension of consciousness refers to the degree of wide-awake attentiveness with which we attend to the

**Chart 1** PERSPECTIVES ON THE LIFE-WORLD: COMMONSENSE, IDEOLOGICAL, AND SCIENTIFIC[16]

| Orientational Aspects | Commonsense | Ideological | Scientific |
|---|---|---|---|
| Tension of consciousness | Fully engaged participation (Practical) | "Interested reflection (Practical-Theoretical) | "Disinterested" observation (Theoretical) |
| Doubt | "Suspended" doubt—"natural attitude" | "Relative" doubt—*adequacy* of symbolic expression, accepting common culture | "Radical" doubt in region of experience, accepting subculture of science |
| Form of spontaneity | Mastery of world in embodied projects (Pragmatic) | Control of ambiguity in identity by symbolic expressions (Apologetic) | Clarification and understanding (Diagnostic) |
| Temporal perspective | Standard time of working world—intersection of inner and outer time (Vivid Present) | Present meaning of the past of society as human project—in relation to fulfillment (Internal History) | Cosmic time as measure of motion before and after (Objective Time) |

**Chart 1 (Continued)**

| Orientational Aspects | Commonsense | Ideological | Scientific |
|---|---|---|---|
| Accent of reality | Unity of world and congruity of experiences (Effects) | Unification of sentiments and beliefs through symbolic adequacy (Aptness) | Warranted by rules of procedure and congruity with scientific corpus or change in corpus (Consistency) |
| Significance to everyday world (Relevance) | Accepted grounds of inference and action (Public World) | Maintenance of commitment and loyalty (Common Sentiments) | Explanatory adequacy in various regions of experience (Understood World) |

[16] On the notion of finite provinces of meaning and their cognitive style, see Schutz, *Collected Papers,* Vol. 1, pp. 229–259. For an exposition of the orientational categories—revising the last two—see Harold Garfinkel, "Perception of the Other," unpublished thesis, Harvard University, 1952, chs. 7–13.

affairs of every day; thus, the commonsense world of working provides a baseline from which degrees of withdrawal of attentiveness can be gauged. Perhaps the furthest remove from the wide-awake attitude would be dreaming while we sleep, since there is no conscious steering of activities of consciousness in this period. We characterize the theoretical reconsideration of the ideological perspective as a practically oriented theorizing. The scientific perspective involves a disinterested observation which is of a much more theoretical character.

The problem of doubt has been discussed at some length; however, we should recognize that the suspension of doubt in the natural attitude of common sense has a counterpart in ideology with its suspension of doubt in the common culture and introduction of doubt with reference to its symbolization; furthermore, the radical doubt of the scientific enterprise touches only a region of experience and does not introduce doubt of the most radical kind into the enterprise of science itself—the doubt of radical philosophizing. Some interpretations of science would insist that the methods of science introduce the most radical doubt, but we have already suggested that this position dogmatizes the methods of empirical science as the only method for achieving knowledge.

The notion of forms of spontaneity is drawn from Alfred Schutz and refers to the deeper interests and systems of relevance with which the world is approached. Schutz postulates a fundamental anxiety over death and contingency which presses the organism toward control of the world in its projects and activities. This principle is, so to speak, the driving force of the "interests" that dominate man's pragmatic orientation in the everyday world. We shall have occasion to reconsider this notion in our discussion of "interest" theories in Chapter 4; the basic notion, however, helps to discriminate the system of relevances with which the particular province of meaning is approached. We have taken the pragmatic orientation of everyday activity as a base line; in relation to this, the ideological perspective is "apologetic"—a term used by Clifford Geertz to clarify this strategy in dealing with ambiguity. When the common culture within which projects are pursued becomes so ambiguous that these projects begin to falter, the pragmatic struggle to cope with things gives way to the imaginative strategy of reformulation "in defense of" the common culture. Clifford Geertz has used the term "diagnostic" for the approach of science, and to the extent that the term carries the full weight of a strategy of clarification, explication, and bringing to light, it affords a nice contrast to the other forms of spontaneity.

The dimension of temporal perspective will be taken up in much more detail under the consideration of our knowledge of the social world and the problem of internal time perspectives. The basic notion informing this dimension is the intersection of inner time and objective, or cosmic, time in the form of standard, or civic, time.[17] The temporal perspectives of ideology and science lack the vivid present in which the intentionalities of consciousness intersect within the everyday world; these perspectives shift their orientation away from the inner flow of meanings. The ideological perspective grapples with the internal history of the society—the present meaning of its past. This subjective meaning of a cultural history employs external history but asks about the meaning of the enterprise in relation to societal fulfillment. By contrast, the scientific perspective brackets inner time in both the personal and the cultural sense, confining its activities to external, or objective, time; in this sense, the struggle of "scientific" historicism with interpretative history can be understood as a conflict of temporal perspectives—each possessing a significance for social understanding within its own cognitive style.

An accent of reality belongs to each finite province of meaning within its own domain. When we attend the theater and feel that we cannot participate in the drama—that somehow the performance does not engage us—the play lacks the accent of reality appropriate to this fictional style. The commonsense world uses rather pragmatic criteria for its sense of reality—the coherence of the effects in terms of efforts and intentions. By contrast, ideological effectiveness, as Geertz suggests, is in the manner of metaphor a question of aptness in contrast to a mere extravagance. By the same token, the consistency of a proposition according to scientific rules of procedure is the criterion of reality within the

[17] *Ibid.*, esp. the essay "Choosing Among Projects of Action" and pp. 218–222. For a detailed analysis of this problem, see Schutz, *Der Sinnhafte Aufbau der sozialen Welt*, esp. Ch. 2.

culture of science; of course, incompatibility with other propositions may mean the rejection of several propositions or suspension of judgment until further testing.

The everyday world is the paramount reality with which other provinces of meaning have to come to terms. This claim rests on the actuality of this world as a field of communication. This is the public world in whose terms and media these other worlds finally participate—bringing new motivation, new direction, new light and understanding, or new questions. A vivid example of this problem occurs in the recounting of dreams in psychotherapy; it is recognized that much is lost in the communication of dreams —much of the feeling and symbolic formation—and yet the therapeutic power of grasping the meanings which are carried in the dream is brought about by the communicative process. Communication occurs in the language of the everyday world, and historical power depends ultimately upon that communicative process both in personal life and in social formation. We suggest, for the moment, that the significance of the ideological sphere as it impinges on the everyday world is in the mobilization of common sentiments —the motivational dimension of the public world as a common world. The relevance of the scientific perspective (and this applies particularly to the social sciences) is to bring regions of the world as experienced into consciousness as an "understood" or a "known" world. In this respect, the "known" world of common sense is constantly in process of modification by the "understood" world of science.

If ideology and social science actually operated in such distinct provinces of meaning as the cognitive styles in Chart 1 would suggest, the controversy between the functionalists and voluntarists would not have assumed such an ideological character. One way of understanding the intersection and conflict of social-scientific perspectives in ideological terms is to consider again the problem of temporal perspectives. Ideology, as was suggested, deals with problems of the future by reformulating the symbols of the common culture in a more apt or adequate expression of the vitalities of the societal process. In this respect, ideology deals with the problem of man's fulfillment within his cultural enterprise; moreover, it draws its materials from his cultural heritage. The sciences of man also come to terms with the values and meanings by which social processes are organized, since the social world is a "meant" world that is defined by horizons of meaning. The sciences of man may operate with objective, or cosmic, time and delineate the external history of society in a sequence of factual states, but this will not be a science of society except as it takes for granted the meanings of these so-called facts within the internal history of that society. Another way of stating this problem is to assert that a science of man must give some account of the significance of values in the constitution of social processes, even if giving an account of these evaluative dimensions means that the science treats them as epiphenomenal or disregards them.[18] We have already seen that this is precisely the position taken by the physicalist approach in the sciences of man; within this approach, the future of the society is determined scientifically by extrapolation from antecedent states of the society; thus, value and meaning are understood as products of underlying or external forces of a different order. Such a position is itself an ideological schema, since it imputes meaning or meaninglessness to the human enterprise in the form of external determination; such imputation is a kind of evaluation which cannot be tested by scientific observation.

These remarks about the intersection of ideological and scientific perspectives in the social sciences already anticipate the fundamental question with which this inquiry must struggle—the nature of the subject matter of the human sciences. So far as a science of man is possible, it will be

[18] See the discussion of physicalist social science in Chapter 1—an instance where value and meaning are treated as epiphenomenal.

developed within the cognitive style of an empirical science as we have attempted to depict it. However, the scientific perspective may intrude upon the ideological province of meaning without any warrant, and in this case it will overreach its limits as a science. We have some hint of the nature of this problem in the consideration of the way in which the sciences of man impinge upon society's understanding of the social world; they may communicate to this society a claim to apprehend its future, when the temporal perspective in which they work is not the historical temporality of society. To this extent, the attempt to translate their findings within the temporal perspective of the everyday world —the intersection of inner and outer history—may lead to false claims for historical determination; hence, a science of man becomes an ideological perspective on the society by substituting objective time for societal time. If this should, indeed, prove to be the source of the ideological conflict, the resolution of the difficulties will come about through a clear identification of the subject matter of the human sciences and a clarification of the relationship between their models of the social world and everyday affairs.

The distinction among cognitive styles makes it possible to identify the perspective of social science on the everyday world. This is a first step toward clarifying the possibility and limits of a science of the social world. However, it leaves unresolved the conflict between various scientific styles; moreover, it provides no criterion for determining the contributions of these styles to an understanding of the social world. This next step in clarification rests upon an understanding of the nature of the social world—the actual subject matter of the sciences of man. This is the social reality which underlies both a social world and any science of that world. It also underlies the everyday world which we have taken as point of departure. This is the "lived" world of interpersonal experience which forms the unreflected background of everyday activity. In turning to the pregiven social world which is taken for granted in any science of that world, we take up in a new way the problem of self and other with which George Herbert Mead wrestled. The divergence of scientific styles arises from different assumptions about the nature of sociality; hence, the clarification of this "lived" ground of the social world should make clear the peculiar contribution of these styles.

# part two

# *a science of the social world*

# 4 *the nature of the social world*

George Herbert Mead's postion on the social self is reexamined, and a balance between human creativity and social patterning is established

THE IDEOLOGICAL CONTROVERSY in the human sciences emerged from the ambiguity in the understanding of social reality; at least, this is the hypothesis which informed our historical treatment of the American development. We traced the roots of this ambiguity to George Herbert Mead's background in behaviorism. We also recognized his struggle to transcend that background in his later work. We do not claim that the present controversies are mere repetitions of Mead's struggles, nor do we assert that a direct historical sequence can be traced from Mead's influence to present discussions. We claim only that the basic problem with which Mead struggled—the polarity of "I" and "me"—has continued to plague the development of the human sciences. The centrality of this problem of "social self" and "intentional self" becomes manifest in the ideological debate between the functionalists and the voluntarists. The functionalists seek the content and enrichment of the intentional self in Mead's generalized other—a social formation of the self. The voluntarists, on the other hand, postulate interests and creativity which transcend any processes of adaptation which the society may have generated. Hence, the problem remains: the nature of the self and the social world in which it appears. In more basic terms, we confront the problem of identifying the subject matter of the social sciences: what is this social reality which they claim to apprehend?

After delineating the ideological controversy in the human

sciences, we proposed the phenomenological method as a way of moving the debate to a methodological level. The first step in this transition has now been accomplished—identifying the difference in orientation between science and ideology. However, even within the broad orientation of science, one encounters diverse understandings of social reality. Here, too, the phenomenological method can help to disclose the aspects of social reality which are systematized within these scientific perspectives. In order to accomplish this, however, that method has to be applied to the social world which forms the common subject matter of the human sciences. What was accomplished in the preceding chapter for the intentional orientation of social science must now be carried through for the object of that intentionality.

In order to clarify what is *given* in the relationship of self and other, one has to go to the "lived" encounter of I and Thou. The world of I and Thou is a relationship of direct and immediate encounter; here, the face-to-face sharing of ideas, feelings, and concerns is spontaneous; this personal confrontation breaks through fixed definitions of status. Dancing together, "making music together," conversing on a personal level—these are ways of sharing internal time in the most concrete way.

Most of social life is experienced through objectified or reflected expectations: how my friend will react to this or that; how the clerk in the store will handle my check; what the policeman will do if I pass the stop sign, etc., etc. This is the world of the social self—the world of the generalized other. This is the world of they, him, or it, but it is not the world of Thou. It is the derived world of social expectations. However, the world of organized interaction arises from and is continually expressed through immediate encounters of person with person in gesture, sign, and symbol. The relationship of self and other is the presupposition and substratum for all derived structures of society. This "lived" world sets the limits to any sociology, since a science of the social world can only generalize the organization of secondary typifications; it cannot objectively grasp immediacy. These "lived" structures of immediacy are transformed as they are objectified in social process and scientific reflection. However, a social science presupposes a social world—the relationship of self and other on which the secondary structures are built. Moreover, the understanding of this immediate structure is decisive for interpretation of the social world by a social science. For example, social science may reduce the social world to the derived structures of expectation, denying any limits to its generalization of social process; then man becomes a mere reflection of the generalized other. Or a social science may grant the limits set by immediate social relationships and postulate certain basic interests, such as the struggle for power as decisive in the social world. In any case, a science of the social world presupposes one or another interpretation of the "lived" primary world of immediate encounter; moreover, this interpretation constitutes the level of abstraction on which the science works and, consequently, the limits of its immediate relevance to concrete social process.

In turning to the "lived" world of self and other, we seek, then, the primary level of social experience from which complex social relationships arise. In order to grasp the basic structure of that social matrix of society, we shall draw upon the researches of Alfred Schutz. We shall develop some implications of this research for an understanding of the nature of social reality and its essential tendencies. This basic structure should provide formal criteria for an evaluation of the understanding of man in the various scientific styles. This basic structure also discloses the norms for an ethic of the social world. Thus, the phenomenological approach to the "lived," or primary, level of sociality moves the inquiry from a debate between styles of social science to foundations for any scientific or ethical reflection on social reality. In this respect, the sociology of the everyday world is itself a style of social science—richer and more concrete, perhaps, but nonetheless a style which presupposes this primary level of I and Thou.[1]

## THE THESIS OF THE ALTER EGO

We shall take as our theme the problem of the "I" and "me" as George Herbert Mead formulated it. This was Mead's way of defining the problem of mind, self, and social reality. It is the core *problem* of social reality, since it is the basis of interpretation of the "social." Thus, the theme of our reflections will be the "intersubjective reality" which is presupposed in any science of the social world. When this theme has been clarified and we have brought into the open some essential aspects of human sociality, we can consider the dimensions of this reality which are categorized in the different scientific perspectives. In this way, we can achieve a systematic ordering of the scientific perspectives in terms of the basic criterion of social reality—the "lived" world of daily life. Hence, we turn to a reconsideration of Mead's thesis within a phenomenological frame of reference.

If we are to take Mead's method seriously and develop it along the lines of phenomenological description, we have to return to the basic unit of self and other with which he started. This structural unit of sociality is categorized in various ways by the human sciences. In recent years, sociologists have talked about interaction; for example, Talcott Parsons' notion of the relationship of actor and social object —the interaction situation—is constructed along the lines of a chess game.[2] This model involves each actor's taking the

[1] The phenomenological method accords with George Herbert Mead's approach, since he investigated the emergence of mind in the experience of significant gesture. The method is used here to identify essential tendencies as well as to develop a description of experience, thus clarifying aspects of the process of communication which remained obscure in Mead's analysis. For a discussion of steps in the use of phenomenological method and varieties of interpretation, see Spiegelberg, *op. cit.*, Vol. 2, Ch. 14.

[2] The concept of "interaction" presupposes a whole social world; each scientific categorization is a way of interpreting the nature of that world.

other into account in his moves, but it also presupposes that the actors work according to shared objectives and the rules of the game. At the root of this model is Parsons' notion of double contingency—each actor is in the position of guiding his own action or response according to his anticipation of what the other may do. However, the notion of double contingency presupposes all the things which Mead attempted to explore; it presupposes gesture, communication, shared meanings, and temporal structure. Moreover, the model for interaction in Parsons' theory, the chess game, is a highly abstracted form of the duality of self and other. The chess model, like the marketing model in economic theory and the exchange model used by George Homans, is a typification of the self and other which presupposes the social relationship. To this extent, we shall see that these models presuppose interpersonal relationship—constructing rational formulations of particular aspects of relationship for particular purposes.[3] Marcel Mauss developed a notion of exchange on a much more profound level in his study *The Gift*, thus founding the exchange model within the reciprocities of the intersubjective world.[4] Each of these models —chess game, exchange, and personal reciprocity—presupposes an interpersonal world or social reality.

Two groups of theorists are making significant contributions to unfolding the presuppositions of the social world

---

Talcott Parsons developed the notion of "double contingency" to suggest the problem confronting each actor in taking account of the alter ego's possible reactions along with the contingent alternatives of his own actions; see *The Social System* (New York: The Free Press, 1951), esp. pp. 36ff. and 94. His use of the chess game as a model conveys even more sharply the instrumental character of this understanding of the basic relationship of self and other; see *Theories of Society*, Vol. 1, p. 41. Hence, the problem is not whether one or another interpretation is scientific but, rather, what aspects of the "lived" world are typified in particular models—disclosing the degree of abstraction and hence relevance to the everyday world.

[3] George C. Homans is fully aware of this process of abstraction; we draw attention to it in order to clarify the status of scientific categorization. See his monograph *The Human Group* (New York: Harcourt, Brace & World, Inc., 1950), esp. pp. 10–21.

[4] Marcel Mauss, *The Gift*, translated by Ian Cunnison (New York: The Free Press, 1954).

as an interdependent, intersubjective relationship of self and other. The symbolic studies in the anthropological field will undoubtedly contribute significantly to this line of theory, since they touch on the roots of the process of communication. The symbolic interactionists who follow in the tradition of George Herbert Mead have continued to amplify his reflections on the social self and have brought to light useful concepts such as the reference group and personal identity.[5] The work in communication by both these groups has made quite clear how profoundly symbolization and sociality are embedded in each other and how important this grounding is for an understanding of human categories in the human sciences. Nevertheless, work in both these areas continues to be limited by the dominance of the behavioristic framework in which so much of symbolic interactionism has been pursued.

We shall turn here to an explicitly phenomenological explication of the relationship of self and other—the intersubjective world. The most important recent contributions to this field were made by Alfred Schutz. His predecessor in this field, Max Scheler, made an early application of phenomenological method to social reality.[6] However, this method never won wide acceptance in the United States, although its place in psychology is growing.[7] We shall draw heavily on Schutz's contributions to elucidating the nature of the social world. However, the particular line of thought in this inquiry will be guided by Mead's original statement of the problem and will consequently reshape much of Schutz's work for this task.

The difficulty of working in the phenomenological tradi-

[5] Reference has already been made to the work of Anselm Strauss, Erving Goffman, and Tamotsu Shibutani in this field.

[6] Most of Max Scheler's work took a metaphysical turn, but his study *The Nature of Sympathy* (New Haven, Conn.: Yale University Press, 1954) is a basic piece of phenomenological research on intersubjectivity.

[7] For these developments, see Wann (ed.), *op. cit.*, and May *et al.* (eds.), *op. cit.*

tion is that from the very first its ambiguities as a method have occasioned harsh differences over lines of development. The differences between Max Scheler and Edmund Husserl, Heidegger and Husserl, and numerous other conflicts over method and lines of development make it almost impossible to speak of phenomenology as one theory or school of thought.[8] No attempt is made here to identify or follow an orthodox line in phenomenology. Once granted freedom "to return to the facts"—to explicate the pregiven in our social experience—we can follow the lines set down by Mead and yet advance toward a more balanced understanding of the self in human science. This will be the path which we shall follow in making the transition from Mead's concept of the "social self" to the root concept which will guide the subsequent inquiry—the "intentional self."

The reflective attitude of human science works against the background of the social world of everyday life. If we turn back to social experience, it is evident that the other person is taken for granted in our commonsense world; we assume another consciousness like our own consciousness, and we engage in gestures and communication upon the assumption that this other person operates much as we do. In Alfred Schutz's terms, the other person is pregiven in our reflections on this everyday world, forming the social relatedness which we take for granted in all our activities.[9] However, what is taken for granted in the natural attitude of the commonsense world cannot simply be taken for granted in a science which proposes to give an explanatory account of events in that world. The existence of the other consciousness thus forms a fundamental problem to social science. Although human science need not resolve this problem, its theory must make some determination of it.

[8] For the difficulties in identifying this movement, see Spiegelberg, *op. cit.*, esp. Vol. 1, Introduction.

[9] See Schutz, *The Problem of Social Reality*, esp. pp. 11f., for the discussion of the reciprocity of perspectives by which "typifying constructs of thought" are built up, creating a common world.

If we introduce reflective doubt about the existence of the other person, then the consciousness of the other proves to be a very questionable assumption on our part. What we take for granted in everyday dealings suddenly becomes highly uncertain in the reflective doubt of a theoretical attitude. We experience another "something" over against us who moves, gestures, symbolizes, etc.; or phrasing it in the dialogue of struggle which Jean-Paul Sartre employs, we encounter the other who objectifies us in his "look." To be sure, in our everyday experience we communicate and manage our affairs, so we can reasonably assume that this person is a consciousness. However, this person is never given to us as immanent in our consciousness; he always stands over against us as transcendent to our consciousness. Here we can follow a distinction drawn by Edmund Husserl between immanent and transcendent objects of consciousness. In discussing this distinction, Alfred Schutz draws attention to the difference between immanently directed acts (in which the intentional objects, if existent, belong to the same life stream as the immanently directed acts themselves) and transcendently directed acts (acts directed toward the conscious stream of another).[10] In my reflections, I can encounter through reproduction of past images the objects which present themselves to me, and I can test these past presentations by perceiving such objects again from this angle and that. In each case, there is given to me in my stream of consciousness both the intended meanings and the presentations through which those intentions are fulfilled. If it turns out that my recollection was actually a dream or fantasy, and thus no such object exists to be presented, I may indeed recollect the dream but not find it fulfilled when I seek the object in perceptual fulfillments. By contrast, the other person as stream of consciousness is

[10] See Schutz, *Der Sinnhafte Aufban der sozialen Welt*, Sec. 19. See also Edmund Husserl, *Ideas*, translated by W. R. Boyce Gibson (New York: Collier Books, 1962), Sec. 38, esp. p. 112.

never given to me in this sense as the fulfillment of an immanently directed act.

Immanently directed acts give their objects, when they are reduced to their essential character, in an apodictic way. Whether these objects exist or not is another question and has to be tested by intuitive presentation, if one follows the phenomenological line of reasoning.[11] The initial task of phenomenological description, however, is to become clear on what is given in consciousness—to make an inventory of consciousness. On the other hand, intentional objects of transcendently directed acts are dubitable. They need to be tested for intentional fulfillment, and even after such testing they remain uncertain. This is particularly true of the other's stream of consciousness, which is never given as object to my consciousness but is only mediated through his disclosures in symbols and gestures. The "other consciousness," to simplify the terminology, is what Gabriel Marcel would call metaproblematic—a mystery in which my being as consciousness is caught up as I reflect on its possibility.[12] The other consciousness cannot be an object to me but is a reality in which I can *participate* by becoming engaged with the other. Indeed, we can follow Mead in postulating this social relatedness of self and other as prior to my experience of myself, to my self-awareness. This other consciousness is present to me before gesture, sign, symbol, and language become my mode of self-consciousness and consciousness of the other's meaning.

The dubitability of the other's consciousness sets sharp

[11] Edmund Husserl's statement of this method is available in his *Cartesian Meditations*, translated by Dorion Cairns (The Hague: Martinus Nijhoff, 1960), the First Meditation and esp. Sec. 6. For a discussion of the metaphysical implications of this view, see Quentin Lauer's Introduction to Husserl, *Phenomenology and the Crisis of Philosophy*, esp. pp. 28–31. The limits on making explicit this pregiven are clearly stated by Eugene T. Gendlin in an essay, "Expressive Meanings," in *An Invitation to Phenomenology*, edited by James M. Edie (Chicago: Quadrangle Books, 1965), pp. 240ff.

[12] See the discussion of this notion in Richard Zaner, *The Problem of Embodiment* (The Hague: Martinus Nijhoff, 1964), pp. 5ff.

limits to our interpretation of the meaning of another person's activity. We shall have to explore this problem of understanding another's acts in considerable detail in the next stage of the inquiry. For the moment, however, the crucial point is that the social relatedness—the presence of the other's consciousness—which we take for granted, confronts us as a highly dubitable existent in the attitude of scientific doubt. Indeed, we work in the human sciences on the assumption that the other consciousness is sufficiently similar to our own for understanding, but this other stream of consciousness will never be given to us in a transparent way. The other consciousness remains an inaccessible presupposition of the social world and sets fast limits to the pretensions of any human science. Edmund Husserl's struggle to found the existence of intersubjectivity in his *Cartesian Meditations*, however inadequate its results, indicates the seriousness of this problem.[13] The intersubjective world is the pregiven reality within which mind, self, and society are possible—the milieu of symbolic activity. However, this intersubjective world resists our attempts to bring it into the category of objects which we can analyze and manipulate. Hence, our grasp of this social reality involves a knowledge through participation rather than through objectification. The intersubjective world is internally related self-consciousness, and this is its difficulty as a scientific field. We ourselves are involved in the reality which we grasp as the consciousness of the other.[14]

Alfred Schutz has formulated our awareness of the other consciousness as the "general thesis of the alter ego." The essential point is an important advance toward a reformulation of Mead's position. If we return to the "lived in" experi-

[13] See Husserl, *Cartesian Meditations*, the Fifth Meditation, in which he attempts to found a transcendental intersubjectivity.

[14] Gabriel Marcel distinguishes the scientific attitude of the observer (first reflection) from the second reflection, which seeks to recapture the unity of the subject by *participation*; see the discussion of this method in Zaner, *op. cit.*, pp. 6ff.

ence of the everyday world—the base line for reflections on the nature of social reality—we recognize that our vivid, living present is not given to us except in reflective acts. I cannot capture my present as an object of consciousness except in reflection.[15] My gesturing eludes my consciousness of it as gesturing. My attention is toward the other for whom the gesture is intended. My awareness focuses on his response to this gesture. This mutual mirroring of gesture and response characterizes face-to-face dialogue. The vivid present is not accessible to the ego in his speaking and acting; he "lives in" this action. However, the other (the alter ego) is present to the "I" in the immediacy of his speech and act. I listen to him and grasp his meaning *as it is being expressed,* in the vivid present. Although his present is given to him only in reflective acts, that vivid present is immediately given to me as I give my attention to it. Thus Schutz formulates the thesis: ". . . the alter ego is that subjective stream of thought which can be experienced in its vivid present." [16]

Schutz radicalizes this thesis to found his social theory, and we shall follow his line of thought. His formulation is particularly valuable because it sets Mead's basic theory in a balanced frame of reference and overcomes its behavioristic background. Schutz gives further specifications of this general thesis in the following terms:

> This experience of the Other's stream of consciousness in vivid simultaneity I propose to call the *general thesis of the alter ego's existence.* It implies that this stream of thought which is not mine shows the same fundamental structure as my own consciousness. This means that the Other is like me, capable of acting and thinking; that his stream of thought shows the same through and through connectedness as mine; that analogous to my own life of consciousness his shows the same time-structure, together with the specific experience of re-

[15] There are three main discussions of this problem in Alfred Schutz: *Der Sinnhafte Aufbau der sozialen Welt,* Ch. 3; *Collected Papers,* Vol. 1, pp. 150–203; and "Symbol, Reality and Society," esp. pp. 315f and 352ff.

[16] *Ibid., Collected Papers,* Vol. 1, p. 174.

tentions, reflections, protensions, anticipations connected therewith, and its phenomena of memory and attention, of kernel and horizon of [the] thought, and all the modifications thereof. It means, furthermore, that the Other can live, as I do, either in his acts and thought, directed towards their objects, or turn to his own acting and thinking; that he can experience his own Self only *modo praeterito,* but that he may look at my stream of consciousness in a vivid present; that, consequently, he has the genuine experience of growing old with me as I know that I do with him.

. . . In so far as each of us can experience the Other's thoughts and acts in the vivid present whereas either can grasp his own only as a past by way of reflection, I know more of the Other and he knows more of me than either of us knows of his own stream of consciousness. This present, common to both of us, is the pure sphere of the 'We.' And if we accept this definition, we can agree with Scheler's tenet that the sphere of the 'We' is pregiven to the sphere of the Self—although Scheler never had in mind the theory we have just outlined. We participate without an act of reflection in the vivid simultaneity of the 'We,' whereas the I appears only after the reflective turning. And our theory also converges (on another level, to be sure) with Scheler's statement that acts are not objectifiable and that the Other's acts can be experienced only by co-performing them. For we cannot grasp our own acting in its actual present; we can seize only those of our acts which are past; but we experience the Other's acts in their vivid performance.[17]

The lack of symmetry in this experience of vivid simultaneity—the "We-relation"—points to the "social" interdependence of self and other which can stabilize George Herbert Mead's theory. In this experience, my vivid present is confirmed by the other's response, even as his vivid present finds recognition in my response. I actualize my "now" as my vivid present through the other, even as he actualizes his "now" as this selfhood through my presence for him. The "We-relation" is the matrix of self-actualization of the "I" as being-in-the-world, but it is a matrix of mutual depen-

[17] *Ibid.*, pp. 174f.

dence. We depend upon each other in the "We-relation" for the confirmation of our being-in-the-world. The possibility of actualization as self-in-the-world depends upon the intersubjective experience of self and other in the "We-relation."

The basic issue is the priority of sociality in the communicative process, where "priority" refers to the founding of the communicative process. Alfred Schutz has clarified, in his essay "Making Music Together," the founding of the communicative process on a sharing of inner time in a vivid present or quasi-simultaneity.[18] He uses the structure of music in this particular essay, since its notations, or signs, are secondary to the mutual participation in the musical event. Schutz defines a piece of music as ". . . a meaningful arrangement of tones in inner time. It is the occurrence in inner time which is the very form of existence of music."[19] He then proceeds to develop the nature of sharing in the temporal process of the musical piece by reading a score, hearing a performance, and playing together. Playing in a duet, in an orchestra, or singing together, the participants live sumultaneously in the inner temporal process of the musical piece and synchronize their activities by sharing in the various dimensions of inner and outer time which characterize the face-to-face relationship. They act "in concert."[20] The example of making music together serves to focus the priority of ". . . partaking in common of different dimensions of time simultaneously lived through by the participants"[21] —the tuning-in relationship—since the sharing of inner time is the essence of participation in the musical event. Alfred Schutz summarizes this priority of sociality as foundation of the communicative process in the following way:

> . . . It appears that all possible communication presupposes a mutual tuning-in relationship between the communicator and the addressee of the communication. This relationship is estab-

[18] *Ibid.*, Vol. 2, pp. 159–178.
[19] *Ibid.*, p. 170.
[20] Alfred Schutz does not use this expression, but it is an idiom which carries some of the weight of his argument.
[21] *Ibid.*, p. 177.

> lished by the reciprocal sharing of the Other's flux of experience in inner time, by living through a vivid present together, by experiencing this togetherness as a "We." Only within this experience does the Other's conduct become meaningful to the partner tuned in on him—that is, the Other's body and its movements can be and are interpreted as a field of expression of events within his inner life. . . .
>
> . . . It is hardly necessary to point out that the remarks in the preceding paragraph refer to communication within the face-to-face relationship. It can, however, be shown that all the other forms of possible communication can be explained as derived from this paramount situation.[22]

The significance of sign, gesture, and symbol need not be underplayed in order to achieve the balance of interiority and exteriority in the emergence of mind, self, and society.[23] The issue is one of foundation, and there seems to be little question that the behavioristic background of George Herbert Mead's analysis led to an unbalanced stress on exteriority. Alfred Schutz's phenomenological analysis, drawing on the work and insight of Edmund Husserl, breaks through the closed circle of external determination in the communicative process. However, Schutz has gone beyond Husserl in laying the foundations for intersubjectivity in the general thesis of the alter ego—participation in vivid simultaneity. The tuning-in relationship carries Schutz's thesis much further, since it goes below the level of significant gesture to a sharing of inner time in the musical event. It is this mutual

[22] *Ibid.*, pp. 177f.

[23] We have no argument with Clifford Geertz's stress on the emergence of man in his symbolic activity; the enrichment of self and cultural world can be seen as correlated when the proper balance of interiority and exteriority of embodied consciousness is preserved. The serious question for this phenomenological analysis is raised by Charles Hartshorne in a critique of Edmund Husserl's notion of intersubjectivity, where he points to a perpetuation of a dualism between the being of the other and the other as given. Alfred Schutz's approach, which we follow, presupposes an *overlap* in experience of self and other, as well as a distinction; symbolization brings this to consciousness. See Hartshorne, "Husserl and the Social Structure of Immediacy," in *Philosophical Essays in Memory of Edmund Husserl* (Cambridge, Mass.: Harvard University Press, 1948).

confirmation of being-in-the-world through vivid simultaneity—most richly experienced in various forms of the tuning-in relationship, such as dance, ritual, music, poetry, and the intimate moments of a loving relationship—which discloses the foundational interrelatedness of personal being.[24] Sociality is not a product of external forces or so-called interaction; rather, interaction, communication, and the emergence of complex social structures are *derived* typifications of the essential sociality of man. Hence, Mead's insightful analysis of the self finds a solid foundation in the "We-relation," through which sign, gesture, and symbol develop and ramify the human "reach" beyond the face-to-face relationship to the most complex possibilities of temporal, spatial, and higher-order relationships.

### *THE EMERGENCE OF MIND WITHIN SOCIALITY*

George Herbert Mead's triadic structure of the emergence of mind can be reconstituted in a more balanced way as the coming to consciousness of the "We-relation." Mead's original formulation, which was discussed in Chapter 1, can be schematized as follows:

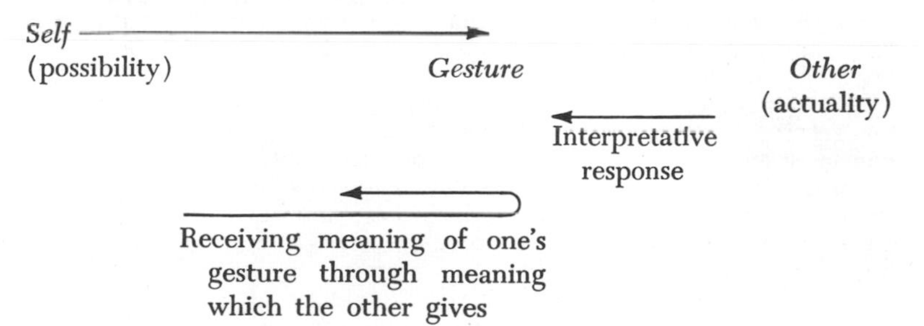


In this schematization, the self is a reflection of society; as the self takes the other's perspective, he apprehends his

[24] Early childhood experiences with the mother could well be explored in this context—holding, rocking, fondling, singing, etc. These experiences are recognized as foundational to psycho-organismic development, but the

fumbling gesture as meaningful sign. On more complex levels of language and culture, he assumes the perspective of the generalized other, achieving mind and rationality by calling out in himself the response which he arouses in others by gesture and sign. The problem with this account, as indicated in Chapter 1, is that the use of an explanatory hypothesis of social determination leads to the paradox of selves emerging from a social process which itself presupposes selves. The problem is how internally related selves can emerge from externally related entities. The evidence of the "We-relation" suggests that selves are internally related on a primordial level; thus, the emergence of sign, symbol, and mind reflects the increasing interiority of this sociality as self-consciousness and the cultural enrichment of this sociality as the shared world of cultural meanings.[25]

A new schematization of the triadic structure can be sketched from the pregiven relatedness of self and other in vivid simultaneity in the following way:

---

sharing of inner temporal consciousness would seem to be fundamental to this early experience of sociality. This analysis could serve to place the affective mode of relationship which has so dominated the developmental theories in a more adequate context. The flux of consciousness and the kinesthetic patterns—shared and developed in this originary "We-relation"—would thus form the ground of the embodied consciousness and its higher level of activity in sensation, apperception, and will. See Zaner, *op. cit.*, pp. 239–261.

[25] The presupposition of self and sociality, of symbol and communication, of the intersubjective world which forms the subject matter of the human sciences is thus the social nature of reality. According to this understanding, we can discern essential tendencies in man which reflect the pregiven structures through which his experience of the other is possible. The accessibility of these pregiven forms to clarification in reflection also implies the accessibility of these forms to elucidation by reason in reflection. The most comprehensive grounding of the social nature of reality has been effected by Charles Hartshorne in the framework of process thought; a conception of God as social being, ". . . as that member of the society which exerts the supreme conserving and coordinating influence," underlies this view, but our concern is to explicate the problem of sociality on a less general level, even while recognizing the essential role of generalization in clarifying the implications of a social world and its scientific illumination. See Hartshorne, *Reality as a Social Process*, Ch. 1 and p. 40.

underlying relatedness

*Self* ⟷ *Other*

Subjective center of relational being

Subjective center of relational being

⟶ (Dynamic) The gesture expresses the impulse to actualization of pregiven sociality through eliciting response of the other

⟵ (Form) Interpretative response actualizing pregiven sociality as meaning (arising in intimacy of "We-relation" of shared inner process)

⟵ (Unification) Empathic sharing in other's interpretative response as meaning of gesture, coming to consciousness of sociality (unification of self and other as "We"), and simultaneous emergence of identity (self-consciousness as unification of gesturing self and expressed meaning in intentionality)

The basic innovations in this model are: (1) the presupposition of sociality coming to consciousness as mind through gesture, sign, and symbol; (2) the balance of the gesturing self (dynamic) with the meaning-receiving and meaning-giving interpretative response of the other.[26]

In this schematization, three basic elements can be identified: dynamic, form, and unification. These are very general elements with a long history in philosophic discussion and most recently developed in the theological milieu by Paul Tillich. There may well be additional structural components

[26] The notion of the "social" presupposed by this statement is clearly expressed by Charles Hartshorne: "Let us define the social as the appeal of life for life, of experience for experience. It is 'shared experience,' the echo of one experience in another. Hence, nothing can be social that is without experience. The minimum of experience, let us further agree, is feeling. Creatures are social if they feel, and feel in relation to each other's feeling" (*ibid.*, p. 34).

for an exhaustive account of social experience, but these elements serve to clarify the triadic relationship in Mead's analysis.

Unification is the crucial element in this analysis: sociality comes to consciousness in the process of gesture (dynamic); concern for response is expressed through the communicative gesture (form), which becomes the basic structure of sociality. Thus, all three elements appear in each dimension of the emergence of mind, self, and society from sociality.

1. The gesture is dynamic, eliciting attention (a standing over against the other and reaching toward the other); however, the gesture itself presents an intention, expresses meaning with some form; it also reflects a relatedness and need for response—an anxiety over a lost unity and a concern for response.[27]

2. The interpretative response is a meaning-giving (form-receiving and form-giving) act; this dominance of form in the interpretative response should not obscure the implicit dynamic of the openness to the other and the reflection of relatedness in the attention to the other.

3. The dominance of unification becomes fully manifest in the reciprocity of perspectives, which is presupposed in seeing the gesture from the perspective of the other; however, this empathic seeing from the stance of the other involves the dynamic of distance from oneself, which is mediated by the other's giving of form to the gesture—making possible a sharing in a common world of form. The unity of self and other is actualized as a social world through the sharing of gestures, signs, and language; the unity of the self is actualized simultaneously, as personal identity in

[27] The notion of fundamental anxiety or anxiety of being can be formulated in a variety of ways according to the context of consideration; the social conception of reality implies anxiety as alienation and distortion of the social harmony; however, alienation itself presupposes something of the basic anxiety of the finite freedom with which Paul Tillich deals. See his *Systematic Theology* (Chicago: University of Chicago Press, 1951), Vol. 1, pp. 190f.

the consistency of the intentionality of the self with the responses of the social world and particularly the world of significant others. The structure of dynamic and form in their unity as self-consciousness reveals man's essential tendencies as: (1) care for response; (2) reflective awareness and openness to form; (3) thrust to integrity and unity.

We could summarize the restatement of Mead's schema as a shift from the dominance of form and social determination to the principle of unification, or sociality, in which internal dynamics (the intentional self) and shared forms (the social self) develop in dialogue and enriching counterpoint.[28] This basic structure thus reflects essential tendencies of the self which are disclosed as fundamental conditions of experience itself. The dynamic freedom of distance and openness to being is an essential element of experience, emerging in the actualization of sociality. The shared forms of a public world mediate the self-consciousness of personal identity and reflect the sociality which underlies the communicative process itself. In turn, the relatedness of being is presupposed in this social process—appearing in the form of immediacy as the "We-relation" and amplified in a social and cultural milieu through the dialogue of gesture, sign, and higher-order symbols. Hence, the "We-relation" is the immediate givenness of sociality and also the matrix of lan-

[28] This position is a consistent explication of the balanced view of mind and sociality which George Herbert Mead was elucidating; see *The Social Psychology of George Herbert Mead*, esp. pp. 256–260. The principal modification which has been introduced to move beyond the vulnerability to social determination in Mead's formulation is to found experience in vivid simultaneity—consciousness of the other in the vivid present (the "We-relation"); hence, self-objectification—the "me"—arises from the sociality of the I and Thou rather than the reverse; the expression of this "lived" sociality in symbolization and a reciprocity of perspectives is an actualization of subjectivity in cultural and social forms. Mead can say that "the individual enters as such into his own experience only as an object, not as a subject" (p. 258), but this social reflection through the generalized other has a deeper foundation in "lived" intersubjectivity which we call the "We-relation"—the "lived" experience of subjectivity which comes to consciousness in reflection and is the presupposition of language.

guage and mind. In this respect, self and symbolization are interdependent expressions of creativity (dynamics) and shared meanings (forms) which emerge as the coming to consciousness of sociality in evolution.

A symbol is a vehicle of conception, to use Susanne Langer's rather general definition.[29] In this sense, a symbol is the mode of the self's openness toward the world; it is also the mode of its distance from the world—distance through which it surpasses the immediacy of its environment and transforms what surrounds it from an environment into a situation. The subject-object relationship implies a standing-over-against the other or the situation. Thus, being "situated" rather than being "conditioned by an enviroment" implies a self which can set itself apart from its world while at the same time being open toward that world. Symbolization is precisely this possibility. Reality is given through the symbol —whatever that reality may be—and the reality is both intended by the self in the symbol and set at a distance from the self through the symbol. Being conscious of the other, to return to the "We-relation," is not merely a matter of being united in a sense of sympathy or common feeling; being conscious is also awareness of this other as that other person who is speaking, gesturing, expressing fear or joy, turning toward us or away from us, etc. Thus, being conscious of the other is grasping the other's meaning. When the other enters into a "We-relation," he implies a willingness not only to give his presence but also to disclose his feelings and thoughts; similarly, the sharing of the self in a "We-relation" is an attempt to enter this symbolic world through interpretative activity. Being conscious of oneself, moreover, is reflective awareness that one is the intentional source of encounter; in brief, self-consciousness, or distance from oneself as acting, thinking, feeling, etc., is dependent upon the

[29] Susanne Langer, *Philosophy in a New Key* (New York: Mentor Books, 1948), p. 61.

symbolization through which the process of consciousness can be given to itself. The self as self-consciousness comes into being not only through the response of the other but also through the process of symbolization.

The "We-relation" can be understood as the social matrix of symbolization, because the self gains distance through the response of the other to its gestures and disclosures; thus, the self receives from the other the meaning of gesture and symbol through which its own consciousness can become an object of reflective awareness. The self discovers its intentional structure through the fulfillment of its meaning-intention in the response of the other.[30] The other is thus a source of distance from oneself through symbols, as well as a source of confirmation of being by his attention in the vivid simultaneity of mutual presence. This second aspect of the "We-relation" is the source of symbolization to which George Herbert Mead's analysis was addressed—the emergence of mind through the recognition of the meaning of gesture in the other's response. Thus, the social character of human being is fundamental to the self in its anxiety for being—the impulse to find response in the other and the impulse toward gesture and language—and also to the intentional thrust of the self toward a consciousness of its own meaning as the meaning of being-in-the-world.

This analysis of the "We-relation" involves two dimensions —"impulse to confirmation of being" and "impulse to meaning"—which can be separated only analytically. The very notion of "anxiety over being," which was introduced as a root of the "We-relation," implies the distance from self and other which arises in symbolization and self-consciousness.[31]

[30] Gesture, sign, and symbol (higher order) are expressions of meaning or, in Husserl's terms, meaning-intentions. Evidence is the harmonious relation of meaning-intention to meaning-fulfillment; in this instance, the mutual mirroring of the "We-relation" is the process of building up typical structures of meaning through disappointments and fulfillments. See Husserl, *Cartesian Meditations,* p. 15.

[31] Alfred Schutz postulates this anxiety as the root of the spontaneous drive to mastery in the everyday world, but he does not seem to ground

The notion of intentional expression implies consciousness of self which is mediated through the distance offered by the other's response. Hence, to speak of the human world is to speak of an intersubjective world which is a world of presence and distance, of impulse to relatedness and thrust to distance. The human world is thus an intersubjective world in which self and other are united in their essential relatedness and yet separate in their actualization of this relationship. In affirming the other, the self expresses its distance and freedom. The self is ultimately, then, a freedom or distance from the self, the other, and the world—a freedom made possible by sociality and yet a freedom through which sociality emerges.

The self as embodied consciousness is thus free in its self-surpassing power to reconstitute any situation. However, this freedom is mediated through the other person and through symbol. Moreover, the content of the self—its structure as a continuing form—is mediated by society and culture. The self is constituted in its biography; the self is simultaneously the intentionality toward the future through which that sedimented past is reconstituted in a grasping at enlarged meaning and fuller integrity. Here again the dominance of unification suggests the essential character of the dialectic of dynamics and form with which the self experiences its identity as given and yet reconstitutes that given selfhood. Unification discloses itself as the internal thrust of embodied consciousness to achieve a richer world and thus an enlarged scope of internal meaning; this thrust to self-surpassing involves simultaneously a reaching beyond any unity of the world which is already given toward a more comprehensive meaning. The reach for embracing unity thus

---

it in any notion of reality; the expansive "search for meaning" and the "creative expression of meaning" which disclose themselves in symbolization can readily be referred to such anxiety, but the anxiety itself presupposes a self-transcending subjectivity, as was indicated earlier (see fn. 26).

includes the self-surpassing dynamic of freedom toward richer experience for the self within a world of more comprehensive meaning.

We have, in this preliminary consideration, focused only upon the "We-relation" in its positive or creative aspect. However, the dependence of the other upon the self's disclosure in the "We-relation," as in all the other relationships which will be considered later, arises from the freedom of the self. The possibility of bad faith also arises in this self-transcendence of the "I." The "We-relation" may be an occasion in which we encounter deceit. Even as the "I" subject has the power to negate every social and cultural form, up to and including his own existence, so the "I" subject may engage the other in a mutual confidence which he intends to betray or may later betray for other reasons. Hence, the "We-relation" is not only matrix of being and meaning but also occasion of man's deepest betrayals. The ambiguity of the "I," and thus of the "We-relation," arises from self-transcendence and belies any social determinism.

When we speak of the "I," then, in terms of its creativity and power, we confront the question of the content of the "I." What can be said about the "I" subject in reference to ultimate fulfillment or meaning? This problem was already suggested in the notion of an anxiety of being and meaning. The self, so far as can be discovered in phenomenological reflection on its intentionality toward the world, reflects a thrust toward wholeness both in its self and in the harmony of the world in relation to which it is constituted.[32] We can speak here, then, of a passion for unity which presses the self beyond any level of integration of self or world which is already achieved; any coherence of the world already grasped is subject to reconsideration and new levels of formulation. These general notions, then, point to the form

[32] See John Wild's discussion of this notion of an "ultimate horizon of meaning" in his book *Existence and the World of Freedom* (Englewood Cliffs, N.J.: Prentice-Hall, Inc., 1963), esp. p. 209.

of the "I" subject as intentionality stretched upon the world with care for response (anxiety of being), concern for meaning (enrichment as self-consciousness), and infinite passion for unity (lured to harmony) in its own being and in relation to an ultimate horizon of meaning. However, the content of this "I" subject is mediated through the physical, social, and cultural world; the enrichment of the "I" is inseparable from the enrichment of its world. George Herbert Mead's insight into the social mediation of the self points to the content of the self which is the objective correlate of intentional being-in-the-world. Much more can be said about the content which is mediated by a particular structure of social and cultural possibilities; in the present context, we need to recognize that the world is always the limited, finite possibility available to this infinite passion for unity. Hence, the social self is the vehicle of actualization of the "I" but is also its limitation and the focus of transcending projection to new possibilities. The key term, however, is "unity," and the integrity of self, social world, and cultural actualization is subject to this principle.

The infinite concern of the "I" for integrity also implies that the objective reality of its ultimate commitment becomes creative or destructive for the content of its fulfillment or defeat. The internal unity of the "I" is inseparable from the richness of its ultimate horizon. The "I" constitutes itself in its intentionality toward the social and cultural world, but it is in turn constituted by the meaning of the world toward which it moves. Bad faith, for example, which arises in the anxiety of being, ultimately reflects the choice of the "I" in its reach toward fulfillment; in bad faith, the harmony of self and other to which the "I" belongs is sacrificed for a lesser reality of the "I's" choice, and the basic relatedness of self and other is denied. This possibility, as indicated, arises in the freedom and distance through which the "I" comes into being in self-consciousness, but its content as bad faith arises in a violation of the essential unity of self and other, in the "false" commitment of the self to its own fulfillment. Hence, the content of the "I" can be discussed normatively; for the moment, it is essential only to recognize that the reality of ultimate commitment—the ultimate horizon of meaning in which choosing and valuing occur—reflects an adequate or inadequate expression of the project of the "I," *i.e.*, its apprehension of fulfillment as particular being in the context of universal being.

## *INTERPRETATIONS OF SOCIALITY*

The problem of human science is to formulate the parameters of the intersubjective world in such a way that the self-transcendence of the intentional consciousness is held in tension with the structures of the social and cultural world. In place of George Herbert Mead's notion of the social self, therefore, we shall use the idea of intentional self. The intentional self is situated in social and cultural worlds through its orientations as a perspective on these worlds. That perspective can never be subsumed under the structures of that world, even though the possibilities and conditions open to that perspective can be detailed through these structures. In social-scientific language, role structures define the "situation" of the "I" but not the "I." The intentional consciousness is a project stretched upon the world, as we have suggested, and is thus an orientation to the future which takes up the past and its structures but can never be exhausted by that past. The intentional self is thus a temporal self, as we indicated in our account of the vivid simultaneity of the "We-relation." The deepest encounter of the intentional self occurs in the "We-relation," because this is the finite matrix in which its struggle with its temporality and contingency comes to focus—the impulse to confirmation of its being as presence-in-the-world and the impulse to meaning as self-awareness. However, the "We-relation" is also the deepest expression of the impulse to harmony as the richest possibility of selfhood in relationship to another self-consciousness.

The nature of the intentional consciousness has been explicated by Maurice Merleau-Ponty in reference to perception. This notion of the self as perspective on the world and embodiment in the world can serve to recapitulate our previous considerations and frame a typology for ways in which the human sciences have interpreted the freedom of the intentional self. Merleau-Ponty points out, and here he follows Edmund Husserl, that the consciousness is implicated in a flux of the world—grasping in sensible profiles from its own perspective a world which is never given transparently.[33] Thus, the perception of a chair is a sensible consciousness of an object in which its profile, texture, color, and distance occur within a horizon of other objects and fields; this particular perspective can be renewed by moving to other locations and glimpsing the chair or by feeling it, sitting on it, etc. In brief, the identification of the chair as chair and the consciousness of its being thus-and-so involve a projection of possibilities which could be completed—a constitution of the world which is intended but never transparently fulfilled. The identification is an idealizing possibility of consciousness through symbols—the vehicles of conception to which reference was made earlier. Nevertheless, this is an idealization and promises more than is given in the perceptual experience of consciousness.

In his discussion of perception, Merleau-Ponty points out that an understanding of man as intentional consciousness

[33] The following discussion is drawn principally from Maurice Merleau-Ponty's *The Structure of Behavior* (Boston: Beacon Press, 1963); however, a concise statement of his view on the paramount reality of the perceptual consciousness as embodied or sensible consciousness—the "lived" consciousness on which all higher order elaborations are founded and which is elucidated in the reflective work of science—is to be found in *The Primacy of Perception*, pp. 3–42; note his remark: ". . . we must rediscover the structure of the perceived world through a process similar to that of an archaeologist. For the structure of the perceived world is buried under the sedimentations of later knowledge" (p. 5).

means that we recognize man as mind which is embodied—as sensible consciousness which is a perspective on the world. There are various ways of misconceiving this intentional consciousness in correlation with a world by the way in which we formulate the theory of man in the world. Man's consciousness can be understood in terms of the ideal significations which are given to him in reflective thought on that world; the consciousness is then understood as ideal. On the other hand, the "lived in" flux of events within which the sensible consciousness acts may be taken as productive of sensations which become consciousness as images or representations; in this latter sense, consciousness is derived from something external which it is not. A more concrete approach to the intentional self attempts to deal with the ideal and sensible aspects of consciousness.

Our examination of expression and interpretation in the "We-relation" introduced the dimension of embodiment into the relationship of self and other. The notion of symbol as vehicle already implied this; gesture presupposes bodily expression. We have moved, therefore, from the cognitive level on which George Herbert Mead investigated the emergence of mind to the "lived" experience of the "We-relation" and its linguistic actualization; now the implications of the embodiment of the "We-relation," not only in vehicles of conception but also in perceptual consciousness, will complete the concretizing of this account. The "We-relation" is possible only because self and other are embodied; I meet the other through his bodily presence, although our relationship surpasses bodily conditions; the "We-relation" presupposes physical or biological processes even though it transcends them. Mead was correct to explore this problem as a question of "intersubjectivity" and consciousness, but his account needs to be extended to the understanding of embodiment.

Another way of stating this final step in the inquiry into self and other is to pose once again Mead's problem of the emergence of mind. Any theory of evolution involves a concept of levels—physical, biological, mental. Mind, self, and society emerged in the course of evolution; at least this is a working hypothesis which underlies contemporary theory in the human sciences. The problem, then, is how one interprets the intersubjective world. On what level of meaning is it to be interpreted? Do we best understand the meaning of self and other—the "We-relation" or some counterpart—from an analysis of external physical forces or from the conditioning of instincts by milieu, etc.? Is the discussion of self and other reducible to genetics or some physical field concepts? Is the interpersonal language of the "We-relation" an illusory language in which we falsify the physically determined character of these relationships? Or, moving to a radically different level, is the embodiment of our meanings little more than a sensuous limitation of the pure grasp of ideas?

Merleau-Ponty speaks of various perspectives of signification within which the unity of self and world can be understood. He treats these interpretations as physical, vital, and mental perspectives of signification.[34] If we treat these interpretative perspectives as abstractions from the "lived" process of sociality, we can distinguish the level of abstraction and the element of basic structure which is emphasized. Chart 2 delineates the basic structure of these perspectives as abstractions from the concrete level of embodied consciousness.

The foregoing analysis has been developed from the concrete level shown at the base of Chart 2—the world of embodied consciousness or finite freedom. The reflections of

[34] The following discussion is an adaptation for the author's purpose of Maurice Merleau-Ponty's discussion of "planes of signification" on which form is disclosed: ". . . In other words, matter, life and mind must participate unequally in the nature of form; they must represent different degrees of integration and, finally, must constitute a hierarchy in which individuality is progressively achieved" (*The Structure of Behavior,* p. 133).

the everyday world may simply be the practical typifications by which everyday activity is organized in the service of various interests. This is the most concrete level for sociological investigation and is best exemplified in the work of Alfred Schutz. The voluntaristic perspective abstracts the dynamic element of interest and develops a typology of the conflict of interests and the dialectic of rationalization and nonrational commitments to value. The functionalist abstracts a relational system from the unification of social process—imputing a trend toward order or equilibrium in the process. The behaviorist abstracts a form aspect and gains a determinate grasp of social process from the laws of exchange. From this difference in abstraction, it is evident that the voluntarists would find themselves at odds with both the functionalists and the behaviorists, as we have already noted in the account of recent controversies in Chapter 2. Behaviorists and functionalists differ primarily in that functionalists purport to account for the internal dynamics of self and world, while the behaviorists treat internal dynamics as products of conditioning. This is a significant difference, since the functionalist operates with a principle of unification which should account for the whole process, but he takes this principle on a very abstract level which makes it comparable to the behaviorist notion of balance. Hence, the functionalist develops a pseudointentionality, while the behaviorist confines himself to external or formal determination.

In Chart 2, the arrow running from bottom left to upper right indicates the increasing degrees of abstraction in these major styles of social science and the focus of the particular abstraction on one or another element of the basic structure of sociality. The concrete style of science of the everyday world may stress unification or harmony (as has been the case in the foregoing analysis) or may shift toward dynamics (as Schutz did under Max Weber's influence) or toward form (which occurs in Georg Simmel's style of social science. There are, of course, various styles of social science, but we have limited this account to those which have become dominant in recent decades.

Although the ordering of the various styles of social science has to be postponed until more has been said about the nature of the scientific perspective, some suggestions on the understanding of man in these perspectives can be drawn from the discussion of sociality. Three essential tendencies were identified in the structure of the "We-relation"—translating the structure to vectors: (1) the gesture disclosed freedom as a dynamic of invocation; (2) the interpretative

**Chart 2** SCIENTIFIC PERSPECTIVES ON THE SOCIAL WORLD (*Revised*)[35]

| Styles | Actor (Dynamic) | Order of Objects (Unification) | Action (Form) |
|---|---|---|---|
| Behaviorist | Impulses | Balance of Forces | Laws |
| Functionalist | Needs | Maintenance of System | Pattern Variables |
| Voluntarist | Interests | Domination/ Compromise | Ideal Constructs |
| Intentionalist | Attention | Reciprocity/ Harmony | Projects |
| (Implicit Level) | Spontaneity | Intentionality (Embodied) | Schema (Body-Subject) |

[35] The author is indebted to Robert Terry for discussion and clarification of this chart; Maurice Merleau-Ponty's characterization of the prephenomenal is basic to this chart; further clarification was derived from Harold Garfinkel's incisive presentation of the Intentionalist style (not his term) in "Perception of the Other," *op. cit.*

response reflected the form as received and constituted; (3) the empathic taking of the stance of the other led to the unification of dynamic and form as sociality and self-consciousness. Much more could be said about freedom as power, which is manifest in the gesture, and about freedom as openness, which is disclosed in the interpretative response. We have already noted the interrelation of these elements in each dimension of the process of communication. The understanding of man as embodied consciousness or finite freedom views him as intentionality toward a world and understands the world as inseparable from the intentionality to which it is related. Abstractions from this self-and-world relationship may serve to clarify certain aspects of the network of intentionality in the world, but they require translation into the context of "lived" experience before their bearing on the everyday world can be assessed. A brief glance at the views of man underlying these interpretations will suggest the problems which arise if they are mistaken for an understanding of concrete sociality.

*The behaviorist style* is the most abstract. What it gains in generalization is very costly on the dynamic side, since the interiority of sociality is reduced to external conditions. So far as that interiority is routinized, an account of conditions can provide useful understanding of determinations and continuities. So far as the behaviorist purports to do more than this, he substitutes his abstracted models of social conditions for the social world; in this case, interiority becomes little more than the preservation of an adequate internal balance in relation to those forces. Whatever particular content the social theory gives to those forces would then become the expression of the human in its field of force —desire, utility, self-interest, pleasure, or any other of a number of variables which the human sciences have introduced on this level of interpretation.

*Interpretation on the functional level*—as, for example,

Talcott Parsons' structural-functional theory—tends to treat fulfillment in terms of maximal adjustment in the release of instinctual or other energies; thus, functionalists impute value by the way in which they categorize the energies of the organism. However, the nature of man and his fulfillment tends to be defined by the cultural and social world in functional theories of the type which Parsons has developed. Hence, an imputation of the meaning of fulfillment emerges from the categorization of the values and structures of the social system; the self has no other content of fulfillment than a suitable internalization of that culture and adequate opportunities to express its possibilities in particular choices and activities. The content of the self—its meaning—is to reflect its culture in its particular location. The social process or the cultural world, as it has emerged in a particular era, thus gives any content to the fulfillment of the self that is worth discussing. This reduction of self-fulfillment to the cultural process follows from the creation of the social self by the cultural world. This is the bias of functionalism to social conformity.

*Voluntarist and Intentionalist,* as we have identified them, open up innumerable possibilities for the exploration of intentional consciousness. The problem of human fulfillment or content of the self arises on this level as well. We have already made some proposals for this content in terms of harmony and integrity; however, the explication of that content means an exploration of the religious, ethical, aesthetic, and other realms of human consciousness. We shall limit much of the subsequent discussion of these problems to ethical values in relation to social science, but the notion of an ultimate horizon of self and sociality implies that reason enters as fully into the explication of these meanings as it does on the instrumental level of means. The significant problem for human science, on this level of interpretation, is whether a science of man is possible at all. We have already noted that the social scientists avoid this concrete level of interpretation because of the ambiguity of the structures which emerge and the difficulty of gaining access to what we have called intentional consciousness. We noted also that human science tends toward situational determinism—for example, in much of symbolic interactionism—once it takes the level of symbol and cultural milieu seriously. The constitutive consciousness of the self, which we have repeatedly insisted is implicit in George Herbert Mead's analysis, including every subsequent attempt to adapt his insights, is active and creative as well as passive in its receptivity to a pregiven world, so that simple determinisms merely obscure the nature of intentional consciousness. If this is the case, we are pressed with the question of whether a science of man can be developed on this level of interpretation and what its nature would be. Can there be human science on the human level of meaning?

Another way of stating this problem is to recognize that the "We-relation" is not accessible to scientific explication; we spoke of the "We-relation" as the "lived in" experience of vivid simultaneity which can be brought to consciousness in reflection but has the character of immediacy. If this claim is accurate and the "We-relation" which we posit as the fundamental experience of sociality and humanness is not accessible to objective study, what aspect of the human process is accessible to scientific investigation and in what sense? We have attempted to bring out the nature of man as intentional consciousness and the central category of his sociality—the general thesis of the alter ego. Have we, in the course of raising this human level of interpretation, simply eliminated the possibility of a "science" of man? If, on the other hand, a science of man is possible, what are the limits imposed upon its concepts and methods if it is to take seriously the intentional consciousness? What is the constitutive character of that consciousness in relation to the social and cultural world? If, then, the subject matter of any science of man finds its grounding in intentional consciousness, what is the nature of a science which is appropriate to such a subject matter? The essence of the human is concern for response, reflective self-awareness, and thrust to integrity and harmony. In what ways do the sciences of man enhance these tendencies of the essentially human? If many of the current theories in social science deny or subvert these tendencies, at least in their theoretical formulations, does this simply obviate their utility, or can society appropriate their findings, with appropriate modifications, in its own decision-making?

All these questions press us to the next stage of our inquiry, which has already been anticipated at several points. We need to characterize a "science" of the human and social world. If we are clearer now on the subject matter of a human science—what the human means in the tension between the "I" and the "me" of Mead's formulation—we seem further than ever from the possibility of a "science" of this human subject matter. In terms of Chart 2, therefore, we face the question of how the structure of embodied consciousness is organized in relation to the cultural and social milieu in which it actualizes its tendencies. The uniqueness of the human sciences stems from their willingness to grapple with such difficulties; they attempt to bring the complex world of the intentional self into the sphere of systematic reflection.

# 5 *a scientific perspective on the social world*

Intentionality is used to develop the nature and limits of social science; various scientific styles are defined in relation to the everyday world of commonsense experience

THE WORLD of the intentional self is not fully accessible to the other in even the most intimate relationship. The other's consciousness always remains a transcendent corollary of our own consciousness; we can never inwardly experience in our consciousness the richness and particularity of the other's consciousness—if only because his "here and now," as well as his total biography, furnishes a unique perspective on the world. We can approximate the meaning of a situation to the other in only a rough way—in the fashion of common cultural understandings and a reciprocity of perspectives, taking for granted that his interests are similar enough to our own so that things appear to him as they do to us.[1]

Chapter 4 has radicalized the creative character of the intentional consciousness and the "immediate" character of the intersubjective world of I and Thou, which we designate as the "We-relation." This radical notion of the subjective meaning of the social world sets the limit for a science of the social world. Social science attempts to grasp this subjective meaning in an objective schema of interpretation.[2] To what extent can there be a science of such a subjective

[1] For a discussion of the presupposition of a reciprocity of perspectives, see Schutz, *Collected Works*, Vol. 1, pp. 11f.

[2] See Schutz, *Der Sinnhafte Aufbau der sozialen Welt*, Sec. 43.

reality? With reference to Chart 2 of Chapter 4, how can the reflected meanings of a theoretical science penetrate to the level of "intentional consciousness"; further, if a science of social reality cannot penetrate to that level of mental integration, to what extent is it a science of the "social" world?

A science of the social world is possible and useful if the ideals of science are pursued with a rigor appropriate to the subject matter. The ideals of science are precision, unity, universality, and pervasiveness of law. These ideals, as Felix Kaufmann notes, cluster around the ideal of truth as the informing goal of science. With reference to the concept of truth in science, Felix Kaufmann remarks, ". . . it is an ideal of inquiry to incorporate into science 'true' propositions, i.e., propositions able to withstand any possible control. And in general we mean by 'ideal' a goal defined in terms of a potentially endless process."[3] "Control" refers to the assumption that any proposition may be eliminated from the corpus of a science according to the rules of procedure in the science. Truth is thus an infinite ideal of science, since it presses toward the "incorporation of permanently valid propositions."[4]

The problem of a social science is to pursue with appropriate rigor the ideals of science in its search for truth. If our explication of the nature of social reality is accurate, there are aspects of the social world which would lend themselves to relatively precise formulation; there are also aspects of this world which elude systematic formulation. If the social world were not predictable within reasonable limits, we could not accomplish a single cooperative act; in fact, the simplest act would be an adventure. On the other hand, those aspects of social reality which are richest in meaning and possibility to the intentional consciousness—the less routinized processes of the social world—are predictable only

[3] Kaufmann, *op. cit.*, p. 72.
[4] *Ibid.*, pp. 64f. and 72ff.

in a limited way. If the ideals of science are pursued with dogmatic rigor, there is a tendency to reduce social reality in order to fit it to a "scientific" ideal; hence, certain aspects of social reality become the preoccupying concern of the social sciences simply because they are more amenable to precise formulation. In either case, the richness of social reality is artificially filtered out, and social science is limited to one or two relatively uninteresting styles. Thus, our task in this chapter is to give an account of the scope and possibilities of a science of the social world. Our aim will be to indicate the relevance of several styles of social science to social experience and the limitation of any social science in comprehending the human world.

Human science is a possibility because human action has objective coherence. The social world is a habitable world for man because it follows typical courses and offers a predictable environment for human projects. The human sciences are creative attempts by man to formulate these coherences in such a way as to account for expected courses of action in this social world. However, every formulation by social science alters the possibilities and expectations of that world; social science is a part of the fabric of the social world. Furthermore, the social world is dynamic, whereas the grasp of that world in human science is fixed. Human action looks forward in its projects; human science looks backward to grasp the meaning of human action in terms of the past. This characteristic of human science marks its limits as a predictive and controlling discipline; human science can talk about the future only on the assumption of continuity of past patterns of action. On the other hand, the value of human science arises from its explication of the conditions of human projects, bringing to consciousness many aspects of the social world which lie hidden from view and identifying regularities which give relative predictability to the social world.

A dramatic example of this work of human science may

help to set the stage for our theoretical analysis. Several social scientists carried out a study of the treatment of mental illness in public clinics in New Haven, Connecticut.[5] In the course of the study, it became evident that established psychiatrists tended to reject lower-class patients in the clinic, passing them over to instructors and students in the lower echelons of the medical hierarchy. This rejection of lower-class patients was apparently caused by the doctors' feeling that psychiatric techniques were incompatible with the mental disorders and personal attitudes of lower-class patients. (Psychiatry has been largely a middle-class style of therapy.) This was only one of several ways in which lower-class patients received less adequate help in public clinics. According to the study, the psychiatrists were astonished to discover that they were shunting these lower-class patients over to students. They were not conscious of this pattern in their handling of cases. What came of this insight was not made clear in the study, but several important possibilities can be noted: (1) a more equitable distribution of cases, for the sake of both patients and medical staff, could be developed; (2) perhaps even more important, psychiatric technique and understanding could be broadened through more systematic application of therapy to lower-class patients.

This rather dramatic example illustrates both the potential of social science for altering the situation which it observes and the account which it can give of human projects. The intentional character of human action does not mean that it is unstructured or lacking in pattern; on the other hand, the dynamic character of that action means that knowledge of the situation forms material for reshaping those patterns. The human sciences, when they deal appropriately with their subject matter, prove to be creative elements in the reshaping of the social world. This at least will be the inter-

[5] See August Hollingshead and F. C. Redlich, *Social Class and Mental Illness* (New York: John Wiley & Sons, Inc., 1958).

pretation that emerges from our attempt to define a science on the human level of the intentional self.

The notion of the intentional self sets marked limits to social determinism and thus presents problems to any scientific dogmatism about human action. On the other hand, this concept furnishes an important key to fundamental issues which have plagued the human sciences. The first issue has already been raised—the problem of the unity of the "me" and the "I," the social self and the creative "I." A second issue is the determination of the structural units of human behavior or action: by what criteria are actions delimited as meaningful units? This problem is seldom discussed in the human sciences, but its resolution is presupposed; to this extent, every behavioral science presupposes the meanings arising from intentional consciousness. We have already referred, for example, to Schnore and Duncan's claim that knowledge of the actor's attitudes is irrelevant to the social scientists; in their view, a science of society need only examine external forces at play on these units, thus calculating the direction in which the configuration of forces will move the process.[6] However, these ecologists presuppose an understanding of the process; the meanings of social structure, technological process, organization, and statistical indices are created in terms of the common culture of the society.[7] Meaning is given to their findings *not* by their scientific work alone but by the presupposed meanings prevalent in the common culture; they take for granted what is meant by members of the society when they do, talk about, think about, and intend certain activities. Schnore and Duncan assume that they *know* what the social process is!

[6] See Chapter 2, fn. 7.

[7] The term "common culture" is shorthand for the framework of typical meanings which is taken for granted in the "everyday" world. Harold Garfinkel defines the "common culture" as ". . . the socially sanctioned grounds of inference and action that people use in their everyday affairs and which they assume that other members of the group use in the same way." See *Theories of Mind,* p. 689.

When one has calculated the forces at work and speaks, as these men do, of the direction of collective movements, one is drawing on the intended meanings of the common culture without acknowledgment or scientific verification. A science which is supposed to explore these problems takes them for granted. Asking "what the social process *is*" leads the scientist back ultimately to the intentions of the actors and the relationship between those intentions and the common culture in which they participate. The scientist can presuppose the meaning or inquire into it; he cannot escape it.

In the following discussion, we shall begin with the social issue—the meaning of action and social process. From this exploration into the theme of scientific inquiry, we shall be led back to the source of the social world in human intentionality.

## *THE MEANING OF ACTION—THE PROJECT*

The ambiguity of the "meaning of an act" can be seen initially in an example from legal judgment. Consider the problem faced by a court in a treason trial. What constitutes the treasonable act; that is, what is the *act* to be judged, or in the customary words of the court, what is "relevant" to the case? Certain activities of the accused may have been treasonable; for example, he may have taken certain documents and transmitted them to foreign agents. On the other hand, these activities gain a very different meaning when they are set within the larger context of his activities, as in the case of a counteragent who has been instructed to divulge unimportant information in order to become acquainted with a spy ring operating within the country. Or, to complicate the picture even more, the common culture within which the court operates may decide that the activities *known to them* are treasonable, whereas the spy may have acted in the best interests of his country according to *his own* understanding; here, then, the intentional meaning, so far as this can be discerned, and the full scope of meaning of the action give a decisive context of interpretation for what was *meant.* To be sure, the official responsibility of the court in preserving the society makes the effect on the society and the understanding in the common culture the decisive criteria for judging the action. In either case, the interpretative context is determined by what was "meant" —on the one hand, meant for the agent; on the other, for the common culture. To the court, the significant criterion of "meant" is the understanding of loyalty in the common culture.[8]

Dropping our illustration, let us explore the notion of common culture and the significance of "understood meanings." In order to gain a clearer grasp of the functioning of common culture, we can turn back to our source of reflection—the everyday world of common sense.

We pursue our activities in the everyday world according to typical processes; thus, most of our activities are of the kind "I-have-done-it-before" or "I-can-do-it-again." The natural attitude of this commonsense world dictates that things will be generally the way they were before and that tried methods will work. There are, of course, shifts of context, and new problems arise constantly, as we have seen, but the course of events learned from childhood retains a certain familiarity and repeatability. We have referred this typical course of events, meanings, and symbols to the common culture; generally speaking, we act according to the possibilities and meanings provided by our common culture, especially in managing the affairs of our workaday world. These understandings of the common culture do not exhaust the meaning of our activities, but they provide a *pregiven typification* of them.[9]

[8] See Schutz, *Collected Papers,* Vol. 2, "Equality and the Meaning Structure of the Social World," for an elaborate presentation of problems in interpretative context.

[9] *Ibid.*, Vol. 1, "Common-sense and Scientific Interpretation of Human Action."

Furthermore, we suggested that the attitude toward this commonsense world is pragmatic. In the everyday world, we are concerned with managing our affairs, getting where we have to go, accomplishing the marketing, or carrying out the productive activity that is expected of us. We turn from this pragmatic attitude distracted, at moments, pausing to daydream, or stopping to sit by a fountain and reflect, but our activities in the working world tend to be problem-solving efforts which are organized according to typical courses of understanding and activity. The typifications of meaning are the taken-for-granted understandings of how things should go. We say ordinarily that such and such "makes sense"; we mean explicitly that it fits the everyday understanding.

This "lived in" experience expresses our spontaneous, unreflected activity in the world. Edmund Husserl describes this experience as "lived" by reference to the inner time-sense of retention and protension.[10] This can be illustrated by the problem of perception of an object—a problem with which Husserl preoccupied himself. We see the object by retaining its presence for us through the stream of time; we reach forward toward the horizon of possible aspects of it which we do not perceive. For example, in looking at a die, we see only the partial surfaces of several sides, and yet we call it a "die"; we leap forward in protension to possible sides which are not accessible. We see the die from our "here and now"—the orientational center where we find ourselves; we retain its content as meaning and reach forward to its possibilities within the vivid present of our perceiving. This "lived" experience of the object in perceiving is different from the recollective process of that experience, and it is different again from a reflected experience of consciousness. We may later, in recollection, turn back upon an experience and bring it to explicit consciousness, but

[10] See Husserl, *The Phenomenology of Internal Time-Consciousness*, esp. Secs. 9–13.

then we reproduce the image of the die as perceived in our recollection. We reproduce the die. Reflective experience makes the objects immanent in consciousness available for conscious attention, but this reflective process is different from the "lived in" experience of retentions and protensions with their inner time-sense; it is an attentional modification of consciousness. This reflective self-consciousness makes the *experience* of the die into *an object* of consciousness; thus our attention is on consciousness of an object of the everyday world.[11]

The "meaning of action" is just such a reflective modification of consciousness. "Meaning" is the unified significance of our action as it appears in the reflective glance of our attention.[12] Our "lived in" experience is meaningful as it *appears* to reflective consciousness; to be sure, much of our activity remains inaccessible to consciousness—activity such as breathing, lower-level sensation of temperature, much of our feeling, anxiety, etc. (The anxiety of loneliness is almost totally inaccessible to consciousness.[13]) Meaningfulness is constituted, however, in the reflective consciousness as it brings to light what was intended or is being intended; moreover, the reflective attention is directed from a later "here and now." This reflective, meaning-giving attention may be retrospective—reconstituting the multistructured building up of spontaneous activity—or it may be a kind of preremembrance which projects itself toward an action

[11] This summary of Edmund Husserl's extensive research on this problem is only intended to suggest the difference between "lived" and reflected experience.

[12] For an explication of the retrospective character of the concept of "meaningful experience"—its presupposition of the "lived" as given in reflective attention—see Schutz, *Der Sinnhafte Aufbau der sozialen Welt*, esp. Secs. 7 and 8. See also Maurice Merleau-Ponty's development of this Husserlian theme on the priority of the "lived" to the "known" in *The Structure of Behavior*, pp. 219f., and *The Primacy of Perception*, esp. pp. 12–27.

[13] There is a difference of opinion on this among phenomenologists—we follow Alfred Schutz on this issue. The reference to loneliness and anxiety is to the research of Harry Stack Sullivan, *The Interpersonal Theory of Psychiatry* (New York: W. W. Norton & Co., Inc. 1953).

to be accomplished; in both cases, the action is reflected on as a completed process. Hence, the meaning of action can be seen as retrospective or prospective; in both cases, however, the reflections are attentional modifications of the "lived in" experience of the everyday attitude. To ask about 'meaning" is to withdraw at least fragmentarily from "lived" experience to reflective understanding.

Alfred Schutz gives a helpful analysis of *choice* which illuminates this distinction between reflective attention and the process of "lived" experience.[14] The problem of human choice, as he notes, is often discussed as an issue between freedom and determinism or necessity. However, the discussion of choice as "determined" arises from an attentional modification; a later "here and now" is taken as perspective, and the spontaneous activity of projecting—choosing—is viewed retrospectively as *selection* among completed alternatives; actually, the alternatives were not yet available in the earlier "here and now"; thus, choice is converted in reflection into a static determination. The prospective meaning of choosing is the spontaneous creation of alternatives; the retrospective meaning is an allocation among fixed alternatives. Since one alternative is of necessity poorer, one's choice is only to err in the retrospective view.

In shaping a project, we build up step by step a course of action; some of that process is pregiven in typical courses of action which we take for granted, and newer typifications are constituted in syntheses which we build; only in the most routine actions are all steps predefined. This shaping process is acted through in the "lived" process of our vivid present, retaining significant elements of the situation in relation to protensions and anticipations. If we convert this projective, shaping process into a *shaped* process by a retrospective glance, we create an illusion of determinism—the shaping process by which alternatives come into existence is converted into a predetermined choice among preset alter-

[14] See Schutz, *Collected Papers,* Vol. 1, "Choosing Among Projects of Action."

natives. Alfred Schutz illustrates this process in the following way: the problem of choice is conceived retrospectively as the traveler at the fork in the roads, where only one road can be a right choice; hence, his freedom is only to err before a preconstituted set of possibilities, and he can thus be rational and determined or free and in error. This is a retrospective picture, however, since choice involves constituting the alternatives in spontaneous activity; this constitution works with pregiven materials of previous syntheses of experience, but it constitutes these materials in a new unity of the project. We shall observe later that responsibility means just this actional freedom of constituting a future.[15]

In sum, the meaning of action refers to the reflective modification of attention and may be a retrospective or a projective glance of recognition. In either case, the concepts of "action" and "meaning" arise from the reflective modification. Moreover, there are orders of synthesized meaning which embrace larger and smaller segments of activity; as we noted in the example of the treasonable act, particular activities may be seen as treasonable, but they gain a different meaning in a more comprehensive ordering of elements within the full project of the action. Alfred Schutz refers to these various orderings as "schemas of interpretation" of experience; in a more comprehensive sense, one can speak of "systems of meaning" which order phases of the cultural and social world—for example, a linguistic system, a scientific system, a legal system, etc.[16] For our present purposes, the essential point is to reckon with what is to be

[15] The notion of rational action—calculation of the most efficient means to an end—is not an exception to this, although it fits the "fork in the road" model more aptly, since the goal is presupposed. In fact, much of technological transformation is a process of reconstituting "the situation" by redefining goals and likewise involves creation of means rather than mere allocation among given alternatives. For example, one could interpret the problem of American railroading as a failure to realize that they were directed to "transportation" and not *merely* to transport *on* rails.

[16] See Schutz, *Collected Papers,* Vol. 1, "Symbol, Reality and Society," which is somewhat elliptic but is one of his most creative essays; and see also the exposition of "domains of relevance" in the discussion of equality, Vol. 2.

conveyed in the notion of the "meaning of action," recognizing that there are limited and comprehensive orderings of meanings by which action is synthesized within an interpretative context. In general, meaning is given in the interpretative glance of the actor or observer, and the meaning which is given depends upon the schema within which the action is understood. The issue, then, is whose schema is decisive for understanding the action.

When we refer to "common culture," we mean the understood typification of modes of acting and "reasons" for acting which are available or "at hand" in the everyday experience of the society. This "common culture" is not consciously intended in the everyday routines, but it serves in reflective consciousness as the formulation of meaning when questions arise. Thus, when a neighbor's action is somewhat bizarre, we struggle with whether to take him seriously, "laugh it off," or call a policeman; we are bringing to consciousness relevant aspects of the common culture as the schema of interpretation—posing the question about the action as to whether it "makes sense" within these understandings of our common culture. Hence, the common culture is the comprehensive system of the meaning of action which is available to reflection as the "understood grounds of inference and action" for the everyday world. However, reference to "meaning" and "common culture" already places us in the context of reflective awareness and is not to be confused with "lived" experience. The common culture, moreover, furnishes little more than rules of thumb for coping with the rich complexities of neighborly relationships; what "makes sense" in that culture has to be reinterpreted in terms of concrete dynamics and circumstances.[17]

"Meaning," as we shall use it, refers to a synthesis of recog-

[17] The reflective character of the notion of common culture indicates that this is a theoretical typification by which the social scientist attempts to typify the structure of that realm of "lived" experience as a world of pregiven meaning.

nition in the reflective consciousness. For example, while touring Isle au Haut one summer, I heard several of the group in the front of the car referring to a teapot in a tree. Upon hearing this remark, I recollected having seen a teapot in a tree. This experience had remained on the periphery of my attention simply because I could not integrate it with the rest of my meaningful understanding in a synthesis of recognition. I could not "have" the experience. Our host explained, at this point, that he had found a teapot (apparently, some campers had left it) and had hung it in the tree. After hearing his explanation, this experience could be synthesized by me within the reflective attention of a total ordering of these events. The experience was too extraordinary to take for granted; thus, it required a reflective awareness. Meaning had to be given to the experience by a synthesizing act of consciousness; in discussing meaning, therefore, we refer to the constitutive work of reflective consciousness.

*The decisive criterion for the "meaning of action" is the project of the actor—the anticipated state of affairs in his own preremembrance or the retrospective recovery of that project as elapsed; that is, meaning is "what is meant" or "what was meant."* To speak of the intentional self on the human level, as we have in the preceding chapter, is to postulate that human action can be brought to consciousness in reflective attention because its integration is on a mental level. *The apprehension of the project may be inadequate, but the project is the criterion of meaning.* Even the subliminal processes which cannot be explicitly made conscious are not alien to consciousness but form the "lived" expression of that consciousness in its attention to the world. The criterion of meaning is the synthesis of recognition of the intentional consciousness, even though any particular person may at one or another stage of his experience be very unclear on his intentions. Action, from the simplest perception to the most complex plan, is protensive—moving in a constitutive synthesis toward the future. In reflection, the project defines the span and unity of what is meant. Usually we assume this span from the common culture, in which meanings are pregiven. We have already seen in the case of treasonable activity that the project furnishes the criterion of what was occurring in the series of events which the court attempts to order under an adequate schema of interpretation. We can say, in this sense, that the project defines the *intended* meaning of the action. Whether that project or intended meaning was fulfilled or not, the court has to decide—whether, for example, the patriotic intention came to fulfillment. In terms of the common culture, the court may decide that the project foundered because the agent did not fully grasp the danger to the society of some of his actions and the priority of the claims of the society over any individual's interpretation of its long-run good. The court necessarily employs the interpretative context of the common culture in evaluating the project. Hence, the court may find the agent guilty of treason, even though the "intention" was not treasonable; the agent is guilty of treason because his project was misconceived and miscarried; however, his project defines the span and sense of what was meant by his act.[18] If his project was treason, the court may concur.

The common culture of the society is the schema by which scientific interpretations can be tested; the coherent ordering of experience and meaning in the society is given in common culture and accounted for by science. *The common culture is, so to speak, the system of meaning of the societal processes—the project of that society in the most comprehensive*

[18] We avoid here the ambiguous terms "objective" and "subjective" meaning, employed by Max Weber, which obviously apply to this situation; such terms are equivocal, since the legal system does not necessarily embody the ordering principle of the common culture, as in the case of "Southern" justice in dealing with the Negro—courts may implement the objective interpretation of a regional culture, although they presumably represent the "common law" of a country within a constitution of rights.

*sense;* how that societal project coincides with what is concretely meant remains problematic; furthermore, every reflection on meaning, as in the trial, is from a later "here and now" and only reconstructs the project. Actors participate in common culture according to their location in the society and the degree of responsibility which they assume; however, their particular projects are judged within the common culture according to the accepted understanding of how things are done and what is or is not done. We take for granted that their projects reflect that common culture which we share. Hence, social action and social relationships presuppose sharing common typifications and meanings with roughly similar systems of relevance. A society is only an "external process" in an abstractive view of scientific observation, and even then it is no longer a society unless it is grasped in terms of its intentional structure—from the inside. Eric Voegelin expresses this understanding as follows:

> Human society is not merely a fact, or an event in the external world to be studied by an observer like a natural phenomenon. Though it has externality as one of its important components, it is as a whole a little world, a cosmion, illuminated with meaning from within by the human beings who continuously create and bear it as the mode and condition of their self-realization.[19]

The task of the human sciences starts with a common culture of understood meanings. The scientist may content himself with certain taken-for-granted meanings; for example, in estimating the redistribution of population in an urban area, he may take for granted that residence and neighborhood association are "understood" concerns of families in finding their location. On the other hand, the scientist may be interested in a specific group and the way in

[19] Eric Voegelin, *The New Science of Politics* (Chicago: University of Chicago Press, 1952), p. 27.

which that group interprets the meaning of residence; he will, in this instance, inquire much more rigorously into the particular interpretation which this group is giving to the common culture; he may discover that residence means primarily being with one's ethnic compatriots.[20]

We find a comparable situation in the more intimate relationship of friendship or marriage; most of the time, we take for granted that the other person is using the common terms and symbols in the ways which fit the common culture and are appropriate to the particular shape which our own relationship has given to that culture. However, in the intimacy of personal encounters, the broader common culture and even the particular culture of our own relationship are undergoing modification. In personal encounter, we engage in a process of redefinition which may lead to sharp conflicts, new understandings, and even a radical transformation of the relationship.

Pregiven cultural meanings thus form a typical world which we appropriate in ways that correspond to our location in the society; this was the common world of the social self with which George Herbert Mead was concerned. Clearly, it is appropriated most significantly through participation in the symbol system of the common culture, although its constitutive power runs much deeper even than this. On the other hand, this common or objective world of cultural meanings is constituted and reconstituted in active syntheses of consciousness which make these activities and symbols an *expression* of the being-in-the-world or project of the subject. The object-world as physical, social, and cul-

[20] Contrast, for example, the views set forth by Schnore and Duncan, *op. cit.*, and the position of Peter Rossi in his comments and in his study *Why Families Move* (New York: The Free Press, 1955). Note also that Duncan cannot give a scientific definition of a Negro but accepts the common culture in his "objective" study *The Negro Population in Chicago* (Chicago: University of Chicago Press, 1957); there is scientific reason to take for granted typifications of the common culture for the pursuit of certain problems, such as spatial location of groups, but this gives no warrant to deny the significance of what is taken for granted.

tural milieu is a world-for-consciousness, even as consciousness is consciousness-in-the-world. It is this correlation of consciousness and world which leads any discussion of common culture back to the consciousness within that culture; to this extent, symbolization provides the vehicle of common consciousness as crystallization of the common culture. The interpretation of action should begin by making objective aspects of the cultural and social world into themes for reflection, but this beginning can find fulfillment only in its referral back to the constituting consciousness in which that world is experienced; hence, the *project* is the total intentionality with which subjectivity as a totality is stretched toward the world as possibility—shaping the future; in relation to this embodied, total meaning of a world, the usual meaning of *intention* is superficial. In this sense, the project is the decisive criterion against which a scientific interpretation has to be tested for adequacy.

The basic analogy for this whole problem is furnished by the notion of embodiment. Richard Zaner's discussion of the theories of embodiment in Gabriel Marcel, Jean-Paul Sartre, and Maurice Merleau-Ponty furnishes a clue to the relationship of common culture to the constitutive consciousness:

> . . . the fundamental relation between my body and surrounding objects is to be conceived in terms of my body's actual and possible action on them and their action on my body. Thus perception as well as being a "power" of my body, one of the modes of my body's action in and on surrounding objects, must be conceived as fundamentally what I would call *actional:* to perceive is to act, not in the sense of effecting a real alteration on objects (though perception is a necessary condition even for that), but in the sense that to perceive is to reflect the possible action of my body on them. Objects are not first of all complexes of physical entities called atoms, nor is perception the reception of sense-data caused by the physical motions of these affairs. Objects, for my experience of them by means of

my body, are essentially connected to my body's action on them, they are "poles of action."

> . . . to consider objects as strict poles of action, and my body as actual, is tantamount to maintaining that objects in the world and consciousness as embodied are inseparable, that they are strict *correlates* of one another, and that, therefore, one must always consider objects strictly *as* correlates of the consciousness of them, and consciousness *as* the strict correlate to its objects. This then implies that objects are strictly "meant," or "intended" as such by consciousness.[21]

This actional understanding of the embodiment of consciousness in the world runs directly counter to the doctrine of sensations which treats consciousness as the passive product of stimuli acting upon it. We can acknowledge the passive or automatic syntheses of sense experience in which the world appears as the pregiven world of our embodiment, but this material basis of our constituting acts is made possible by kinesthetic flow-patterns which reveal a certain "if-then" style:

> . . . "If" I set in motion certain kinds of kinaesthesis (say, "opening my mouth," along with other types, "raising my hand," and so on, moreover in a very particular manner and order), "then" certain sensuous contents will be actualized (say, tasting sweetness, pulpiness, and the like, correlated with "apples"). But, on the other hand, and just because of this functional correlation, the organism is itself co-experienced (co-intended) simultaneously with the sensuous perception of a content: every sensuous perception, to speak at a higher level, necessarily involves a co-perception of the organism itself as that with which I perceive and that by means of which what is perceived is perceived.[22]

The reciprocal relationship of passivity and activity, of automatic and intended syntheses opens the way to an under-

[21] Zaner, *op. cit.*, p. 248.
[22] *Ibid.*, p. 257.

standing of the object-world as pregiven to consciousness and yet constituted in the syntheses of consciousness. The regularities of the object-world and the understood typifications which we designate as common culture form the milieu of typical meanings with which the sciences of action are preoccupied, but these regularities are not made once for all; they reflect the "mundanization" of consciousness which may properly be called the process of embodiment. We may for certain purposes abstract that object-world or common culture in its typifications from this process of embodiment, but if we convert it into a "causal force" which is producing consciousness through sensations or association of physical stimuli, we break the intentional character of that reality; in other words, we introduce the anomaly of meaning and correlated consciousness as a *product* of nonconscious physical forces; the fact is that the world appears to consciousness as a world of colors, shapes, etc., which cannot be reduced to the products of nonqualitative sensations.[23]

This understanding of the regularities of the object-world as corollary to consciousness of that world grounds our interpretation of the relation of consciousness to common culture and thus of the possibility and limits of a science of human action. *Science deals with the typical courses of action and the accepted grounds of inference and action which occur within a particular society or culture.* It attempts to account for these regularities. These objective meanings, symbols, and styles of embodiment, to use the analogy of the mundanization of consciousness, are the shaping milieu of consciousness; they are also the vehicles of disclosure of intentionalities. In other words, the criterion of adequacy for any scientific grasp of these typical patterns is the projected meaning of this world for the consciousness of that

[23] The epistemological problem arising from such causal notions—the undermining of all thought by reducing it to external causes—was the preoccupying concern of Edmund Husserl in his development of phenomenology. See Merleau-Ponty, *The Primacy of Perception*, pp. 43f.

world. The self-interpretation of consciousness as the meaning-giving synthesis of recognition—the project—provides the ultimate limiting condition of any systematization of the meaning of action in a society. Hence, the unity of action, social structure, and cultural forms is not an objective unity which can be formulated as objective regularities or sequences; it is a unity *meant* in the intentionality of a particular group or society. For many purposes, this intended meaning can be taken for granted on the basis of the common culture, but the presupposition is that this meaning is in fact the intentionality of participants in that culture; furthermore, the culture is the sedimented project of the society and is the decisive criterion for the adequacy of any interpretation of societal processes.

Regularities of gesture, symbolic meaning, action, and expected forms of behavior furnish the coherence of the social world; this sedimentation of meaning makes *possible* a science of human action. In retrospective, meaning-giving reflection on the processes of society, science attempts to formulate these typical patterns according to its interests. Since these scientific formulations are abstractions from the concrete and infinitely rich horizons of regularity in any phase of social process, we recognize that scientific constructions of typical patterns are *idealizations* of these regularities. These idealizations are constructed with reference to scientific problems; they constitute what Alfred Schutz has called second-degree constructs of typical patterns.[24] This was in essence Max Weber's understanding of the ideal-typical method of social science.[25] In its simplest terms, this is a method which has its counterpart in our everyday experience, since we ordinarily represent certain kinds of object-identities or patterns of activity by idealized images

[24] See Schutz, *Collected Papers*, Vol. 1, "Common-sense and Scientific Interpretation of Human Action," pp. 40ff.

[25] See Max Weber, *The Methodology of the Social Sciences* (New York: The Free Press, 1949), esp. Ch. 3.

which we can reproduce as meaning a particular object or activity. The practical interests of everyday life determine the systems of relevances with which these regularities are reproduced; the problem, for example, of the stereotype in social life arises from this idealization of the social object (where "idealization" means removing much of the concrete richness of particularity and "intending a generality"—a class of persons as having these or those characteristics). The interests determining the particular idealization may be of such a kind that a stereotype emerges which resists change under the impact of concrete experience; for example, the stereotype of the Jew in Nazi Germany accumulated typifications which had no warrant in empirical experience—thus conjoining fantasy to everyday typification.[26]

The ideal-typical method of human science formulates patterns of activity and cultural understanding according to its scientific interests. The criterion of adequacy for the scientific interpretation is the actual pattern dominant within a society or culture; however, science attempts an objective formulation of the societal process, understanding action in the society or in a segment of the society within an objective schema of interpretation. This is what Alfred Schutz called the attempt to grasp the subjective meaning of action in an objective schema of interpretation. The subjective meaning—the project—remains the limiting condition of the adequacy of the scientific grasp, since the project constitutes the active synthesis of meaning in the dynamic process of society. We can call this a limiting condition in the sense that no adequate grasp of what is meant would be possible except for the self-interpretation of reflective consciousness, and this grasp would always be limited by the shift of position to a new situation at the time the meaning is opened to reflection; thus, my grasp of a past experience at time $t_1$ is distorted by the perspective of the "here and now" of $t_2$.

[26] Alfred Schutz discusses this problem of ingroup and outgroup typification in the essay on equality, *Collected Papers*, Vol. 2.

This limiting condition—subjective meaning, or project, as constituting the unity and span of meaning of the action —does not destroy the possibility of a science of human action, but it does dictate both the appropriate method and the proper limits of understanding. A social pattern or symbol or institution can be viewed as a sedimentation of meaning through which consciousness is shaped and may thus form a theme for scientific schematization. The particular social science will then proceed to idealize elements of this pattern and the occasion of its occurrence according to its own interests. However, the understanding of the meaning of this regularity is ultimately verifiable only by exploration of the intentionality in which it is constituted and actualized.[27] Whether we consider an artifact from a prehistoric period or a linguistic usage in a modern society, in every case the cultural regularity *discloses an embodied consciousness* and leads the reflections of the interpreter back to some grasp of that consciousness.

The regularities of the culture shape and reshape consciousness in passive syntheses of a pregiven pattern, but they are simultaneously the vehicles of expression and disclosure of the embodiment of consciousness in its being-in-the-world; hence, these typifications cannot be understood apart from the grasp of that intentionality, although for certain purposes this intentionality may be presupposed. Even as the regularities and coherences of common culture make a human science possible, the dependence of these regularities on a consciousness which cannot be objectified as an immanent object of reflection for the observer limits human science to an interpretative role. In giving an account of these regularities, the human sciences find themselves engaged in retrospective reflection on a social reality which is prospective in its dynamic character. To explicate this

[27] Scientific models have internal criteria as well which are determined by the principles of method of science as a discipline—itself a cultural tradition. For an elaboration of the ideals and preference rules of the culture of science, see Kaufman, *op. cit.*

limitation, however, we have to shift our attention from mere typification to the temporal modes of social and cultural process.

## *PROJECT AND CONDITIONS*

Our suggestion that the *project* defines the span and meaning of the action marks the prospective, historical nature of human action as the expression of meaning in a social and cultural milieu. Project means, therefore, more than the goal or end of action in a limited sense, although it includes such goals and the dispositions that support them. Project is used here to define the meaning of the action in the most comprehensive sense—including the meaning of the total movement of a group or societal process in the realization of certain values. The project is a reflected aspect of the flow of processes and events; projects on certain levels, for example, may be relatively conscious in conception and calculated in execution, but this usually refers to the simpler means-end sequences of action. We can categorize projects on a series of levels, from relatively unaware execution of somewhat routinized processes to expressive movements to instrumental processes and even to the comprehensive level of the projection of the meaning of a life as a realization of value or the actualization of a culture as an embodiment of cultural values and meanings. The notion, therefore, of an intentional self and the intentionality of social process implies that meanings and values are being actualized in the spontaneous flow of inner creativity and socially pregiven structures. To indicate the direction of flow of this process in its temporality and to preserve the meaning structure which gives it coherence, we use the generic term "project"—classifying with this term an extremely complex network of intentionalities and domains of relevance within which multiple temporal structures and overlapping contexts of relevance are ordered in personal, social, and cultural worlds. The projects of a person or group or society thus come to consciousness in a reflective awareness which brings the span and course of forward movement to clarity. This reflective process, in this sense, brings to clarity the embodied, pregiven world as experienced.

Concern with the project in human action is an attempt to illuminate what is being actualized within a set of events, requiring that that project be interpreted within a comprehensive schema of meaning. We shall return to the nature of this task in the following chapter. The immediate problem is to clarify the work of social science in "giving an account of" the project—accounting for its constitution. In a general sense, the task of social science is to "explain" the project —indicating *why* this project is what it is in this situation. We have suggested that the sciences of man attempt to account for the constitution of the project itself in the light of the conditions in which it emerges. This is the retrospective character of their reflective elucidation of the meaning of personal, social, and cultural processes. We should guard against the notion that we are solely or primarily interested in individual actions when we consider the conditions underlying projects, although roughly similar problems would occur in dealing with individual events—for example, in a jury trial. To speak of social and cultural events as expressions of meaning in a spontaneous flow of creativity in the context of pregiven structures does not mean that order, determinateness, and coherence are absent from this process. If the process is meaningful, it is more than a concatenation of discrete forces, whether these are interpreted in a reductionistic way or on the highest level of personal and moral freedom. The social world is given and experienced as a coherent reality, even in the midst of conflicts and ambiguities. The projects of persons and groups are coherently articulated with their biographies and histories as well as with uniformities in the relationships between classes of phenomena underlying them. The task of social science is to illuminate the constitution of these projects in the impingement of prior conditions and through the regularities of underlying conditions. In this account of the project or projects, according to domains of interest and relevance to the particular scientific disciplines and the specific epochs of social and cultural development, the sciences of man explicate the actual content of the project in the course of relating it to prior conditions and underlying regularities. We said earlier that the human sciences take the project for granted, and they do so in the sense of postulating from within the common culture a set of events significant to their interests—economic, political, educational, etc. However, they fill out the meaning of the project as they ground it in constitutive processes—explicating its meaning in relation to whole sequences of events within a particular population and preferably in comparison with similar events in other populations. As we look more carefully at the relationship between conditions and projects, we can begin to specify the sense in which the social sciences give an account of the project; hence, we can define the meaning of cause and explanation as they bear on the social world.[28] We shall

[28] Robert Brown's analysis of this problem is extremely illuminating; see *Explanation in Social Science.* His use of intention is relevant but somewhat narrower than the notion of project in our intentional analysis; nevertheless, the development of the importance of moving from types of explanation which give clues to classification rather than testable propositions—from intention, disposition, reason, and function to empirical generalization and corresponding theories—is an important step in clarifying the nature of the science of social reality. Brown takes a more hopeful line than Felix Kaufmann on the possibility of establishing what Kaufmann calls strict empirical laws which are negated by counterexamples; however, in principle the two are in agreement on the necessity of establishing testable hypotheses on the regularities of relations between classes of events, whether in simultaneity or in sequence. Our principal reservation on both analyses has to do with the style of social-scientific work, since it is evident that richness in the explication of the project and interrelatedness of dimensions in human process have to be impoverished in order to achieve this degree of determinate uniformity in the association of properties among classes of events—the kinds of uniformity, for example, appearing in economic analyses. We shall indicate subsequently the reasons for the success of economics with its particular subject matter and the necessity of similar developments in other disciplines of social science, but we shall also make clear the limitation of this style for the total scope of contributions which social science can make to the clarification of social processes.

have occasion to reconsider the illumination of the project by social science in the concluding chapter, since this is the most direct point of intersection between social science and social ethics. For the moment, however, our principal task is to clarify the sense in which a science of the social world gives an account of that world.

We have used the term "giving an account" to indicate the attempt of human science to place human action in an understandable context. Various terms are used to designate this type of understanding; some human scientists refer to "causality" and others to "motivation" or "motivational forces." Some have contented themselves with functional analyses, but the implication of such analyses is that activity or process is "understood" when its function within the total system has been identified. We shall follow Alfred Schutz initially in referring to "motives," since this term indicates the problem of causation and yet places it on the human level of intentionality.[29] Once the nature of "motive" is clarified, it should be possible to interpret the account of action on other levels.

A "motive" is a system of meaning which arises in reflection on our everyday experience. For example, a friend may ask why we are going downtown, and we answer that we are going downtown "to shop." "Going shopping"—the *project* which determines our decision to make the trip by car, bus, or train into the central shopping area—is understood to be a sufficient reason for what we are doing. Reflective consciousness may take a *prospective* direction and look upon the project as the causal principle of our activity. We are going downtown "in order to" do some shopping. The project is thus the motive of our action in prospective reflection; hence, the project provides a system of meaning which formulates the protensive movement of our "lived" experi-

[29] See Schutz, *Collected Papers*, Vol. 1, "Choosing Among Projects of Action," esp. pp. 69ff.; see also *Der Sinnhafte Aufbau der sozialen Weltz*, Secs. 17 and 18.

ence. The project is, therefore, what Alfred Schutz has called the in-order-to motive of our action.[30]

Prospective reflection on the meaning of action—turning toward the future—conceptualizes in the *future perfect tense*; it reflects in consciousness a state of affairs to be accomplished as it will be when accomplished. We translate a projected state of affairs in terms of *what it will be* when it *will have* happened. This anticipation of a state of affairs expresses the meaning of our action; this meaning-intention will find its fulfillment or disappointment in the actualization or failure of that project. Referring, then, to our earlier discussion of meaningful experience as reflection on elapsed experience, we see that the project as motive is a "past" which we create in the future perfect tense—anticipating a possible state of affairs in our *imagination*.[31]

So far as one can speak of *the project as a motive* or cause, the grasp of the meaning of action for the actor and the cause of action come together; from the actor's perspective, when he reflects in prospective terms on the state of affairs toward which he shapes the flow of experience, the project of his action is the motive for his acting—the *why* of his action. The actor may suggest something which has occurred as the motive for his action, again referring, however, to his prospective orientation; for example, he may say that he is going shopping because he needs a new hat—the *reason* for his appearance on the bus at three o'clock in the afternoon. However, this is a modified in-order-to motive, since projects orient to the future, but this manner of speaking looks at a prior need. In the future perfect tense, the meaning of action

[30] The in-order-to motive is the project on the level of "lived causality" in a reflected sense; hence, our broadening of the concept of project embraces more than Schutz's conception of the in-order-to motive, even as it includes more than Robert Brown's notion of "intention" (see fn. 28).

[31] We shall expand this more limited definition in Chapter 6, but for the moment, our focus is upon the temporal character of the reflective consciousness; and in this respect, concern with the project is attention to the meaning and values to be realized when an action is conceptualized "as if" it were fulfilled.

and the motivation of action ("lived" causality) take the character of an in-order-to motive or a project; from a given "here and now," the actor leaps into the future through imagination and views a possible state of affairs as already elapsed. We shall extend this later to project in an inclusive sense.

Reflection on the meaning of action may also, as was suggested, take a retrospective view on the conditions leading to the action. We have already noted that viewing action as a reflection of the common culture is an objective understanding of the meaning of action; in this sense, action is viewed in the past tense as already constituted. The understanding of the social self—or the "me," in Mead's terms—is such a retrospective view—the self as constituted. This is the finished state of affairs, viewed retrospectively, which accounts for the way things are. This retrospective view on the meaning of experience or action treats the project as completed, even if only in fantasy, and attempts to give an account of the *conditions* leading to the project. For example, the retrospective view on going shopping for a hat attempts to account for this recollectively in terms of prior experiences. The shopping trip is itself viewed in past terms, and the conditions leading up to this project are viewed in the pluperfect tense—he made the shopping trip because he *had* lost his hat. Alfred Schutz treats this retrospective view of motive as the genuine "because" motive. In a sense, "losing the hat" is the immediate motive constituting the project, but a horizon of biographical features comes to focus in this project, including the custom of wearing hats, thus accounting for the *what* of the project. The perspective of "because" is the observer's view.

The distinction between the in-order-to motive and the because motive is clearly stated by Alfred Schutz when he notes that the in-order-to motive starts from the project and explicates *the constituting of the action,* while the because motive starts from prior experience and explicates *the consti-*

*tution of the project.* This is an extremely useful distinction because it formulates the temporal modes of a motivational understanding of the meaning of action. In these terms, there are three temporal dimensions which need to be distinguished. The inner time of spontaneous activity directs itself toward the future in constituting its world—drawing upon passive syntheses of experience in which the pregiven world furnishes materials for this creative flow. This inner time moves in protensions and retentions which are unreflected, though much of this process can be brought to consciousness in reflection. We have, secondly, the self-interpretation of action arising from *prospective reflection* in which states of affairs being projected are brought into consciousness as "they will be" when they have elapsed; this type of preremembrance is necessarily vague, though in fanstasy both the projected possibility and some of the steps may be visualized. In the course of experience, both the projects and many of the constituting steps are rather clearly formulated and become matters of usage or custom; they are routinized. The project expresses in a reflected consciousness the meaning of action and the motive of the action as it looks forward. Thirdly, there is the *retrospective* self-interpretation which views the experience in full pastness as "motivated" and links the project as elapsed to antecedent circumstances and experiences. These three temporal dimensions yield different kinds of explanatory understanding. The internal temporal process, in which action is constituted, is accessible to phenomenological analysis only through reduction. We have already drawn on the results of such analyses to establish the nature of social reality. In this respect, the reflection on the constitutive processes of the self and other—the "We-relation"—formed the frame of reference for defining the theoretical modification in scientific explanation. Hence, the problem of explanatory understanding in social science refers to the project and its underlying conditions.

For simplicity, we shall speak of the *project* as the system of meaning in which action is viewed in its orientation to the future and therefore in its subjective meaning. All action can be illumined as project, although such elucidation usually occurs in the context of problems. Project, in this inclusive sense, is the meaning and realization of value which is expressed in the action or social process. To give an account of action, one must grasp the project of the action or at least presuppose it, since taking the system of meaning which arises from prior conditions assumes a grasp of the project—the *what* that is constituted. We shall refer to genuine because motives as *conditions* within which the project is constituted. This retrospective system of meaning is, in the way we shall designate it, an "interpretation of the situation." The ambiguous term "motive" will thus be dropped, but Schutz's distinctions should not be lost; the *project* expresses the prospective reflection on the intention of the actor (in-order-to motive), whereas the *conditions* express the retrospective reflection on the constituting conditions of his project (because motive).

If we go back to the nature of reflected meaning in action, it is evident that the project can never be a fulfillment of the conditions or the situation; the conditions are grasped from a "here and now" later than the conception of the project and thus furnish only interpretative illumination. The conditions, especially as they disclose regularities, constitute the project as a biography constitutes a person; it is *fabric* of his *identity* but not external to it.[32] This is the temporal character of intentionality which can never be reduced to the actualization of certain prior conditions; however, the action of the intentional self occurs in the context of past conditions—it is "situated" action. We have already seen in the discussion of choice and freedom that a spurious sense of external determination can be created by viewing the

[32] See Schutz, *Der Sinnhafte Aufbau der sozialen Welt*, Sec. 18. In this respect, social science explicates the fabric of the society—the process of constitution of the project—disclosing the identity of the society.

protensive character of action as retrospective meaning, since the constituting action of the self is converted into external determination by elapsed alternatives which did not exist prior to the constituting action. A similar illusion of external determination arises when a project—the intended meaning and motive for action—is treated as the fulfillment of prior conditions or circumstances; the conditions only illumine the project by bringing identity to awareness as the meaning of these events.[33]

In explicating the notion of the intentional self, we have raised "causation" to the human level and spoken of "project" and "conditions." This conversion of the term "motive" was made largely to avoid ambiguities, but it also protects the consideration of motive from reductionistic interpretations. One of the major problems in the human sciences has arisen from the notion of unconscious motive, which reduces "cause" to the nonhuman level. This understanding of the "unconscious" derives from the Freudian tradition. Talcott Parsons has given currency to this understanding of uncon-

[33] The actor, group, or society can seldom bring the project to light; the elucidation of the project in terms of its conditions is a work of clarification for the society—a coming to awareness. To claim that these conditions are not *externally* determinative is not to suggest that the process is random, incalculable, or indeterminate; if this were so, the process could not make sense. However, the meaning of the process is not separable from the identity of the intentional reality which brings it to expression as actualization of meaning and value. The classic instance of the role of social science in clarifying self-identity is the work of psychotherapy; in one sense, the person is a product of his environmental situation and constellation of relationships; on the other hand, he is the meaning-giving source of the pregiven structure which we call his biography—he constitutes it in its course, and he reconstitutes it in the reflective awareness which he gains. This total coherence of identity in a situation through the course of realizing meaning and value can be and is evaluated in the context of an ultimate horizon of meaning. This is the religioethical task of every person; on the societal scale, it is a task which is borne generally by writers, artists, statesmen, legislators, judges, and, in our context, social ethicists. There are a variety of styles on the social-scientific level through which the conditions are determined and the project elucidated, even as psychotherapy is only one style of dealing with the constituting of personality. Each of these styles contributes aspects of this illumination, although the precision of some styles is gained at the cost of abstraction from the cultural and social nature of the project.

scious motive in the development of his theory of action.[34] We can see from the foregoing discussion that the notion of unconscious motive is a contradiction in terms, since the grasp of motive is an interpretation of action within a system of meaning; it is thus necessarily a reflected grasp of experience in consciousness. The flow of the inner time in its spontaneity is at least quasi-unconscious, though one may "feel that one is feeling" without the full reflection which Schutz seems to imply; "lived" experience is quasi-unconscious in that its meaning is not reflected prospectively or retrospectively. When Talcott Parsons speaks of "uncon-

[34] The transition to a Freudian model of man was a crucial transformation in Talcott Parsons' theoretical construction; in this way, he was able to handle the motivational aspects of his theory by positing an internalization of the goals and norms of the social system; the Freudian model provided the mechanisms for describing this socialization process and for detecting the parameters of deviance; in this understanding, personality can be interpreted in "structural categories" rather than in dynamic processes, and these categories can be treated as an equilibrium system, oscillating between tensions raised by deprivation and return to a gratification-deprivation balance through achievement of consummatory states. In the light of our foregoing discussion, it is evident that the behavioristic dimension against which George Herbert Mead's theory was struggling has gained a total victory in Parsons' model; moreover, a reduction occurs from the cognitive level employed by Mead to the cathectic level introduced by Parsons. We have suggested earlier that the need to deal with these dynamic processes of the self in a way to include somatic processes was a crucial advance; here a consideration of embodiment is a unified development of the notion of the person in the social context. The transition in Talcott Parsons' theory was signaled by two essays in *Working Papers in the Theory of Action* (New York: The Free Press, 1953), "The Superego and the Theory of Social Systems" and "The Theory of Symbolism in Relation to Action." A somewhat clearer exposition of the postulates is found (from the same period) in *Toward a General Theory of Action*, edited by Talcott Parsons and Edward Shils (Cambridge, Mass.: Harvard University Press, 1951), esp. pp. 110–158. A systematic attempt to analyze the socialization process within the Freudian framework is to be found in Talcott Parsons and R. F. Bales, *Family, Socialization and Interaction Process* (New York: The Free Press, 1955), Chs. 2 and 3, where Parsons takes Mead's notion of internalization and Freud's theory of libido as dimensions to be assimilated into his functional analysis of a series of steps of differentiation and integration. The significance of this mechanistic approach—an attempt to analyze a developmental sequence—is actually undercut by the over-all reduction of personality and its activity to a tension-reduction model. This deficiency plagues the Parsonian analyses on the highest cultural levels as a built-in deformation of the cultural process,

scious goals," he is in fact looking at the prospective thrust of action as an internalization of a culture through socialization. The unconscious motives in action theory are the movements toward a gratification-deprivation balance in the personality system; hence, the projects of the actors are determined by the objects and expectations around which this balance has been developed. This is a thoroughgoing attempt to account for the project—the identity—through internalization of culture whether in the actor or in the society.

Parsons' theory is a remarkable advance in systematization

---

treating transcendence of the cultural system in social critiques as a sign of strain (see Chapter 2) and viewing cognition in an instrumental way. The inadequacy of this concept of goal-orientation—and especially the "slipperiness' of the notion of "unconscious goals"—and indeed of the motivational constructs in the theory is cited by Max Black, *Social Theories of Talcott Parsons* (Englewood Cliffs, N.J.: Prentice-Hall, Inc., 1961), pp. 278-281. Robert W. White's critique of the Freudian model in "Competence and the Psychosexual Stages of Development," *op. cit.*, rests on two theses: that the libido model is not adequate to conceptualize the child's emotional development and that the translation to the interpersonal level still does not make the prototypes in this model adequate. White's principal thrust is against the passivity in the conception of man which informs the model. When the theory of action is taken on the complex level of cultural analysis, the debate becomes merely ideological; the difficulties, however, arise in the basic postulates of the theory and especially in the understanding of the personality system. Since the theory is so comprehensive, its proponents have become resistant to critiques and thus find themselves defending an inadequate notion of man for the sake of a heuristic model which has some useful functions. The notion of goal is not only inadequate for scientific theory, as Black notes, and the model for development inadequate on the interpersonal level, as White notes, but the very notion of a pleasure-gain balance or gratification-deprivation balance is an unwarranted imputation. Pleasure and pain are not contraries in this sense, as Paul Ricoeur has shown in *Philosophie de la Volonté* (Paris: Aubier, 1949), Vol. 1, pp. 100ff. The significant contribution of Talcott Parsons in pressing toward the interrelation of meaning and organic processes can be retained through the notions of passive *synthesis* and *embodiment* without the unwarranted skewing which is introduced by libido theory; however, this radically alters the status of the action model. In general, the comprehensive status of the theory for cultural and social analysis collapses if this linchpin is pulled. To use Maurice Merleau-Ponty's understanding of the Freudian model, its utility is maximized when men are caught in pathology and act least humanly; see *The Structure of Behavior*, pp. 178ff.

of the relationship of personality and society. The principal limitation of this style of analysis is the ambiguity and inadequacy of the notion of equilibrium and gratification-deprivation balance. In these terms, the constitutive character of the ego is reduced and the systematic interrelatedness of variables is enhanced, but a spurious sense of external determination is introduced. This limitation is especially marked in the ambiguity of the notion of function, since little more than tendencies can be derived from the concept; the testable generalizations of conditions which constitute the project are slighted for a comprehensive theory which is not comprehensive enough. The functional style of analysis depends upon a context or system frame of reference, and our principal claim in Chapter 6 will be that such a context must be comprehensive enough to order the various domains of relevance in a way that is adequate to personal, social, and historical experience. Although the functional style is enormously helpful in systematizing complex processes and indicating regularities which can be explored empirically, it loses the vitality of the constitutive processes of the project and lacks the empirical lawfulness of the more external analyses. We have introduced this issue around the notion of unconscious motives because the theory of action has rightly pointed to the conditions below the level of awareness through which the project can be elucidated; but in turning to the Freudian model, the constituting of meaning and value in the conjointly rational-emotive dimensions of personality was lost. Some of these deficiencies in the theory of action can, in fact, be overcome by loosening the model considerably and treating the components as ideal typifications rather than on the system level; indeed, this is the way the theory is being used, and it is making considerable contributions.

This critique of unconscious motives is directed against the reductionist attempts to convert intentionality into the product of social and cultural conditions by substituting systems of interpretation for the protensive thrusts of inner spontaneity. Much of our experience remains below the conscious level. Moreover, our mental integration of experience is limited and fragmentary. There are aspects of our experience which remain alienated from the integrity of consciousness. Psychotherapy enhances human consciousness and freedom by helping to recover these alienated fragments of experience; it brings them into the sphere of consciousness—particularly by disclosing the ways in which our projects have involved interpretations of the situation which were distorted for one or another reason. We recover the meaning of the distortion and thus transcend its power. The self gains distance from its own existence and particularly its past through the recovery of alienated elements in a context which is meaningful for consciousness. One is not speaking, however, of unconscious motives in considering such alienated fragments; in order to interpret the experience of alienation, the meaning of one's own project in these conditions and the constituting of the project in relation to these conditions have to be grasped; through this process, aspects of the spontaneous process of the inner time which had remained monotonously repetitive in new situations, where they were inappropriate, become meaningfully integrated in a later stage of maturity of the intentional self.[35]

The further implication of this understanding of the self is that enrichment and fulfillment of the self come through reflective appropriation of all facets of experience in con-

[35] The problem in the science of human action is to work, as Talcott Parsons has attempted to do, on a deep enough level of embodiment in order to deal with the integration of motility, sensation, and perception with the higher-level cognitive processes. In order to deal adequately with the shaping of the present by the past, we can acknowledge and seek to clarify various levels of pregivenness in the self-world correlation, recognizing that it is the task of science to clarify this intentional structure without distorting it, to illuminate it without reducing it. (See the previously cited discussions of this problem by Maurice Merleau-Ponty.) It is not the biographical determination in Parsons' model which limits its adequacy but the deficient principle of integration—equilibrium is not adequate to the variety and unity of social experience.

sciousness; the enrichment of mental integration and the corollary enrichment of the meaning of the cultural and social world are consequences of this reflective work of consciousness. Psychotherapy enhances this maturation not by reducing consciousness to a product of meaningless conditions which are alien to consciousness but by bringing into reflective awareness aspects of experience which an anxious consciousness feared to integrate in its own system of meaning. In this sense, we can say that Freud presupposed an intentional consciousness. That which was unconscious thus becomes "motive" through becoming accessible to consciousness. When the Freudian tradition is reinterpreted in terms of the intentional self, the deterministic aspects of unconscious forces can be set in their proper perspective.

The project, in the richest and broadest sense, is the clue to the constitutive role of the self in action. We said that the project constituted the unity of the action as meant; we can also say that the project discloses the identity of the self as constitutive source of action and, by analogy, of the society in its actualization of value. The social self and the constitutive ego thus come together in the comprehensive notion of the project. Viewed *protensively*, the project is that limiting condition of any discussion of the meaning of action, since its roots lie deep in the constitutive movement of inner time and disclose essential tendencies of the self which we postulated in the preceding chapter. Viewed *prospectively* as a system of meaning or motive, the project is the reflected meaning of that protensive movement—set in terms of a posited or fantasied state of affairs in the future perfect tense; thus reflected, it shifts from vivid present to reflected pastness.[36]

[36] The reflected character of the notion of project should be kept in view, since it merely attempts to typify "lived in" experience in a model which is more appropriate to the human level of integration; hence, the situational determinations of the content and possibilities of the project enable a science of man to clarify conditions in the manner of "afterthoughts" without confusing its grasp of conditions with a determination of human action.

The project is always constituted in the context of passive syntheses—pregiven meanings and possibilities; it is also limited in its actualization by conditions and possibilities, including the resistance of sedimented meanings to new demands imposed by the project. The freedom of the intentional self in its project is enhanced by its increasing grasp of the conditions entering into the constitution of its projects; its responsibility for the reconstituting of a situation in the light of meaning is enhanced, moreover, by grasping the limits and possibilities of these conditions. Hence, the retrospective view of constitution of the project enriches the unity of the self. The self may, of course, gain a false sense of determination and defeat from a misunderstanding of these conditions as externally determinative forces; however, the actual spontaneity of the self soon becomes restless with such spurious interpretations of the constituting of the project. Setting this whole summary of the notion of motive in the context of psychotherapy, we can say that alienated elements of the self perpetuate the past into new projects without regard for the actualities of the situation; to this extent, they represent elements alienated from consciousness or intentionality and from the meaningful present; thus they deprive the project of adequacy to the situation.[37]

[37] This alienation comes about through the violation of the fundamental tendencies of the self (see Chapter 4), particularly the violation of the essential sociality of the self in its search for response—to oversimplify, in a violation of love; however, the alienation itself presupposes a self-transcending freedom and its corollary of anxiety, since the unity of the total personality is broken and fragments remain unrelated to its intentional organization of a world. If one proceeds from a recognition of the isolated fragments on the lower levels and constructs a human or mental order on top of this as a kind of superstructure upon instincts, the cognitive structures become instrumental modes of more efficient adaptation rather than a new constitutive level of integration; the latter idea is the basic fallacy of the Freudian theory, as it is of later derivations. The idealistic solution is a distortion in the direction of mental structures, even as the Freudian solution distorts on the instinctual side. As Maurice Merleau-Ponty puts it:

> Man is not a rational animal. The appearance of reason and mind does not leave intact a sphere of self-enclosed instincts in man. . . . But if the alleged instincts do not exist *apart* from the mental dia-

The task of psychotherapy (and, to this extent, the task of all the human sciences in different ways and for different regions of experience) is to bring to consciousness the relevant aspects of the past and present situation so that they can be integrated into the human project as meaningful elements. In this sense, social science is the systematic openness of the self to its situation.

## *THE SCOPE FOR HUMAN SCIENCE*

With this paradigm of the role of human science, we can attempt to be somewhat more explicit about the possibilities and limits of these sciences. We have already made clear that the project as the intended meaning of action sets a limiting condition on the knowledge to be achieved by the human sciences. We need now to recognize that the human sciences have to start with this project or some presupposition about it. We have already explicated this presupposition of meaning in another context. Now it is evident that a science of action in "giving an account" of the project is concerned with delineating the conditions and "interests" which entered into the constituting of the project. This is not a causal task in the sense of identifying antecedent forces and subsequent effects; that retrospective illusion should have been dispelled by now. However, it is an interpretative attempt to bring the project and its conditions more fully

---

> lectic, correlatively, this dialectic is not conceivable outside of the concrete situations in which it is embodied. One does not act with mind alone. Either mind is nothing, or it constitutes a real and not an ideal transformation of man. Because it is not a new sort of being but a new form of unity, it cannot stand by itself (*The Structure of Behavior*, p. 181).

The issue, then, is the nature of unity on the human level—the meaning of integration; the centrality of this issue suggests the import of the motivational base for the theory of action; however complex the higher levels of analysis in the theory, it is no more adequate than the instinctual level from which it was constructed.

into the scope of meaning for consciousness and the society. Hence, the human sciences are concerned with systems of meaning in which projects can be understood in their situational context; for example, the decisive situational context is the state of the culture, but demography and ecology are also relevant aspects.

The decisive point is the temporal mode in which the human sciences work. Whereas intentional action is prospective, the human sciences work retrospectively—viewing the project as elapsed and accounting for its constitution in terms of prior conditions and experiences. The prior conditions are normally the sedimented meanings and styles of the common culture. These are viewed retrospectively as having had this or that effect on the development of this or that action. For example, the studies of prejudice begin with a delineation of one or another perception, categorization, discriminatory practice, etc., and set that variable in the context of varying conditions with which it is associated—social class, ethnic background, etc. In the case of prejudice, the intentions of certain terms have to be explored, but the temporal mode of the human sciences is to give an account of the conditions within which those meanings appeared. We state the matter in these intentional terms, although the human sciences often claim to give an account of causal forces of prejudice from external conditions. It is clear from the foregoing analysis that "lived causality" on the human level is a question of the meaning given to particular conditions in a situation; for example, encirclement of Germany after World War I did not *cause* prejudice against the Jews, but the "meaning of encirclement" and the "meaning of Aryan autonomy" were elements which were articulated in the German project—mastery of the world by the so-called master race.

In general, the human sciences attempt to bring to consciousness the meaning of the human project in terms of the conditions in which it is constituted. To this extent, they "take the project for granted" and view it as elapsed; in turn, they work in terms of the past or the elapsed state of affairs and attempt to account for it. This explains the widespread feeling that the human sciences only *explain* the obvious and spend most of their time giving an account of why things are the way they are (viewed in terms of the elapsed state of affairs). The work of the human sciences, on this basic level of giving an account of action, as we have seen, will necessarily have this character of bringing the situation of the person or society to consciousness. History is, in this respect, the prototype of the human sciences, as well as one of the leading and oldest of the human sciences. The basic distinction between history as ordinarily understood and the human sciences or so-called behavioral sciences, according to the interpretation of this analysis, is that the subjects of the fully historical interpretation are no longer accessible to the scientist—the scientist cannot alter the consciousness of those subjects; the human sciences usually deal with contemporaries, having access to the subjects of action and thereby altering the understanding of those subjects both through their inquiries and through their findings. However, the human sciences interpret action as elapsed and face problems similar to the historical disciplines. Obviously, this close alliance of the disciplines means that they can be mutually helpful in many areas of inquiry.

Much of our experience is constituted in passive syntheses. This sedimentation of experience is so much taken for granted that we seldom bring it consciously to awareness in interpretation. Various regions of experience can be explored as sedimentations from the past and yield high degrees of regularity. This applies to everything from cognitive styles to marketing procedures. These regions can be broken down into human projects, and we can view these typical courses of behavior (the common culture) as conditions that constitute these projects. So far as we postulate the continuity of these routinized patterns in any region, we can speak of predicting future states of affairs; in this sense, social science operates as a predictive science.[38] The scientist projects a typical pattern of activity or meaning to the future on the basis of an interpretation of the past; he has no "control" over this pattern, since he cannot manipulate the processes of meaning in which these patterns are held within the society as the way things should be.[39] However, his illumination of the project for the society and of the regularities which underlie it immeasurably increases the society's control of its world; in this sense, the construction of laws and predictability in social science will be important advances in the constitutive power of society.

In addition to persistence of sedimented typifications, many projects of action can be fitted to calculable models of efficiency in the pursuit of ends. This is the model of rational action which Max Weber developed as a key to his interpre-

[38] The issue is not, as indicated earlier, that prediction and control are absent from human affairs or human science, but only that the terms change meaning on the human level. Concrete levels on Chart 2 of Chapter 4 indicate both enrichment of milieu and increasing centeredness of dynamic unification and creativity. This transformation by levels does not eliminate a science of human action but converts prediction to grasp of the meaning of courses of events and the likelihood of persistence of that meaning. "Control" of process, of course, requires a stability of conditions which is seldom available except in the most routinized processes. The problem is not simply one of complexity of variables, which might be handled by more and more powerful mathematical methods and computers; the problem is the meaning of science on the human level. Furthermore, the distinction between physical science and social science is not essentially in terms of experimental and nonexperimental sciences. Much can be learned in the human sciences by contrived situations, although stabilizing conditions becomes very difficult on the societal level; nevertheless, even on this level, a comparative social science provides the facsimile of experiment. As for the claim that social science is reflective and retrospective in understanding, the notion of experiment only *seems* to contradict this; experiment anticipates an outcome in the future perfect tense—a project—and attempts to establish the conditions under which certain typical processes will occur, thus eventuating in the fantasied state of affairs. Experimentation is thus a theoretical modification of the practical attitude in a simulation of human projection and fulfillment; so far as the model gives some predictability, certain regularities can be identified under prescribed conditions, even as in everyday affairs we take it for granted that calling to a friend will gain his attention—a retrospective reflection provides a conscious interpretation of the course of events which we usually take for granted. Hence, the orderliness of human affairs, such

tative sociology.[40] It is true that many realms of action fit such rational models, since projects are constituted with a relatively definite awareness of the state of affairs to be achieved and some sense of particular steps to be taken. Both the completed state of affairs and the steps may be rather vague, but these become more definite and routinized with time; and in particular regions of activity, such as economic behavior, such activities can become quite predictable. Models of rational behavior can be constructed to fit certain regions of routinized activity, and to this extent the project of a firm or group of clients may be anticipated. To the extent that certain elements of the situation are significant in that project, these can be manipulated in accord with the theoretical model and the project can be altered; for example, the manipulation of interest rates has been used to alter economic projects. In economic behavior, rational models can be constructed, routinized anticipations can be calculated, and some manipulation of elements is possible. The appropriate regions of such activity are limited, at this stage, though there may be calculable regions which have not yet been explored.

---

as it is, allows scientific predictability as *likelihood* and control as anticipation rather than as determination. By the same token, this orderliness may be tested in limited kinds of expectations, and certain tendencies of man may be tested by providing occasions in which they may manifest themselves; see, for example, Harold Garfinkel's experiment, which is discussed in his article "Knowledge of Social Structure," in *Theories of Mind*. The issue on prediction is similar to that on empirical laws (see fn. 28); actually the more prediction that can be achieved in social science, the more societal *projects* will be clarified and control enhanced.

[39] The level of predictability appropriate to studies of voting behavior illustrates the values and limits of this type of analysis; social heritage and interests persist with high degrees of regularity in this domain of relevance; see the study of these phenomena in Bernard Berelson, Paul F. Lazarsfeld, and William McPhee, *Voting* (Chicago: University of Chicago Press, 1954).

[40] As suggested before, this is a reflected model and thus has heuristic value for typifying certain kinds of outcomes; it is not, however, an account of "lived" experience, although it has certain analogues in those experiences. See Schutz, *Collected Papers,* Vol. 2, "The Problem of Rationality in the Social World."

We have distinguished, along with Alfred Schutz, three temporal dimensions of experience and attempted to place the human sciences within one. We distinguished the *spontaneous level* of inner time, which is the level of "lived" experience. This is the level of being-in-the-world—or the "corporeal scheme," in Maurice Merleau-Ponty's terms. It is the sphere of the constitutive syntheses of the active "I" and furnishes the unity of the self in social process. We have identified *the project* as the reflected meaning of this constitutive self in its prospective interpretation of meaning; even in its prospective character, we found this reflected meaning as set in terms of the past—specifically the future perfect tense. The implication of this understanding is that any interpretation of the meaning of action is in terms of the past. Experiment in human science simulates this prospective orientation by projecting a state of affairs and identifying typical processes which would antecede it. Finally, we identified *retrospective reflection* on the conditions in which the project arose: an interpretation which *presupposes the project* and attempts to account for its constitution and to elucidate it. In this latter sphere, the human sciences are systematic attempts to bring the situation of action to consciousness. To this extent, they are disciplines of reflection on the situated character of action.

Interpretative understanding of the meaning of action is the presupposition of various types of social-scientific method: (1) the experimental model which *simulates projective action* presupposes the meaning of a situation around which a constellation of typical processes and motives will function—for example, Kurt Lewin's classic studies of types of leadership presupposed a whole range of interpretative understandings of contexts in which leadership is significant and then imposed selected typifications of leadership in order to discern fixed outcomes; (2) theoretical models such as the theory of action and less elaborate models on the middle level of theory are built around *retrospectively constructed* principles of organization; principles such as a "strain to consistency" or pursuit of "interest" are interpreted as accounting for one or more realms of human activity, so that typical courses of events may be set in determinate relations and projects may be anticipated; these theoretical constructions should also be testable when conditions can be controlled. Alfred Schutz has noted that the everyday world operates with a set of "recipes," or "cookbook knowledge," by which courses of events may be anticipated on the basis of *understood projects*. The theoretical constructions of human science are of a similar type but clearer, more abstract, and logically more consistent; hence, they are models of a somewhat higher predictive power under certain limited conditions. In both cases, the meaning of action is presupposed, since it is *imposed* on the experimental situation by the scientist and used as the context of retrospective construction by the builder of theory. Talcott Parsons, for example, in building a pattern-variable schema by reflective construction of choice alternatives which "might have" preceded an orientation to a goal-object, reconstitutes the possible choices by a schema of typified alternatives.

The principal differences among social-scientific theories arise from the degree to which they attempt to take account of internal dynamics as an independent variable. Theories on the physical level work with external variables, taking for granted the meaning of contexts; hence, they are most useful in clarifying highly routinized processes, such as organic functioning of the psyche and population movements, where the taken-for-granted cultural meanings are relatively constant. Theories on the vital level work with cultural meanings as they are institutionalized and attempt to handle internal dynamics as a *function* of this system; thus, this type of theory makes it possible to establish the systematic interrelation between certain cultural values and typical motivational trends; however critical one may be of the reductionistic notion of internal dynamics in such theories, much can be gained from the delineation of systematic relationships among typical values, organizational forms, motives, and situations. Furthermore, conflict-of-interest theories consider dispositional dynamics and correlated values as a principal determinant and attempt to account for projects as typical outcomes of these ideal-typical relationships; the utility of such theories lies in thematizing differences in values and interests. Each of these styles of social theory seeks to give a determinate account of the course of social process by establishing retrospectively a set of determinants and projecting their continuity. These theories represent *styles* of social-scientific theorizing arising out of different interests and clarifying different aspects of the intentional self in its social and cultural world. They are not mutually exclusive alternatives. It is evident from Chart 2 in Chapter 4 that these theories abstract on different levels: the physical theories sacrifice adequacy on the intentional level for the sake of quantification and precision; the functional theories sacrifice physical lawfulness for adequacy in systematic ordering, but achieve an exaggerated sense of system by reducing intentionality to a function of the social system; the voluntaristic theories sacrifice lawfulness and system in order to approach the dispositional dynamics of intentionality. In each case, we deal with retrospective determinations which can provide valuable perspectives on the conditions of action in the society. When such reflective interpretations are confused with the prospective movement of the intentional self, a retrospective reflection creates an illusion of social determination.

We are not yet in a position to evaluate these styles of human science within a comprehensive scheme. That task will be undertaken subsequently. However, it is evident that more exploration is needed on the projective level of action —the intentional level seen in its variability and modifications. The interest theories have been too rigid in exploring the intentional consciousness; much can be gained by a more open and flexible inquiry into human intentionality.[41] The values of this style of social science become very apparent when we turn to the moral aspects of human action and the problem of ethical reflection. Nevertheless, the various styles of social science contribute to an understanding of the identity of the society.

The contrast between "lived" process in its orientation to the future and objective reflections on process in social science could be summarized somewhat in this fashion: action as lived is intentionality which is stretched toward the future, giving shape to history by reconstituting a given identity; action as observed is objectively generalized to an identity which is already constituted. The future character of "lived" process as opposed to the past character of objectively reflected process marks the difference between the subjectively engaged meaning of events and the objectively observed characterization of events. The virtue and limits of social science are found in its objective characterization of events.

The objective conceptions of identity in social science bring to awareness the constituting conditions in which social action occurs. This is an important resource to social ethics and to social policy, as we shall observe in the concluding part of this inquiry. This detachment from "lived" process also presents special problems in translating social-scientific findings to everyday affairs. This problem is particularly acute because the social sciences often project their findings directly into the world of everyday affairs. Every comprehensive ordering of human affairs involves some understanding of what is being produced in the social process; some end or goal is imputed to the process, even if this

[41] There is undoubtedly more research going on in this sphere than is generally thought. Phenomenological studies have become relatively widespread in psychology; there is interest in this method in social science, but preoccupation with large-scale quantification and use of computers make such painstaking and costly research (in time and effort) seem insignificant.

end is merely the extension of what has already been determined by previous states of the society. Each style of social science has an explicit or implicit understanding of the meaning of the social process, since social process cannot be thought or ordered without some implication of meaning or directionality. If social-scientific models are imposed directly upon the everyday world, their imputation of meanings to the social process is arbitrarily translated from abstract models to practical projects of the society; in terms of the foregoing analysis, the models of the constituted identity of the society are substituted for the projected meaning of the society in its shaping of its future. This is the basic source of ideological controversy among the scientific styles; these styles impute opposing meanings to the course of events in the society. When the meanings imputed to social process by these scientific styles have been clarified, it should be possible to order these styles according to their relevance to particular kinds of problems confronting the practical world of decision-making.

# 6 *order and evaluation in human science*

The evaluative or ideological aspects of scientific styles are clarified, and a case is made for giving more attention to an "intentional style"—especially for use on ethical issues

THE SOCIAL SCIENCES make explicit the identity of the society. They accomplish this task, according to the foregoing interpretation, by clarifying the conditions within which this identity emerges, bringing to light the sedimented experience of the society. However, the social sciences work with abstracted formulations of these processes, which need translation into the context of the everyday world. The distinction between theoretical and everyday perspectives in Chart 1 of Chapter 3 made it evident that the theoretical perspective has to be translated in terms of the paramount reality of the everyday world. The discussion of the relationship between retrospective reflection and prospective interpretation in Chapter 5 was an attempt to indicate the differences in temporal structure between the theoretical work of the sciences and the practical orientation of the human project.

The work of social ethics is to clarify social identity more concretely than is possible or warranted in social scientific work. In this sense, social science is neither predictive nor determinative enough by its nature as a theoretical science of the social world; hence, the task of social ethical reflection is to translate the scientific formulations with reference to specific problems confronting the society. Social ethics translates the discerned regularities with which the social sciences clarify the human project into the practical context of societal responsibility. Social ethics converts an account of conditions into discernment of a situation; it translates an illumination of social identity on the basis of past conditions into an awareness of social possibilities in light of a human future.

Two basic problems confront society and the agents of its ethical reflection (legislators, political leaders, judges, the informed man in the street, and specialists in ethics and social philosophy) when they undertake the translation of scientific accounts into social possibilities. They must reinterpret the project in the light of a comprehensive hypothesis of the meaning of the human enterprise. If they do not carry through this kind of reinterpretation, they are borrowing the hypothesis of meaning which is implicit or explicit in the social scientific framework without clear understanding of its congruity or conflict with the social enterprise. The first concern need not be self-conscious except for specialists in this field, since the reinterpretation is usually carried through automatically in terms of the meanings and values which are taken for granted in the common culture. This is a problem of interpretative context, and that context is imposed by the society upon its members as a way of ordering the relevance of aspects of the situation. The second problem is somewhat more difficult and is perhaps the special burden of those who work in social philosophy and social ethics: the weighting and evaluation of the perspectives and findings of social science as they specify the immediate identity of the society. This second problem becomes somewhat clearer if we consider briefly the enlarged meaning of "project" as we have been using it. What specifically is the content of this term as we think of the human sciences making the project explicit?

The social world is a valuing world in which meanings are expressed and values are actualized. This world is not, as we have seen, a simply haphazard affair of incalculable value-realizations but is, rather, an ordered, meaningful world in which typical processes and understood inferences guide and direct our activities. Our interpretation of this world—the hypothesis informing this analysis—is that it is a dynamic process of creation and reconstitution in a changing milieu, so that every illumination of identity opens the way to a new grasp of the future and its possibilities. Scientific clarification of identity helps to dissolve the rationalizing self-deception which characterizes much of our self-understanding; it also counters our tendency to cling to our meanings and values despite the profound problems which may beset us. The sciences of man make explicit the kinds of values that are operative within the society, as these are concretized in distribution of income, resources, knowledge, power, prestige, and rewards. These sciences make explicit aspects of the common culture, although they do this with reference to specific problems and concerns within their disciplines. For example, political science may be preoccupied with problems of decision-making in the urban areas, exploring issues which do and do not come into the arena of decision-making, inquiring into participation in political processes. The nature and operation of the political process—the political identity of the society—become explicit through these studies. However, various approaches in these sciences illumine different aspects of such a problem and stress different dimensions according to the principle of relevance by which they select their categories and make their analyses.

The selectivity of perspectives does not mean that one view is wrong and another correct; it means only that varying perspectives on a problem illumine different aspects. The task of social ethics is to weight these perspectives on social meanings and values in accord with pressing problems and in terms of issues that confront the society. This weighting is not a simple task and is always done with reference to a hypothesis about the shape of human possibility and fulfillment; in fact, political and social debate can and should pose alternative hypotheses in which self-understanding comes to concrete decision about future courses of action. The task of weighting and decision (the appropriation of social-scientific clarification of identity) gives specific determination to the scientific diagnosis as it comes to bear on the situation of the society. In this sense, social ethics (using the term for this whole range of practical concerns) transforms the generalities of a theoretical understanding in the social sciences to the concrete, practical considerations of the everyday world. This social-ethical task is sometimes carried through by social scientists; and, in fact, some of the ideological debate in these disciplines arises from the differences of perspectives with which they pursue their explication of the project and their interpretation of its bearing on the everyday world.

The task of weighting the various perspectives of social science requires some understanding of the styles which dominate these sciences and the specific contributions of these styles to an understanding of the human project. Such a weighting may, of course, be done on a rough-and-ready basis by simply drawing what is most at hand for a decision-making situation. This seems to be the way that businesses and some governmental agencies employ the consultative work of social scientists. If the scientific findings prove useful in operations or decisions, these styles gain credibility and are used. The implications of many of these models need much more careful scrutiny than has yet been used, but it is difficult to introduce this level of sophistication in so-called practical areas of activity. For example, the kinds of testing which have been used in selecting business executives need evaluation in terms of the notions of leadership and value-realization which inform them. By the same token, the ideology of the theory of games could be made much more explicit with reference to the understanding of international relations. To clarify the project, in brief, is also to furnish an implicit understanding of the nature of the social world. That understanding becomes a significant problem in decision-making only when the translation is made into the practical terms of the everyday world, when the constituting of identity clarifies the situation within which social values are to be actualized; at this point, the perspectives which inform the various styles of social science can clarify the relative values which are at stake.

Another way to state this problem is to suggest that social science and social ethics have a common stake in a social philosophy—a common stake in the meaning of the social world and its realization of value. The social sciences usually work with implicit social philosophies. Since the social world is a world of meanings and values, even the denial of the significance of valuing for an understanding of that world is itself a social philosophy. Hence, our present concern is to discriminate the interpretation of value and meaning in various scientific perspectives. The determination of the identity of the society, at any point in its movement, is not a neutral task, although the empirical regularities which science formulates may be of an order of generality which would be useful within various perspectives.[1] By the same token, various hypotheses may guide the ethicist in weighting the perspectives; no final claim is made for the hypothesis informing the present analysis beyond its comprehensiveness and adequacy in organizing the styles of scientific work in the social field.

The ethicist weights the findings of various styles of social science with respect to specific issues and problems of the everyday world. He specifies social identity more concretely than the theoretical framework of social science would allow. However, this gives no warrant to social ethics to determine

[1] So far as the human sciences can establish empirical laws—and this should certainly be their aim—the implications of these laws for the realization of value may shift with interpretative contexts, but the regularities in association of properties of events retain their scientific significance. For example, the laws of mechanics retain their scientific value even with a shift in interpretative context from Newtonian theory to the theory of relativity, but the interpretation changes.

which style is most appropriate within the social sciences or even what problems should be at the center of attention in a particular discipline. The style, problems, informing models, and testable generalizations which guide a specific discipline cannot be determined by any criteria other than the inquiry and state of the discipline. Hence, the task of social ethics is to select and appropriate in order to bring to full clarity the nature of social identity in its struggle for human and social fulfillment.[2] We shall consider in Part Three some of the specific problems confronting social ethics. For the moment, our task is to identity the perspectives and styles which guide the social sciences in clarifying the identity of the society.

Two major issues arise in translating social-scientific understanding into the categories of the everyday world. These issues are closely interwoven, but they can be treated somewhat independently for the sake of clarity. Every typification of experience arises from a selective principle of interest. This is as true of a scientific perspective as it is of our ordinary experience.[3] In order to clarify the systems of relevance within which the social-scientific perspectives operate, we shall first have to make explicit the ordering principles with which they shape the social world. These are the unifying principles which make an understanding of social phenomena possible; on a scientific level, they are the implicit or explicit hypotheses of coherence with which the human sciences operate. These are the principles which

[2] On the issue of the "big problems" and the debate over the "relevance of social science to society," we would guard the disinterested work of science and see the task of social ethics coming to focus around the relevance of findings to the everyday world. The ethicist or political leader may request the exploration of certain problems in the light of issues confronting the society; on the other hand, the social scientist may assume ethical responsibility in pursuing certain problems, but he then strains his role as disinterested observer and diagnostician—much like the doctor who operates on a member of his family.

[3] For a discussion of this problem of "interest," see Schutz, *Collected Papers*, Vol. 2, esp. pp. 229–238, on the general concept of "problem-relevance."

generate what we have called styles of scientific inquiry. Secondly, the theories with which the sciences of man work imply some notion of human fulfillment in the context of social unity and order. This follows logically if our interpretation of the nature of social reality is valid, since man is a valuing and meaning-realizing being who struggles to make sense of his world. When a social-scientific perspective brings to light the identity of man or society, it has to make some sense of his wrestling with values. Different models control the selective work of the sciences in defining problems and interpreting the significance of processes. The adequacy of these models varies according to the interests and problems of the sciences at any point in their development. However, the relevance of the models to an understanding of human fulfillment *in everyday terms* is of crucial significance to social ethics and to the society which employs these findings. Consequently, we shall consider the problem of models and human fulfillment as an independent aspect of the scientific perspectives. The weighting of scientific understanding for the sake of translation to everyday terms will be determined largely by the dimensions of social reality which are relevant to the ethicist; these are determined in the sciences by the ordering principle. On the other hand, the significance of that weighting for the values which are dominating the social identity arises from the implicit notion of fulfillment in the models. Once these two issues in scientific perspective have been clarified and ordered within a comprehensive hypothesis, we shall be in a position to look at the collaborative tasks of social ethics and social science.

## *ORDERING PRINCIPLES IN THE HUMAN SCIENCES*

The elements and individual units of the social world gain their significance from the ordering principles by which that world is interpreted. When we look at a room, for example, we perceive its order or disorder according to some interpretative principle which shapes our expectations. The professor sees the arrangement of his papers and books as a meaningful expression of the sequence in which he hopes to "clean up" his work or as reflecting the accumulation of his projects. The housewife entering the study sees papers and books in disorder. If she can gain access to the room, the professor's order will rapidly be replaced by his wife's order; it then becomes disorder for him. In each case, however, the meaning of the elements—books, papers, equipment, etc.—arises from the ordering principle by which parts are related to one another and given coherence in the total process.[4]

The example of order in a study illustrates the way in which an ordering principle determines the significance of the elements within a whole. The papers, books, correspondence, equipment, etc., have their particular values to the professor according to his total schema of research, writing, and teaching. By the same token, the books, papers, etc., represent units of dirt or disorder to be placed in symmetrical piles for the maid or housewife; their values do not arise from an order of research but from an order of neatness or symmetrical distribution. Neither order is exclusive or absolute; each represents a perspective on the situation and a principle of coherence. A schema of interpretation imputes value and meaning to part-processes by ordering them within some coherent system. It is precisely this imputation of meaning or value which is accomplished by the common culture. In turn, the ordering of elements in the social world by a scientific schema attributes significance to the various elements, including the attitudes, activities, and structures which make up the social world. The formulation of coherence is simultaneously an attribution of value. For example, the ordering principle is decisive in evaluating the meaning of individual activity and fulfillment; one interpretation may see individual fulfillment as the actualization of interests

[4] For a discussion of ordering principles, see *ibid.*, Vol. 1, esp. pp. 300f.

against the interests of others, while another ordering of the social world may interpret such conflict of interest as pathological or maladjustive. A schema of social order evaluates elements by arranging them in the context of a whole.

In developing this notion of perspectives of order, Henri Bergson originally distinguished between spontaneous order and the automatic order of intellection.[5] He was proposing a normative interpretation of ordering, although he recognized the variety of orders with which we organize experience. We recognize that a variety of ordering principles may be used to establish the relations between elements of the social world; we also recognize that these principles illuminate different aspects of that world. Thus, we acknowledge the importance of a variety of perspectives according to the diverse interests of social-scientific traditions; even though we shall attempt to order these perspectives in terms of human intentionality, we see them as perspectives on intentionality. We insist in the present context only that *every ordering principle is an imputation of values* to the parts. We shall attempt to show in Part Three that these principles of order can be relativized in terms of the three essential tendencies of the intentional self which we have already explicated. Thus, some relative ordering of these various schemas may be achieved without insisting dogmatically on a single perspective; indeed, various perspectives illuminate the social world by bringing to light certain aspects of these essential tendencies.

Our first objective is to make clear the main principles of order which have gained currency in the human sciences. Even if we grant that a variety of possibilities may emerge in these sciences, the experience of the discipline has indicated the viability of several main alternatives. Furthermore, we wish to clarify the values of part-processes which arise from these principles. This imputation of value expresses the social scientist's project—his interpretation of the mean-

[5] *Ibid.*

ing of the societal enterprise; it reflects his way of evaluating the elements in a social whole.

At the risk of oversimplifying the analysis, Chart 3 sets forth four alternative principles of social coherence. This typology is drawn from Chart 2 of Chapter 4 and expresses the principles in terms of comprehensive models (column 3) and ordering principles (column 4). There are, of course, other possibilities for arranging these principles, by combining several in a complementary or dialectical relationship, but we are concerned with the main alternatives and particularly with those which have wide currency in contemporary social science. For present purposes, we can identify four ordering principles and corollary models of social reality.

We have already discussed the broad lines of interpretation which are associated with the perspectives of signification (physical, vital, and mental). We can now consider rather specifically the imputations of value which arise from accounting for human projects by ordering principles which are appropriate to these perspectives. The principles may develop on any level, as we shall see; but, empirically, certain principles have emerged in correlation with particular levels of interpretation. Another dimension of the typology arises from the starting point of the scientific schema: the structural units (individual orientation, etc.), the social and cultural whole, or some relationship between them; this dimension can be used to crosscut the levels and extend the typology. We shall indicate these alternative starting points but shall avoid extensive discussion of them; such a discussion would be useful only for a systematic typology of the disciplines.

## *BEHAVIORISM*

If we begin on the abstract level of signification, we recognize the schema of behaviorism; this schema uses the

**Chart 3** ORDERING PRINCIPLES OF SCIENTIFIC PERSPECTIVES (*Revised*)

| **Style** | **Dynamic structure** | **Principle of unification** | **Ordering principle** |
|---|---|---|---|
| Behaviorist (Physical) | Impulses (Pleasure-Pain) | Balance of exchanges | Adjustment to external conditions |
| Functionalist (Vital) | Social self (Needs) | Equilibrium (Order) | Adaptation by internal and external transformation |
| Voluntarist (Subjectist) | Interests | Conflict and compromise | Domination and rationalization |
| Intentionalist (Existential) | Intentional self | Harmony | Continuity as meaning |

physical sciences as *the* model for the human sciences in a literal sense. The search for predictive hypotheses has led to significant attempts to formalize models in this style of work. Within the levels of abstraction in the far-left column, the conditions determine the meaning if the physical level is taken as home base. Whether this analysis proceeds from an imputation of instinctual forces which produce a set of calculable effects (individual starting point) or starts with a field of external forces which produce calculable internal effects, the basic notion is one of "conditioned response"; internal meanings are representations of external forces. Ecological determinists and behaviorists use similar principles of coherence, but they employ different fields of force to account for human behavior; the informing notion is that the "intentional self" of whom we have spoken is a mere reflection of nonintentional forces—*the project is the product of the conditions.* Given sufficient facts, every discussion of values can be reduced to a calculation of facts.[6]

The imputation of value in these theories derives from notions such as adjustment. The stimulus-response school talks about rewards and punishments; this interpretation of human activity imputes a pleasure-pain balance as the internal economy of the structural unit—an economy which can be altered by manipulation of sanctions. Pavlov's experiments would be the type-case. The principle of adjustment suggests that the field of force is "given" and calls for accommodation on the part of the structural unit; the field is not constituted by intentionality but is given "in itself," so to speak. However, the relation of responses to external forces occurs with friction, particularly on the human level, since the conditioning factors are never evenly distributed and since the particular location of the unit makes its demands on the field of force somewhat unique. Hence, every point in the system suffers a certain friction in the associational process; the anticipated rewards are chained to particular types of behavior, but the chains have broken links. Reconditioning can occur, and much of contemporary behaviorism is busy at the task of clearing up associations between anticipated rewards and specific types of behavior. In any case, behavior which does not fit the expectations

[6] In addition to previous references to behaviorism, the author is indebted to William H. Heid for his discussion of these issues in his paper (mimeographed) "Carl R. Rogers and B. F. Skinner: Ethics and Social Scientific Analysis," May, 1965.

and demands of the social milieu is a product of inadequate conditioning; however adjustive such behavior may be in the economy of the structural unit, it needs reconditioning in order to achieve maximum rewards in the given field; in this sense, the unit is a complex of forces whose content is externally determined.

The adjustive or maladjustive response is determined by the conditions of the milieu; these conditions are interpreted by the scientist, who is the only one with objective knowledge; hence, what the scientist infers to be the "meaning" of the milieu—usually a reflection of the common culture as he participates in it—provides the principle of value with which behavior is evaluated. The scientist knows what is *really* happening, because he knows the determinants in the field of force; the subjects of the action merely respond to determinants and operate with ideologies instead of knowledge. The behaviorist implicitly makes the project of the common culture (as "he" interprets it) the criterion of value by which he judges the adjustive or maladjustive response. Whether a particular behavior would transform the culture in the direction of new values which might preserve or even "save" it is irrelevant on this level of interpretation, since there is no principle of evaluation; the future is simply a product of past conditioning.

Behaviorism is not, of course, the only type of human science that has worked on the physical level of interpretation. The Freudian theory of instinct operated on a similar principle of adjustment and accommodation; however, it took the organism in its pleasure-pain economy as the basic principle and determined the resolution of forces under various conditions. This Freudian conception also appropriates meanings from the common culture in order to interpret the symbolic activity of the structural unit; however, a radical Freudianism unquestionably sees the social and cultural world as a sublimation of libidinal forces. In contrast to behaviorism, the *real* forces are the internal impulses rather than the social conditions. The meaning of adjustment is inverted in this Freudian theory, since the organism is not simply conditioned by external forces; the social and cultural worlds are themselves the reflections of libidinal expressions and conflicts.[7] The conflict between the behaviorist and psychoanalytic traditions does not arise, therefore, from a difference of principle in relating the parts in the whole but from a difference of fundamental starting point; both perspectives are concerned with *accommodation* in quasi-physical terms, but the Freudian tradition gives far more significance to the internal drive of the units, while the behavioristic tradition sees the internal structure as a mere reflection or product of external conditions. Later developments in Freudian theory have shifted levels and complicated this picture; however, the principal shift has been to the functional level. The key here is the place of reason, which will be considered subsequently.[8]

The ordering of the social world as adjustment of units to a field of force and the attempt to establish equations of equivalence between external conditions and internal movements form a fundamental schema of human science. This style has been extremely productive in dealing with certain types of problems, and balance is one of its basic principles. Whether this style focuses upon symbolic interaction, libidinal expression, search for identity, maintenance of a pleasure-pain balance, or adjustment to rewards and punishments, similar principles are employed and similar imputations of value are made. For example, an organism is conceived as adjusted when a compromise or balance is hit between the impelling internal forces and the set of conditions in which those forces can be released. Such theories deny that the scientist imputes values, but this is only a way

[7] See the discussion of the elements of Freudian theory in *Handbook of Social Psychology*, edited by Gardner Lindzey (Reading, Mass.: Addison-Wesley Publishing Co., Inc., 1954), Vol. 1. For the understanding of culture, see Sigmund Freud, *Civilization and Its Discontents* (London: The Hogarth Press, Ltd., 1957), esp. on the pleasure-pain principle of the individual and the institutional restrictions of culture, pp. 133f.

[8] See Chapter 5, esp. footnotes, for a discussion of this problem.

of saying that the possibilities available in a particular milieu at a given time (as interpreted by the scientist) are taken as the basis for evaluation of what is an adjustive response. Goodness, then, is maximal pleasure or libidinal expression in a given field of conditions.

Before turning to the functional level, the relative significance of *adjustment* as an ordering principle should be recognized. Our previous discussion of the commonsense world indicated that man's projects orient toward the future under constituted conditions—his biography or history, the social and cultural milieu, his location and his "interests." The project of the intentional self is "conditioned" by the situation; this conditioning applies, moreover, to future limits as well as to past determinations. We can now add the point that intentional consciousness is *embodied consciousness*—a psychophysical process in the natural world. From the perspective of the intentional self and his projects, embodiment is opening on the world—participation in the world; it is having a world. From an external point of view, the reflexes and conditioned aspects of the corporeal schema—the pattern of embodiment as lived, according to Maurice Merleau-Ponty's interpretation—form the limiting and partially determinative substratum of intentional consciousness. These are the passive syntheses which are pregiven for intentional consciousness. Freudian therapy and behavioristic reconditioning have amply demonstrated the significance of these embodied patterns of response. On this level of interpretation, the principle of adjustment or conditioning proves useful for interpreting aspects of human behavior which are taken for granted and undergird our having a world. The effectiveness of these interpretations, however, derives from bringing to consciousness alternative possibilities as well as the actuality of certain pregiven patterns of embodiment; this is particularly true of responses which are alienated from the intentional self, since the conditions of our projects can be alien determinations when they are not integrated on the level of consciousness. Thus, the physical and organic conditions of embodiment are crucial *aspects of our situation;* the fruitfulness of this perspective diminishes, however, when it loses sight of the intentional consciousness and converts the "situation of action" into a set of determining conditions; indeed, this transformation makes the project of psychotherapy or reconditioning completely unintelligible, and social process devolves to a vicious circle of external conditioning and internal adjustment.

Adjustment or conditioning can order many of the associative processes of consciousness; however, attempts to universalize this ordering principle in order to account for the constitutive syntheses of consciousness prove totally inadequate to human experience. Bruno Bettelheim has made this point in a different way in his volume on experiences in a concentration camp, *The Informed Heart.*[9] Dr. Bettelheim is a Freudian in basic orientation, if he can be classified at all, but he notes that this schema is more useful for coping with pathology than in offering a model of human fulfillment. Under the pressures of the concentration camp, more was at stake than adjustment to the environment, since the milieu was itself destructive of human value and meaning. Bettelheim deals creatively with the important role of a reality-sense in making suitable adjustments, but he also points toward the intentional self and its own integrity in achieving internal coherence despite the destructive milieu. Thus, *The Informed Heart* furnishes an excellent account of the values of the adjustive principle as a style in interpreting human experience, while indicating the limitations of the schema in clarifying the human project and the search of the self for integrity and meaning. Adjustment formulates passive synthesis but simply misses the active synthesis of constitutive consciousness.[10]

[9] Bruno Bettelheim, *The Informed Heart* (New York: The Free Press, 1960).

[10] The regularities discernible on this level of abstraction may have to be transposed to different interpretative contexts in specifying a personal, group, or societal identity, but they furnish extremely important generalizations of substratum processes. The principal difficulties of this adjustive

*FUNCTIONALISM*

The human sciences have seldom worked consistently on the physical level of interpretation. Talcott Parsons' study of some major theories in social science traces the instability of interpretations on this level.[11] This instability of physical interpretation leads to ambiguous formulations; the psychoanalytic tradition is an outstanding example of the ambiguity of levels in its interpretation of psychic processes. The principal clue to a shift from the physical to the vital level is the postulation of a structural whole and the use of functional adaptation to account for the meaning of part-processes. On the physical level, the scientist calculates the movement of forces and attempts to infer direction from past states of the field. On the vital level, a totality of organism and environment is postulated in a kind of moving equilibrium, and part-processes are evaluated as they contribute to the maintenance of the stability of these relationships and the increase of the mastery by the internal system over the conditions imposed by the environment. The ordering principle on the vital level, therefore, is functional adaptation rather than adjustment to a given field of force; moreover, functional adaptation is increasingly used in a sophisticated way to account not only for accommodation to fixed conditions but also for *active transformation of the organism and its conditions with a view to actualizing internal needs.*[12]

In considering this alternative, we shall confine our attention to the theory of action, since this is the best-known form of functional theory. Actually, functional theory has a

---

style arise from its imputations of value to external conditions, but these are seldom explicit and have to be elicited by the ethicist.

[11] See Parsons, *The Structure of Social Action*, esp. Part 1.

[12] Talcott Parsons developed a sophisticated reinterpretation of adaptation in his article "Evolutionary Universals in Society," p. 340. The principle of adaptation is used in a similar way here, since it is defined in the "contextual framework" of a patterned system that is changing both internally and with respect to its situation.

long history in the human sciences and need not be equated with the structural-functional approach which Talcott Parsons has developed.[13] For example, Bronislaw Malinowski used functional categories in his interpretation of Trobriand culture, but he started with individual units and their instinctual drives, interpreting the cultural traditions and institutions as functional solutions to human problems. Despite the simplicity of this schema of interpretation, it enabled anthropologists to systematize masses of data from other cultures. Elaborations of this type of theory, particularly in the theory of action, have attempted to meet many of the criticisms which were leveled at earlier functionalism. If we consider the most sophisticated statement of this schema, we can recognize both the strengths and the limitations of this ordering principle.

Functional theory on the vital level, even in its most refined formulations, is circular in its reasoning; it postulates a functional whole and explains it by the functioning of its parts; a system is postulated as a going concern in an environment, then the part-processes and structures are interpreted as contributing to the maintenance of this going concern and its adaptation to the environment. Such a schema of interpretation proved extremely useful in the morphological stage of biological research, and there is no reason why it should not be applied on the human level of evolution for certain purposes. However, there are important value-premises in this ordering principle; these values are presupposed in the postulation of a going concern as the whole within which functioning elements are identified. The continuity of systems and their increasing mastery over their environing conditions become the criteria of evaluation of the positive or negative contributions of particular units.

[13] To mention only a few, see the work of Robert Merton, Clyde Kluckhohm, Bronislaw Malinowski, A. R. Radcliffe-Brown, and W. Lloyd Warner. Each of these versions of functionalism has its own variations, but the principle of coherence is essentially the same.

The equilibrium of the social process is taken for granted; then, the meaning and value of units are stated in terms of their contribution to that moving equilibrium.[14] If one asks why a part is considered in functional terms, the answer is that it is a part and thus either maintains the whole (functions) or disrupts (dysfunctions).

The basic difference between functional theory and the stimulus-response model on the physical level is the importance given to internal structure by functional theory. Earlier applications of Darwinian notions viewed instinct as a set of blind forces; more sophisticated biological theory has indicated the extent to which instinct selects from its environment and even effects internal transformations of structure in order to cope with given conditions. The theory of action, and particularly the style of action theory which Talcott Parsons has developed, uses the organism-environment model but introduces dynamic transformations in both the internal and the external structures. This is the source of the complexity, as well as the difficulty, of the categorizations which Parsons has introduced. When organism-environment is complicated by the notion of actor-situation and both internal and external aspects are treated as dynamic and changing, the complexity of the model increases rapidly. The basic pattern of the construction is to take three orientational principles which link actor and situation—cathectic, cognitive, and evaluative—then to construct the variety of possible organizations of relationship that emerge with combinations of these relationships. We are concerned here only with the implicit values in the ordering principle, but this is a sophisticated model with a variety of uses, as we shall note subsequently.

Functional theory in the human sciences has generally followed biological models and imputed certain need-dispo-

[14] The equivocal character of this notion of equilibrium is underlined by Robert Brown, who gives a series of uses of the term. See *Explanation in Social Science*, p. 117.

sitions to the acting agents. Thus, Talcott Parsons speaks of the integration of personality as a balance of gratifications and deprivations—an essentially biological notion of the meaning of personal identity; personality is, then, the internal equilibrium of need-dispositions in a given field of forces; however, the self is constituted by culture as a form, the social self. On a somewhat higher level of unit analysis, social systems are viewed as interactive networks in an equilibrium; the functions of various elements are understood as actualizations of values of the system, increase of the facilities of the system, and normative regulation of interactions within the system. On each level of analysis, in brief, the ordering principle is functional adaptation within a postulated equilibrium, so that the final level of evaluation is in terms of the values which are pregiven in any particular system. In more recent years, Talcott Parsons has extended this analysis to the evolutionary process by formulating a set of evolutionary universals which mark transitions in systems toward the maximization of the differentiation of units and functions, on the one hand, and toward more comprehensive organization, on the other; in general, evaluation between various systems becomes possible, since it is assumed that maximizing the mobility of particular units and increasing facilities in a more comprehensive equilibrium actualize the potentials of the evolutionary process; this, then, is the directionality of the evolutionary process by which evaluative comparisons can be made among systems.[15]

Alternative social theories differ with the theory of action over its imputation of value; the theory of action gives positive evaluation to units and processes which enhance the values of a given system; it takes a negative view of conflicts, protests, or withdrawals from values of that system, viewing them as signs of tension and maladjustment. On a certain level of analysis, this may be a useful way to look at a situation of action; for example, Neil Smelser has applied this

[15] See fn. 12.

theory to collective movements.[16] This functional analysis diverts attention from the substantive challenge which is embodied in protest movements; protest often brings fundamental values into question, whereas the functional perspective organizes the social world entirely around established values. Conflicts of value, incompatibility of values, struggles for power, etc., are categorized as signs of tension or deviance in functional theory; the substantive issues in conflict of interest are passed over and attention is focused on the growth and reestablishment of the equilibrium of a given system. Here, the theory of action approaches behaviorism, since protest reflects inadequate conditioning. Perhaps this states the imputation of value in the functional principle somewhat strongly, but incompatibility of values is not taken seriously in this type of theory; hence, the struggle over values tends to be viewed as symptomatic of maladjustment.

This basic limitation of functional theory has even deeper roots; values are viewed as nonrational; they are taken for granted with the social and cultural system, but they are not subject to rational adjudication. Reason is viewed as *instrumental* in this type of theory; it functions to map out terrain and achieve goals, but the goals are furnished by instincts, need-dispositions, and cultural inheritance. Reason is technical, a consistent calculation of means and ends; it contributes nothing substantive to the grasp of ends or values. The adjustive principle of behaviorism views reason as a "set of associations" or neural paths which are produced by external forces through internal sensations. Functional theory on the vital level is somewhat similar in its view of reason, but the analysis is complicated by the introduction of internal forces which modify the environing field of force. In both cases, however, values are nonrational

[16] See Neil J. Smelser, *Theory of Collective Behavior* (New York: The Free Press, 1963). The movements are interpreted in terms of strain (cf. Ch. 3) but are incorporated in the functional context of growth.

expressions of desire and are taken for granted; hence, the *scientist's interpretation* of the basic values of a given system becomes *the criterion* of what is functional and dysfunctional about a particular attitude or movement. Values are placed outside the purview of rational understanding; the scientist's interpretation of the values of a given system is taken as the decisive criterion for what contributes to the equilibrium of the system.[17]

The peculiar character of the theory of action, as an instance of functional theory, can now be identified. The functional principle may be employed to order human experience on any level; for example, sensory processes could be viewed as subordinate functions of a rational being in a functional order on the mental level. The theory of action remains, however, on the vital level and thus denies a substantive role to reason in the pursuit of value or meaning. However, this theory also takes its departure from the social and cultural system which it postulates; unlike Bronislaw Malinowski's functionalism, one does not question the adequacy of institutions to meet postulated needs and instincts; indeed, action theory conceives the organism to be sufficiently malleable to receive its substantive meaning and values from the social and cultural whole of which it is a part. Therefore, the functional principle is employed in the context of a collectivist or totalitarian view of the given cultural system; the actor has no leverage against these cultural values except his idiosyncratic impulses, which reflect inadequate socialization or certain "religious" experiences whose referent is the nonempirical and whose sources are nonrational. The theory of action employs the functional principle, therefore, to order social processes within the interdependent whole

[17] The issue is the unity of cognitive and affective dimensions in the "lived" or pregiven experience of embodied consciousness. The functional theories in different ways break up this unity so that values and meanings issue from an instinctual level, while cognitive processes perform mapping operations, the ideal expression being the operations of empirical science in mapping relations between things.

of the cultural and social system; on the one hand, it denies the role of reason in constituting and adjudicating between values; on the other hand, the theory itself *purports to grasp* the nature of the social process and thus makes its own imputations of value about various elements on the basis of a rational, scientific theory. The obvious question arises about the validation of a functional principle when evaluative principles fall outside the purview of reason, but here we recognize that a schema of interpretation rests upon ordering principles which it cannot validate.

This brings us to the decisive limitation of functional adaptation as an ordering principle. The theory of action postulates a given state of a system; thus, its analysis is retrospective, attempting to account for a state of equilibrium from antecedent allocations of energy. Talcott Parsons' theory of evolutionary universals is an interesting example of this type of analysis; he starts with modern, complex societies and then looks backward to identify structural emergences which marked stages on the way to these societies. He postulates certain values which characterize complex societies and then retrospectively characterizes the adaptive processes through which such values were developed. The baseline of value is taken for granted in each case of functional analysis; the scientist attempts to account for those values by retrospective interpretation; given the project, he asks what conditions were prerequisite to its emergence. Those elements and processes are viewed as "functional" which contributed to the emergence of these values; those processes were "deviant" which failed to fit the configuration of value which has been postulated. Social process is actually constituted in prospective intentionality; functional analysis objectifies this process in retrospect and then makes functional evaluations as though this were a prospective analysis, creating a retrospective illusion of evolutionary determination. If we treat this functional ordering as a retrospective analysis of conditions, the illusion can be avoided and *conditions* of human intentionality—*the constituting of social identity*—can be grasped. Hence, our critical considerations touch the interpretative context in which the principle is used; the organizing power of the principle in synthesizing a number of variables in the social milieu is a remarkable achievement on the theoretical level; difficulties arise with translation to the prospective intentionality of the everyday world; as suggested in Chapter 5, functionalism develops a pseudointentionality.

The utility of such an analysis is obvious; it brings to consciousness the prior states of a system with reference to certain values which are selected by the scientist; within this context of values, an appraisal of constituting conditions is possible. For example, action theory is interested in differentiation of functions, mobility of units, and increase of facilities. These values could be actualized in different ways; viewed in the past tense, they emerged in given ways in the Western world. Furthermore, values are actualized in the context of prior conditions: state of language, level of legal development, available governmental structures, state of class differentiation, level of technology, etc. The intentional self is situated with a particular history, in a given time and place, in a specific cultural milieu, etc., etc. The retrospective recovery of the complex of conditions in which particular values were actualized brings to consciousness not only the prerequisite conditions for such an actualization of value but also the limiting conditions which confront further attempts to actualize such values in the future.

The most graphic illustration of the utility of such analysis is the growing knowledge of factors which limit the development of productive potential in so-called underdeveloped areas: conditions of housing, capital development, population growth, etc. Here too, however, the retrospective illusion of determination by conditions needs to be avoided or creative alternatives in constituting new social orders will be erroneously discounted.

The limitation of such functional analysis is just as striking as its utility. The values of units and of total cultures are not simply static; they emerge in the course of development and could not be anticipated from prior states of the system. In Western history, the role of freedom and equality is an excellent example of the unfolding of values through emergence, conflict, and gradual transformation. Those forces which disrupted the social system in the nineteenth century actualized values of the system which were implicit and unacknowledged; a functional ordering of social phenomena would ignore or discount such movements. The human project (cultural values in the most comprehensive sense) is not given at any point in the evolutionary process and cannot be read from previous states of the system. Talcott Parsons' evolutionary universals may simply mark stages in personal degeneration along with technological advance; most of us would deny this, but we do not *know*. Whether this is asserted or not depends upon the ordering principle and its implicit values; merely recognizing certain structural changes in retrospect furnishes no criterion for a positive or negative evaluation of their "meaning." The social scientist operating with a functional theory may make helpful retrospective analyses of the conditions antecedent to the emergence of certain states of the cultural system—analyses which are relative to his particular interests as scientist. If he conceives this account to be an explanation of the future (what is functional and dysfunctional to the actualization of the essential meaning of the culture), then he substitutes his own project for the culture; his own theory becomes an expression of the *essential* movement of the culture. This is to ontologize the theory. Functional theory is a useful method for systematizing certain aspects of the social web with reference to a common culture in prior states of a system. The functional principle is misleading if it purports to evaluate the meaning of current processes and projects. The basic problem is to keep the theoretical and everyday perspectives distinct and to recognize the point at which translations need to be made.

We recognized the importance of physical theories and their adjustive principle by acknowledging the situational limitations on human intentionality; internal constitution of meaning occurs in a field of prior determinations and achieves actualization through embodiment in a particular time and place. In that context, we relativized this adjustive principle by noting its presupposition of meaning and value both for action itself and in its own schema. We also need to recognize the importance of the functional principle in formulating the interdependence of the physical, social, and cultural world. Theories on the organic level rightly stress the systematically related and interdependent nature of social process. We have already suggested that functional analysis explicates the coherence of social reality and the way in which future states of social reality are embedded in antecedent conditions. We also need to relativize this perspective in terms of intentionality by identifying the functional principle as a particular version of the order of social reality—a version stressing functional continuities and scanting the incompatibilities of interest and value which characterize the network of human intentionalities. For all its values in systematization, the functional principle underestimates conflicts of human interests. For this latter level of analysis, in which the variety of human interests is taken seriously, we move to a level of analysis which is much closer to human intentionality.

### *VOLUNTARISM*

On the mental or intentional level, interests and values are treated as constitutive elements in the social world. A major style in human science has developed this interpretation. Max Weber is the most noteworthy exemplar of this style, and his influence has fused with many of the sociological developments in the United States. We place this schema of interpretation on the mental level because the conflict of interests and the incompatibilities among values, as well as the rational calculation of courses of action, play a dominant role in the theory. This is not actually an intentional analysis in the phenomenological sense, but it uses intentionality as its point of reference. In one sense, Weber systematizes the pragmatic interests of the everyday world in developing his typologies of social organization. Adjustment and adaptation play a less important role on this level of analysis, although they are not entirely discounted; the basic categories are conflict, compromise, influence, and domination. In essence, this is a political conception of the social world as a conflict of interests, powers, and values. Weber recognized the conditions of action and their importance, but he was more concerned with values and cultural direction; hence, his focus turned upon the *projects* and their variability rather than the conditions, although he never analyzed projects apart from their situational milieu.[18]

We can contrast this general tradition with the functional ordering of the social world by noting that interest theorists take human projects as their central theme, whereas the functionalists take the process within which projects emerge as the central concern. Max Weber is concerned with the origin of the preoccupation with rationality in the Western world, while Talcott Parsons is interested in the structural conditions within which this change occurred and its structural ramifications. Whether interest theory is adequate to deal with intentionality is a serious question, but it takes the human projects as explicit themes instead of treating the

[18] It is difficult to find an adequate treatment of Max Weber, perhaps because this voluntaristic analysis is alien to all but our pragmatic tradition. Talcott Parsons' stress on the voluntaristic side of Weber is certainly legitimate, although Parsons was primarily concerned with the development of a theory of action in *The Structure of Social Action*, Part 3. The two essays which reflect Weber's mature thought and perspectives are "Politics as a Vocation" and "Science as a Vocation," in *From Max Weber's Essays in Sociology*, Part 1.

social identity as a mere function of the process. Interest theories investigate the variety of projects in terms of competing dynamics and relate these to situational conditions. However, they usually treat interests and values as unaccountable or irrational; consequently, they impose upon the social and cultural world a notion of radical disharmony. The difficulty with interest theories, therefore, is that their recognition of the struggle for power readily elevates that struggle to a final principle.[19]

Interest theorists have a perspectival view of reason; the scientist gains little more rational comprehension than the groups he attempts to understand, since he too is engaged in the social process and grasps it from particular interests and cultural limitations.[20] So far as the social theorist attempts to interpret given projects in the light of antecedent conditions, he can be more neutral than the more interested reflection of politicians; but so far as he enters the lists for one or another project, he has no more claim to objectivity than other interested parties. For perspectival reason, all truth is propaganda; C. Wright Mills held to this view with some consistency.[21]

The perspectival character of reason is not a serious problem to the thoroughgoing interest theorist, although it was deeply disturbing to Max Weber, who sought to develop an objective science of the social world. For true interest

[19] This aspect of Max Weber's thought, as well as his stress on power as domination, is ignored in most American appropriation of Weber, and yet it is fundamental to his theory. For a notable exception, see the brief critique by Carl J. Friederich in *Reader in Bureaucracy,* edited by Robert Merton (New York: The Free Press, 1952).

[20] See Weber, *Methodology of the Social Sciences,* esp. Ch. 1, on the problem of ethical neutrality in the social sciences.

[21] There is wide variety among interest theorists, or voluntaristic theories, as we have called them. C. Wright Mills is almost prototypical on the American scene; his differences with Talcott Parsons become quite understandable in the context of Chart 3 in this chapter. Basic terms such as "power," "freedom," "responsibility," and "value" shift meaning with these contexts, so that Parsons' charge against Mills centers around his "zero-sum" notion of power. See *Structure and Process in Modern Societies* (New York: The Free Press, 1960), pp. 219ff.

theory, perspectives are generated by location, cultural milieu, and interests. Interests are *practical* and shape every apprehension of social reality. Since the clarification of perspectives and the achievement of values can come about only through a pursuit of projects with rational calculation, interest theorists acknowledge the relativity of the social sciences and treat them as important elements in the self-consciousness of the society. So far as society can comprehend its situation in the light of its projects, it can move more adequately and clearly to the actualization of its interests. Such theorists never hesitate to challenge the given values of a particular period in the light of more adequate values, since they understand history and social change as a constant struggle between conflicting interests and values. Conflict between Winston White and C. Wright Mills was inevitable, since White was working with a functional principle, while Mills understood social process as conflict and domination. White takes values as given and then asks what processes contribute to their actualization and stability.[22] Talcott Parsons says that he does not care who "has the power" so long as power is increased in the total system, while Andrew Hacker sees the problem of politics precisely in "who has the power."[23] The principles from which these theories develop yield quite different interpretations of power and impute different values to the elements in social organization. For the functionalist, power is a facility to be utilized in a system; hence, its increase at any point in the system will in time benefit the whole system by raising its level. For the interest theorist, power is domination and control; hence, possession of power by one class or interest group will mean the subjugation of other groups. The interest theorist looks at the distribution of power, and the functionalist looks at the release of power as a kind of energy in the system.

22 See the discussion of the ideological debate in Chapter 2.

23 See Hacker, "Sociology and Ideology," in *The Social Theories of Talcott Parsons*, esp. pp. 304ff.

We have a variety of interpretations of social process under this principle of conflict of interest. The dualistic understanding of man in Max Weber's theory led him to a tragic sense of the incompatibility of interests among classes and nations; values were ultimately irrational; reason was technical or calculating; thus, he was torn between a sense of the importance of ultimate values and a resignation to *Realpolitik*.[24] The utilization of Weber's concepts in American social science has glossed over this fundamental dualism, so that appeals to his name are usually of a superficial kind. C. Wright Mills, for example, is close to Weber's position on many points, and yet Mills had an optimistic attitude toward the possibilities of democratic process.

C. Wright Mills' harangues against the power elite issued from a fundamental optimism; Max Weber's melancholy reflections on Western bureaucratization signaled a deepening despair. The Weberian line, however, is only one path for interest theorists. The theory of the social world developed by Alfred Schutz is deeply rooted in Weberian analysis and is essentially an interest theory; however, Schutz drew more rational components from the influence of Edmund Husserl and shifted to a concern with intentional analysis. This combination of elements in Schutz's theories raises some difficulties in the grounding of the theory, but it contributes to a more balanced relationship between a constitutive reason and a variety of interests and perspectives. In this respect, Weber was the inheritor of the two functions of reason—critical and practical—which flowed from the Kantian constructions.

One would also have to classify Marxist theories within this tradition of interest theories; again, the differences with Weber and American theorists are marked. The similarity among these theories arises from the notion of power as domination or exploitation as well as from attention to the

[24] See Weber, "Politics as a Vocation," in *From Max Weber's Essays in Sociology*.

human *project* in history; these theories also recognize basic incompatibilities among the interests and values of competing groups. Max Weber's disagreement with Marx was actually over the relative importance of ideas, values, and conditions in the emergence of human projects; in contrast to Marx's monolithic concern with modes of production, Weber considered interests, meanings, and ultimate notions of order as constitutive elements in history. Whereas Marx was optimistic about social evolution toward a classless society in which exploitation would be overcome by the elevation of the totally exploited, Weber saw an increasing conflict of cultures within the Western world. Weber was no more optimistic about proletarian domination than he was over *Junker* militarism; he could not visualize a resolution of these conflicting interests. In this sense, Marx is more than an interest theorist; like the functionalist, he postulates a comprehensive system which is evolving in history and creating man in its image—creating the social man. The interest theorist is too pragmatic for such grand schemes; he refuses to propose *his* project (theoretical schema) as the ultimate meaning of the societal enterprise.[25]

The significance of the interest theorists is clearly to be found in their stress on the human projects and values through which social processes are shaped. In contrast to the reduction of the project to a consequence of external forces or antecedent states of a system, these theorists focus on the constitutive role of human interests in shaping history; they reveal a sense of man's historical nature as self-consciousness; the ambiguous term "interest" thus refers without specification to man's constitutive role in history. The difficulty with interest theories is that they claim a more rational comprehension of the human situation than

[25] It is difficult to find comprehensive interpretations of the Marxian theory, obviously because of its subsequent political expression; the most systematic treatment is given by Jean-Yves Calvez, *La Pensée de Karl Marx* (Paris: Éditions du Seuil, 1950). This study places the Marxian analysis in its Hegelian context.

their perspectival notion of reason warrants. This is not always true, of course, and is indicated by Max Weber's resignation to human fate—to a leader whose demon will move him to give direction to Western history. Nevertheless, this style of scientific work brings the creative and transformative role of man's interests into the center of the stage, providing a significant corrective to adjustive and functional theories. If one affirms more for the role of reason in social process than the interest theorists, it needs to be affirmed in the context of the struggle for power and the thrust toward domination. The remarkable achievement of Reinhold Niebuhr, for example, was his capacity to develop an interest theory in the context of a more embracing harmony.

## *INTENTIONALITY*

We gain a more adequate appreciation of the relative significance of conflict theories if we set them in the more comprehensive framework of intentional analysis. We already noted that interest or conflict theories systematize the pragmatic struggle of the everyday world; hence, they abstract a *dimension* of the network of intentionalities with which the self-and-world correlation is constituted. Conflict theory focuses on the human project in its aspect as spontaneity, struggle for mastery, and projection of interests. These interests reflect the perspectives of self, group, or society. This view of human struggle is accurate for much of the everyday world, especially in the political realm. Nevertheless, when conflict is made the universal principle of social process, the common elements and harmonies within which conflict can occur are scanted. The possibility of a society ceases to be comprehensible. Pursuit of interests by the self or the group is understood within too limited a context; such interests must in time lead to compromise, since human reality is interrelated and interdependent, as the functionalists have indicated; thus, a more comprehensive principle of integrity or social unity is presupposed in the conflicts of interest and the struggle for power which characterize the everyday world.

This attempt to relativize the perspective of interest theories in terms of essential tendencies of the intentional self should not be misinterpreted as a desire to eliminate this type of analysis. Pragmatic interests constitute the political dimension of the social world; conflict theory carries through this dimension of the intentional self and enriches society's comprehension of its own projects by bringing the struggle for power to consciousness. The perspectival understanding of reason in these theories is in turn belied by the therapeutic effects of bringing this struggle to consciousness; despite his reservations about the significance of reason in dealing with questions of value, Max Weber had profound confidence in the importance of rational comprehension of the human situation and its projects. The essential tendency of the intentional self toward apprehension of meaning is thus presupposed in his whole project. Hence, we include interest and conflict theories within a more comprehensive understanding of the intentional self without any desire to eliminate their significant role in the interpretation of social reality.

Intentionality is man's living toward the structure of his world in the unity of caring, hoping, conceiving, feeling, and meaning. Its subjective dimensions are the constituting intentionalities of embodied consciousness. Its objective dimensions are the forms in which the world appears for this consciousness. These forms take relatively permanent shape in the typified meanings of the everyday world—the sedimentations of social experience. The ordering principle in this commonsense world is adequacy: adequacy of the sedimented forms for the shaping of vitalities in a changing milieu; adequacy of the allocation of resources for the values which shape the common culture; adequacy of the common culture itself for reflecting the ultimate horizon of meaning toward which the society is oriented; adequacy of the typifications of everyday experience for the changing interests and opportunities of a dynamic world. The term "adequacy," as suggested by these examples, refers to a harmony of meaning-intention and meaning-fulfillment—the fit of the constituted form to the constituting power.

This style of scientific analysis is very rich in qualities, since it approaches the "lived" world, at least in its more reflected levels of typification. For this reason, a science of the intentional world has proved uninteresting to those who wish to see the sciences of man quantified. The typifications of the everyday world form the stuff upon which the sciences of man are built as abstract perspectives; moreover, the adequacy of these scientific perspectives is testable only by the account which they give of this world. Those scientific styles which develop predictions must ultimately test their predictions within the commonsense world. By the nature of the social world, predictability may be limited to the most routinized and peripheral aspects of experience, such as spatial and physiological movements, technological processes, and habitual performances; however, such predictability is of significance to societal projects. Consequently, the refinement and testing of predictive models must ultimately come to terms with the highest ordering principle of typified experience—the principle of adequacy for everyday experience.

The sciences of man are at a kind of crossroads in the development of styles of work. A psychology of intentionality, a sociology of the everyday world, and an anthropology of the common culture are all developing to some extent. Men like Ludwig Binswanger, Alfred Schutz, Oscar Lewis, and Harold Garfinkel have contributed, each in his own style, to a new scientific orientation to the human world. This intentional style has two principal functions to fulfill in the development of social science. First, the richness of the social world and its "significant" problems are accessible only to such a phenomenological method. Alfred Schutz discovered this gradually and played down his Weberian style in later years for the sake of exploring the dimensions of the everyday world. Precision and quantification can be achieved in the social sciences only by screening out the richness of experience and the problems of significance to man; for certain purposes, this reduction of social phenomena may be useful, but what it gains in precision, it will lose in adequacy. Consequently, the decisions on style have to be made with a view to the problems which are of interest to science but without dogmatism about "hard" or "soft" data; in each style, certain problems come into prominence and important aspects of the social world are reduced.

The second function of a science of intentionality is the critical task of setting other scientific styles in perspective and testing their relevance within the everyday world. This task would be insignificant if other scientific styles recognized the limited relevance of their perspectives. As we have seen in the ideological controversy, each of these styles claims to be *the* perspective on the social world. Furthermore, proposals for social policy in everyday affairs are repeatedly made from these reduced perspectives, as though the abstracted model gave an account of *the way things are*. If scientific generalizations were actually testable under controlled conditions in the social world, these proposals would not need translation into everyday terms; they could be tested and verified. As things stand, most of the scientific generalizations about the social world are hypotheses which are actually accepted or rejected, at least implicitly, by a criterion of adequacy for commonsense experience. In fact, this kind of intentional critique is constantly made by legislators, political leaders, and planners in sifting social scientific data. Hence, to say that a function of intentional analysis is to evaluate more abstract perspectives is merely to underline the place of commonsense experience as the criterion of adequacy for any social scientific perspective.

The work of social ethics, as should become evident in Part Three of this inquiry, requires a grasp of the identity of the society—its constitution as a typified process. Although social ethics has its evaluative tasks and develops an understanding of the project of the society, it also has to develop a critical appropriation of the human sciences. Consequently, the discipline of social ethics needs to develop an intentional style of scientific work both for clarifying the ethical dimensions of social experience and for developing a critique of alternative perspectives. This is a task which is only beginning in social ethics. Without the cultivation of an intentional style of scientific work, the discipline of social ethics will remain a formalistic "value game." However, this problem will be interpreted in the next section, where the nature of ethical interpretation is clarified. Now we need to clarify the evaluative aspects of the scientific styles. Every social science involves an evaluative perspective on the social world; this makes the intentional critique of scientific findings even more crucial in policy decisions. We shall also see in Part Three that an ordering of values in the social world —an essential task of ethics—makes possible an ordering of these scientific perspectives. At this stage, we shall confine ourselves to the clarification of the values implicit in the perspectives.

### *EVALUATIVE ASPECTS OF SCIENTIFIC MODELS*

Every ordering principle also refers to a model which expresses the social whole in a comprehensive way. Moreover, these models project a meaning of the total human enterprise and its values. These models reflect what John Wild would call "ultimate horizons of meaning" or versions of order in terms of which the human enterprise is grasped and interpreted.[26] Hence, where the ordering principles

[26] See John Wild, *Existence and the World of Freedom* (Englewood Cliffs, N.J.: Prentice-Hall, Inc., 1963), esp. the final discussion.

impute certain values to the part-processes, these comprehensive images impute value to the total enterprise and its direction.

The significant issue for society is the idea of social fulfillment which informs a scientific model. These ideas are decisive for social interpretation. They are the ideas, moreover, which come to expression in the models of social process. We shall briefly consider several of these models and the way in which knowledge enters into social fulfillment in these alternative formulations.

The comparison of basic models is largely a matter of inference, since the human sciences usually refrain from systematic formulation of their ideas. Furthermore, the notion of a comprehensive model would be rejected by many social scientists, since they often assert that their models are simply heuristic and need have no relationship of analogy to actual processes; for this type of theory, the only test of adequacy of a model is its utility in making certain systematic formulations with some predictive power. And to make the issue even more ambiguous, a comprehensive model of social reality and fulfillment is actually a metaphysical concept, since it is a formulation of the most general structure of social and cultural reality. Our concern, however, is with value implications as the models are translated into the everyday context; their internal consistency and utility in the discipline are the relevant criteria in the theoretical realm.

An alternative approach to this whole problem can be developed out of Edmund Husserl's notion of meaning-intention and meaning-fulfillment.[27] We have already indicated the sense in which the scientist's schema of interpretation is his own project for the society, since it imputes values to the part-processes and to the meaning of the total enterprise. We can refer, then, to a scientific theory as a

[27] See Marvin Farber's expositions of this in *The Foundation of Phenomenology* (Cambridge, Mass.: Harvard University Press, 1943), esp. Ch. 13.

meaning-intention, by analogy to any expression. The verification of meaning-intentions such as perceptual judgments, wishes, etc., requires fulfillments which can validate their adequacy or achieve their resolution. In a perceptual judgment, we verify by the sense of harmony between the meaning as intended and the self-giveness of the object in perceptual intuition. We can perform an "as if" test with these models by projecting their fulfillment in the everyday sphere; this should give us some grasp of the values implicit in their interpretation of social process.

A certain self-correction goes on in natural science in the development of comprehensive models, since some formulations prove less adequate than others to account for processes in the natural world. The higher level of predictability and broader scope of the theory of relativity gave it precedence, as a more inclusive theory, over classical mechanics. Predictability in the human sphere is relatively low and confined to the most routinized aspects of social experience; consequently, debate in the social sciences is not resolvable by operational testing; meaning-intentions cannot be tested for harmony with appropriate fulfillments. These retrospective interpretations of conditions are usually debated in terms of explanatory adequacy. In view of this situation, we are concerned with seeing the relative significance of alternative models; moreover, this purpose can be achieved by testing the grasp of human intentionality which the models evince. From the perspective of the ethicist, the value-implications in the models are of first importance for making his translations to the everyday sphere; however, this level of appropriation of social-scientific findings presupposes adequacy on the theoretical level in terms of internal logic and organizing power. The models with which we are concerned make a legitimate case within the discipline in these theoretical terms; hence, our concern with their implications for the everyday sphere is focused on their explanatory adequacy in coping with the world.

Four basic models are presently dominant in the human

sciences: (1) a mechanistic model of balance of forces, in which the adjustment principle is grounded; (2) an organic model of dynamic equilibrium, from which functional adaptation arises; (3) a master-slave model, in which domination is central; and (4) an aesthetic model of harmony, in which the norm of adequacy finds its comprehensive expression. These images or models are suggested in column 3 of Chart 3. Since many of these problems have been considered in terms of the ordering principles, this analysis can be confined to profiles by which the models can be identified and located. The basic principles of this hierarchy, as already hinted in the notion of harmony in the "lived" world, are of increasing comprehensiveness and richness as we move from the abstract perspectives to the "lived" world, where harmony and fitness furnish the model and criterion. On this intentional level, there is increasing inner determination.

If the hierarchy expressed in column 3 of Chart 3 is adequately formulated, each of the models should be an expression of harmony on a somewhat abstracted level. This is true of the notion of balance in the mechanistic models, since there is a notion of harmony implicit in this model, but it lays stress upon the equivalence of inner and outer structures rather than upon internal determination.[28] The behaviorists have stressed this equivalence in developing their notion of conditioning. However, this basic model is much more widespread than associationist thought; it finds currency in exchange theories of human groups, cybernetics and information theories, and generally in theories which stress feedback processes. Neoclassical economic theory is constructed around such notions of exchange. The utility of the model arises from the typification of experience in passive syntheses. The typical processes in which much of our social experience is pregiven undoubtedly constitute a

[28] See, for example, the discussion of Boyle's law on the inverse variation of the volume and absolute pressure of a gas, in Robert Brown, *op. cit.*, esp. p. 151.

broad range of conditioning in social reality. The limitation of the model arises from the understanding of the intentional self as passive. The active, mastering, creative syntheses of experience and the reshaping of the environment by constitutive rationality are simply passed over by these abstract theories. This model systematizes the passive aspects of intentional experience; however, it is inadequate to cope with the enormous variety and creativity of social and cultural experience. Mechanistic balance is harmony on a very low level of differentiation; as an account of the intentional self and its fulfillment, the model is too limited. For specific regions of experience, the model obviously has important advantages and appropriateness; for example, in the field of economic exchange, it permits considerable formalization.

Social fulfillment emerges in these theories as actualizing impulses, interests, or instincts. Little attention is given to the content of these interests or instincts, since they are simply inputs of desire or energy which are determined in content by the external stimuli and conditions. A science of the social world contributes to social fulfillment by overcoming inadequacies in the external conditioning and by facilitating the responses of the units to the external forces. Man is a simple product of his environment. Fulfillment means actualizing one's instincts or impulses as the external conditions determine them; therefore, a science of the human world is knowledge of stimulus-response sequences.

Knowledge is an ambiguous aspect of social fulfillment within this mechanistic model. Since knowledge is actually an adequate set of associations in which internal circuits reproduce external forces, knowledge only enhances conformity of the inner to the outer. This is clear in the cybernetic notion of society in which feedback creates a more efficient process but introduces no creative transformation in direction, value, etc. Actually, values and meanings are simply taken for granted by mechanistic theory. The inadequacy of the basic model is reflected, then, in terms of knowledge; we find in social experience that knowledge of social conditions alters the meaning of the conditions and leads to a reconstituting of the situation. Knowledge is never simply reproductive of the "given" as mechanistic theory assumes. If this is the case, and widespread social experience supports this proposition, then the notion of equivalence between inner and outer is an inadequate expression of the harmony that operates on the intentional level. Every scientific formulation of the typical conditions in the environment increases the transcendence of selves and groups over their external conditions and alters the nature and meaning of those conditions for them. Apart from such self-transcendence, mechanistic theory itself could not appear. The intentionality of man's action is constantly re-creating the meaning of conditions in the light of his knowledge and the projects which he is shaping. A determinate knowledge of the social conditions increases freedom rather than conformity to external processes; in this sense, social determinism, even if conceivable, would dissolve as soon as it had been formulated in scientific theory. Social science thus transforms its subject matter as it inquires into it and formulates it. Human science finds itself in the reflexive circle which broadens with each new step of knowledge; this reflexive circle has its source in the correlation of increasing internal determination with every enrichment of the cultural milieu—consciousness is self-conscious being.

The organic models of functional adaptation are much more complex, since they stress the increasing complexity of the internal process in relation to the external conditions. The theory of action has developed this model but kept it closely allied to the mechanistic notion of equilibrium; the notion of a boundary-maintaining system is a modified mechanistic idea. This combination of levels makes it difficult to place the theory of action neatly, but the ambiguity arises primarily because Talcott Parsons aims to get his theory down to the physical level; he states his organic theory in terms that draw on the physical models of equivalence, balance, and equilibrium.

We have already considered the utility and significance of organic interpretations of social reality. This functional model stresses the differentiation which is implicit in the more comprehensive notion of harmony, and to this extent the equilibrium model is a more adequate expression of internal determination than the mechanistic theory. In his earlier formulations of this model, Talcott Parsons seems to have been far more tied to mechanistic ideas. Robin Williams expresses this vividly in formulating the notion of societal fulfillment which is implicit in Parsons' understanding of equilibrium:

> . . . In the theoretically perfect case, conformity to institutionalized role-expectations brings gratifying response from alters, is instrumentally effective, and is a source of direct gratification as well. Everyone wants to do that which others want him to do, and others always act as he expects and wishes: ". . . the interest of the actors . . . [are] bound to conformity with a shared system of value-orientation standards." [29]

This formulation reproduces the mechanistic model; to this extent, the theory of action is fundamentally mechanistic in its roots. Parsons has been moving away from this base, however, in his more recent work on cultural systems. His notion of evolutionary universals obviously moves toward the vital level with emphasis upon internal and external transformations defined as a total context.

We have already considered the limitations of this functional approach. It formulates two aspects of harmony—interdependence and mutuality. Parsons postulates a trend toward consistency which implies a lure to harmony; his notion of equilibrium gives no real support to this, so it appears as a hypothesis; to this extent, he has to presuppose

[29] Robin M. Williams, Jr., "The Sociological Theory of Talcott Parsons," in Max Black, *op cit.*, p. 75.

a more comprehensive harmony than his model can formulate. The criticism leveled against Parsons for the passivity in his understanding of man is justified, to this extent, since his model stresses passive conditioning by a total context.

Knowledge of the social process should enhance conflict and increase the level of potential harmony by introducing new levels of transcendence beyond the given social identity; in this respect, Parsons deals with change by interpreting new information and understanding on the instrumental level of scientific knowledge and technological innovation, but he scants the new perspectives of value and shifting horizons of meaning which accompany developments in science as well as in other cultural disciplines. The structural-functional analysis recognizes these other dimensions of change, but it treats them largely as adjustive in the assimilation of scientific and technological transformations. The equilibrium model is dynamic, and in this sense the critiques of its static character do not seem warranted. However, too many dimensions of human dynamics are held constant in order to achieve control in the model; this is particularly true of the creative role of man's apprehension of ultimate horizons. The richness and conflicts within human harmonies are impoverished. Equilibrium *is* a kind of harmony; it treats differentiation on the level of functions and scants the differentiation of perspectives, values, interests, and ultimate horizons in which the full richness and diversity of the *Lebenswelt* is being created. As a relative formulation of interdependence, the organic model is useful; as a total theory, it is quite inadequate for the social experiences of intentionality.

The master-slave model takes the diversity of human projects seriously. We have already explored this problem in considerable detail and indicated the complementary place of mutuality in the struggle for power. Nevertheless, an adequate grasp of harmony should include conflict of interest. Perhaps social process can be systematically understood only as conflict of interest; certainly, political theorists such as Hans Morgenthau have made a good case for conflict of interest as a model on the international level. The theory of games has also used this model. The unity of social experience is scanted by this model, but the radical differences which crosscut social experience find full expression in these theories. The mechanistic and organic models underplay differences; they lose sight of the depths and heights in the human struggle for fulfillment. When Ralf Dahrendorf balances the equilibrium model with conflict of interest, he is arguing for both dimensions of social process on an equal footing.[30] The master-slave model reflects particularities and differences; the organic model reflects common elements in social intercourse; an inclusive notion of harmony synthesizes both dimensions.

With a master-slave model, science of the social world is different from physical science; hence, human science is differently conceived on the intentional level. Max Weber's long struggle to find a middle ground between radical historicism and idealism reflected this basic difference. Weber's ideal-type constructions were an attempt to achieve this middle ground; he was the first to admit that they were developed from the particular perspectives of a discipline and the particular milieu in which it operated. So far as typical processes give a certain shape and continuity to history, science may achieve relatively high levels of consistency in ordering social data; however, prediction and control are limited for the more significant levels of human activity. Human science may play a significant role in societal fulfillment; men gain transcendence over the conditions in which their projects arise as they comprehend the typical patterns in which values are actualized or obstructed. Hence, a science of the human world becomes an important ingredient in the creative struggle of man for

[30] See Ralf Dahrendorf, *Class and Class Conflict in Industrial Society* (Stanford, Calif.: Stanford University Press, 1959), esp. Chs. 5 and 6.

richer meanings and possibilities. Instead of conforming man more closely to the given processes of his social world, science becomes another aspect of the creative and constitutive reason with which he reshapes that world.

We indicated earlier that Max Weber's conviction about the significance of rationality presupposed more reason in social reality than his theory acknowledged. The master-slave model is, in this respect, too limited to comprehend our social experience; it is founded in an irrational voluntarism. Perspectival reason is grounded in a more comprehensive harmony which is not alien to reason; hence, the struggle for domination is a significant but relative perspective on social reality. Max Weber's stress on the universality of logical norms would be an indirect acknowledgment of this more inclusive reason.[31] Any claim that man can understand his fellowman in another culture also presupposes a common ground in reason; however inadequately that universal order is conceptualized, even the antagonism of the master-slave model presupposes it. Hence, we find ourselves pushed toward a more inclusive notion of harmony in which the diversity of perspectives, interests, values, aspirations, and cultural forms obtains coherence and unity. This harmony and the lure to actualize it point toward a social fulfillment which embraces adjustment, adaptation, and conflict but includes them in a more comprehensive order.

We recognize that many models have arisen in human history to formulate such a notion of harmony. The aesthetic formulation has many advantages, especially as it is being developed by Charles Hartshorne.[32] Nevertheless, as already indicated, we do not propose to impose a single perspective on the human sciences, although we have imposed an interpretative context on these models. We have indicated value-

[31] See Weber, *The Methodology of the Social Sciences*, pp. 58f.

[32] See Hartshorne, *Reality as a Social Process*, and *The Logic of Perfection* (La Salle, Ill.: The Open Court Publishing Co., 1962), esp. Chs. 7 and 13.

implications of these models in the light of a notion of the intentional self. We acknowledge that the rich notion of intentionality that has been developed here points us toward a model of harmony in which diverse interests and perspectives are lured toward common interests and universal aspects of reason; man actualizes his search for integrity in particular perspectives and forms, but he is never content with any created levels of personal community or culture; he is ever drawn toward a more inclusive community and cultural expression. An ultimate unity forms a horizon of meaning toward which human creativity moves. The order of the everyday world is simply the crystallization of that dynamic process in any phase of social development.

This brief reference to a principle of harmony suggests the possibility of ordering these scientific perspectives within a hierarchy of social values. Scientific models of the social world have different evaluative emphases, as we have seen: the mechanistic model of exchange stresses the lawfulness of social order; the organic model of equilibrium stresses the orderly interdependence of social elements; the master-slave model of conflict stresses the dynamic thrust of particular interests; the intentional model stresses the harmony of typical courses of action within a common culture. Where mechanistic theory evaluates social process as a flow of exchange, treating constraint of the flow as deviance, the master-slave model would take constraint on the flow as characteristic of social process and open exchange as the extreme case. How, then, is one to select among these evaluative perspectives for an understanding of "what is the case"? If one is unwilling to be dogmatic and claim a single and sovereign theory, then criteria must be found for adjudicating among the styles. These scientific perspectives have to be ordered in such a way that their fitness for particular problems can be determined. At this point, the complementarity of social ethics and social science emerges: social science impinges directly on the understanding of human fulfillment in the evaluative perspective of its models; social ethics selects among these evaluative perspectives for the clarification of specific problems, relying on norms or a comprehensive notion of human fulfillment to make its selections.

We turn, then, to an ethical perspective in order to determine the criteria for selecting among scientific models. Once these criteria have been clarified, we can grasp the evaluative implications of these models of social process. The social world is a complex and highly diversified reality. A multiplicity of perspectives may be taken on this reality; each, in turn, will yield certain returns and entail certain costs. Our task is to gain a comprehensive perspective on human fulfillment within which the relative perspectives of these scientific styles can find their place. The problem of fulfillment, then, is one nexus between a science and an ethic of the social world—a nexus in which the human project and its evaluation must have the decisive voice.

# part three

# *ethics and society*

# 7 *an ethic of the social world*

An order of the social world is developed on the basis of man's social relationships; this is used in turn to indicate the problems for which the scientific styles are appropriate and the ways in which they need to be modified for application to problems of social policy

AN ETHICAL CONCERN has informed this inquiry from the start, so that the appearance of the ethical question is not a new dimension in the discussion. The ethical concern provoked the basic problems: the nature of the social world, the possibility of a social science, and the evaluative implications of scientific models. However, the ethical issue becomes explicit fully where the sciences of man project their understanding of the past into the future as a definition of human fulfillment; these projections disclose the evaluative or ideological aspects of scientific models. These projections can be evaluated only from an ethical perspective. Science and ethics are different perspectives on the everyday world; they clarify different aspects of that world; however, they intersect as they attempt to define the course of human fulfillment.

Although the ethical concern and even basic concepts of ethical order, such as harmony, have emerged in the discussion, the nature of ethical interpretation has not been clarified. This is a necessary step in establishing norms by which the various scientific perspectives can be ordered. Social ethics limits its critique of science to the evaluative implications of scientific models; only in this restrictive sense does social ethics attempt to order these scientific styles and clarify the appropriateness of their interpretations. Ethics asks about the adequacy of a model for the everyday world and for specific problems under consideration. This is an important distinction, since the utility of various scientific styles has to be defined by the problems with which the science is wrestling and the adequacy of a particular style to cope with those problems. The problem of ethical evaluation arises in the translation of the implications of these scientific findings (the limitations of the specific style) to the everyday world; at this point, the evaluative issues are central and the task of ordering falls to the ethical perspective. To be sure, the ethical perspective is only rarely exercised by a special discipline; it is normally exercised by the practical man through evaluations which are imposed by the common culture. Social science has precedence in determining the logical adequacy of its models; ethics and practice take precedence in drawing out the implications of the models for the future orientations of the everyday world. This is the logical implication of the claim that "lived" experience furnishes the criterion of adequacy for social science.[1]

Two elements are needed to order the scientific styles in terms of human fulfillment: the nature of ethical interpretation needs to be clarified, particularly in distinction from the science of man; in addition, the essential norms of the social world, so far as these are present in social experience and shaped in the common culture, need to be made explicit, since they provide the evaluative framework for ordering the scientific perspectives. It was noted in Chapter 6 that the scientific models impute particular values to social process. If these values can be ordered from the essential nature of the social world, these scientific models can be ordered as perspectives on that world. The clarification of the nature

[1] The failure to make this discrimination between scientific models and "lived" experience accounts for the application of an ecological model (behavioristic) to problems of the ghetto in Daniel Moynihan's report *The Negro Family,* U.S. Department of Labor, Office of Policy Planning and Research, March, 1965. See Benjamin Payton, "New Trends in Civil Rights," *Christianity and Crisis,* December 13, 1965.

of sociality (see Chapter 4) furnishes the groundwork for interpreting this essential structure.

From this foundation, it should be possible to delineate the framework of a social ethic; such an ethic would require an ordering of the norms and a hermeneutics of the ethical problems of a complex, high-technology society.[2] These are tasks for a constructive ethic; they lie beyond the boundaries of the present work. Nevertheless, the basis of the ethical construction is already present in this analysis—the ground on which the selection of norms would be made. The detailed exposition of this ground would carry the present work far beyond an introductory level. Consequently, the ethical perspective is developed on a formal rather than a substantive level. However, this formal analysis provides an adequate framework for defining the functions of social science and social ethics in social policy.

## *THE NATURE OF ETHICAL REFLECTION*

In Chart 1 of Chapter 3, the scientific perspective was distinguished from the practical concerns of the commonsense world. In the everyday world, objects are distinguished and ordered by pregiven typifications (dogs, tables, and human activities are largely typified experiences); moreover, culture and its imperatives for acting express these typifications in ordinary language. Daily experience is a preordered experience. This world of values, norms, patterns of behavior, social roles, and corresponding sanctions is already there before our birth and persists with gradual modifications during the span of our lives. It is a pregiven world of ethical, aesthetic, technical, and social understandings. The massive presence of this societal reality impressed Émile

[2] "Hermeneutics" is a word which indicates the use of phenomenological method beyond description and intuition to a grasp of the *meaning* of the historical situation; hence, it is interpretation with a presumption of historical meaning. On this level of phenomenological analysis, see Spiegelberg, *The Phenomenological Movement*, Vol. 2, Conclusion.

Durkheim so much that he took it to be the ultimate source of man, knowledge, and religious reality; society was for him *the* reality. His interpretation was one-sided, to be sure, but he recognized a fact of great significance: the pregiven structure of man's social world.

With a pregiven social world, ethical reflection does not start in a vacuum; values need not be sought out in an ideal world apart from man; values are the pregiven stuff of social process. The subjectivist and objectivist theories of ethics, as H. Richard Niebuhr noted many years ago, abstract from the relational character of our social experience; we are related to one another—existent being to existent being; value (positive or negative) is present in the fulfilling or crippling relations of being to being.[3] This understanding coincides with all that has been said about the sociality of man and the correlation of self with world. The "lived" world is a horizon of meanings, valued relations, and possibilities.[4] The question of value or moral concern is not something imposed on this "lived" world by subjective emotion, reasoned judgment, objective ideas, or external sanctions. The social world is a valued world of meanings. It is moral through and through, since it is from first to last a world of demands, claims, rights, approvals, punishments, imputations, and obligations. Society, as Durkheim recognized, is a moral reality. Hence, ethical reflection starts within the "lived" world of experience—a pregiven world of valued relations. Ethics seeks to clarify the logic and adequacy of the values that shape that world; it assesses the moral possibilities which are projected and betrayed in the social give-and-take. Ethical reflection may take one or another abstract perspective to clarify the moral order, much as social science abstracts from the everyday world, but the criterion of adequacy for ethical interpretation is to be found in the "lived" experience of the social world.

3 See H. Richard Niebuhr, *Radical Monotheism and Western Culture* (New York: Harper & Row, 1960), "The Center of Value," esp. p. 107.

4 One of the clearest expositions of this view is given by John Wild in *Existence and the World of Freedom*.

This reference to "lived" experience raises the question of the nature of ethical reflection. If values and norms are present to varying degrees in the relatedness of the social world, then ethical reflection is viewed as a science of human intentionality; its task is to clarify the moral claims and rights of the social world and their proper ordering in the structures of social organization. The principal category of ethical reflection, then, is history; its task is to comprehend its heritage, to decipher the emerging "sense" of that history, as John Wild has put it.[5] Such ethical reflection presupposes participation in the cultural heritage and its meanings. Ethical reflection also presupposes a kind of distance from this cultural heritage, since it reflects objectively on the meanings implicit in that heritage. The style of ethical interpretation is thus historical in the profoundest sense: it grapples with the present meaning of the past (evaluating the constituted social identity); it considers the moral possibilities of the future in terms of human fulfillment (evaluating the social project which is being constituted). Ethics introduces a radical kind of doubt into the everyday world: it questions the adequacy with which social forms embody the moral intentionality of the culture; moreover, it questions the goodness of those cultural intentions, setting the cultural horizon of meaning within a more universal and ultimate context.

The historical character of ethical interpretation can be highlighted by distinguishing the ethical modification of the everyday world from science (see Chart 4). A science of man has dominant theoretical interests, though it presupposes participation in the common culture. Ethics has dominant practical interests, though it requires theoretical, reflective distance. The basic distinction, however, is in the temporal orientation of the two modes of reflection. Ethics looks to the future; it is concerned with the goodness and rightness of man's doing and making; it is concerned with

[5] See John Wild, "Authentic Existence: A New Approach to 'Value Theory,'" in *An Invitation to Phenomenology*.

the constituted social identity only for the sake of the project being constituted; it looks to the past for the sake of the future. It judges the past, because the future bears new possibilities. Social science, on the other hand, focuses on the constituted identity and attempts to determine its pattern as precisely as possible. It is concerned with the future only as an extension of the past. In ethics, social identity is potentiality to be reshaped for man's fulfillment; man needs to grasp his past and his situation in order to remake them on behalf of a more human world. By contrast, a science of man apprehends the human project itself as a means of clarifying the conditions in which it arose; social science depends upon history for its grasp of the common culture, but it is preoccupied with the historical regularities which persist through historical changes. Social science participates in history for the sake of *knowing* more clearly and precisely that which is not subject to historical change or is at least predictable. Ethics reflects upon history in order to evaluate what needs to be changed and can become the stuff of history-making.

The difference between a science and an ethic of society can also be clarified by distinguishing their handling of intentionality. A science of man meets its limit and judgment in human intentionality; this is the criterion of adequacy for its constructions; whether a particular scientific style acknowledges this or not, its models are testable only by the account which they can give of the intentional world of everyday. Human intentionality interests the sciences of man only as that which they have to explain. Ethics, on the other hand, is concerned with intentionality in itself—with the moral quality of its orientation to the future and to relationships. Science is concerned with the conditioning of intentionality by the past. Ethics is concerned with the quality of this intentionality which has been shaped by the past and the possibilities of its reshaping by moral concern.

**Chart 4** PERSPECTIVES ON THE LIFE-WORLD: COMPARING SCIENTIFIC AND ETHICAL REFLECTIONS

| Orientational aspect | Everyday | Ethical | Scientific |
|---|---|---|---|
| Tension of consciousness | Engaged participation | Interpretative participation | Disengaged observation |
| Form of doubt | Natural attitude | Doubt of moral intention and fulfillment | Permanent control of all propositions in sphere |
| Form of spontaneity | Mastery (Pragmatic) | Understanding (Evaluative) | Inquiry and clarification (Diagnostic) |

Much more could be said about the cognitive style of ethical reflection, but this should suffice for our immediate task of clarifying the norms of sociality. No claim is being made here that this is the only style of ethical reflection or even that all problems of ethics have to be handled by a single style. An idealistic understanding of reality would lead to a different style of ethical reflection; formal or rational structures, accessible to reason, would express the normative principles of morality. A positivist understanding of reality might try to make sense of the systems of sanctions and accountability which operate in society, but it would have to evaluate such a morality on the basis of consequences rather than rationality. However, even those ethical styles which opt for the intentional, historical character of man's existence may develop the reflective style in different ways. Jean-Paul Sartre's existential analysis accepts this general style but develops the dynamic, subjective aspect. Max Scheler also accepted this starting point but developed the objective aspect of the value elements. We have already indicated that this inquiry develops the relational, social, unifying dimension of self and world. This style of ethics rests upon the basic principle of sociality which was developed in Chapter 4. The significance of this principle becomes quite explicit as we turn to the clarification of the norms of sociality.[6]

## THE NORMS OF SOCIALITY

The basic structure of sociality has already been discussed in detail in Chapter 4. Our task now is to generalize from this to norms of sociality as disclosed in the "We-relation." Reflections of this kind, although they draw upon what is given in experience, are undoubtedly shaped by a cultural tradition. Man is in history and cannot rise above history in order to gain an absolute or universal grasp of the structure of his existence. He can, nevertheless, gain a grasp on the universal from within his historical situation. It is this latter grasp which we now attempt. Furthermore, the work of existential and phenomenological research on these problems lies behind this formulation, so that much of the experiential formulation depends upon this century of work.[7]

[6] For discussions of various lines of development in the phenomenological movement, see Spiegelberg, *The Phenomenological Movement*, Vol. 2, and Wild, *The Challenge of Existentialism*. Our remarks are meant to be only suggestive, since a critique of these ethical styles would require a review of this whole movement, from the skeptical ethic of absurdity to the ethic arising from the thought of being, in the line of Heidegger's later work. Our interest here is to elaborate as briefly as possible the ethical perspective and structures which are implicit in the preceding steps of the inquiry.

[7] Two general summaries of this research were mentioned in the preceding footnote. The works of Maurice Merleau-Ponty and Alfred Schutz have been noted. In addition, the special contributions to the author of the following monograph should be acknowledged: Roger Mehl, *La Rencontre d'autrui* (Neuchâtel: Delachaux et Niestlé, 1955). See also F. J. J. Buytendijk, *Phénoménologie de la rencontre* (Paris: Desclée de Brouwer, 1952); Jean Nabert, *Éléments pour une éthique* (Paris: Aubier, 1962); and Georges Gusdorf, *L'Expérience humaine du sacrifice* (Paris: Presses Universitaires, 1948). There is no intention to reproduce the various perspectives in this phenomenological literature, but the author's debt to this research on man's social being is gratefully expressed.

If this analysis is pushed to the level of ultimate grounding, it would become evident that several themes in the Jewish and Christian traditions shape the selection of certain tendencies for special consideration. The biblical tradition affirms the disclosure of the Holy One in the events of human history, taking up nature into the whole course of creative work. Furthermore, this tradition affirms man's calling within the sphere of history—the place of his fulfillment. Whatever other perspectives may have entered the total tradition—and these subthemes may carry important perspectives on the truth of man's existence—we can recognize these two themes as fundamental.

This is not the occasion to develop the foundations of these themes, though they need to be acknowledged in the kind of selection that is being made from our experience of social existence. For present purposes, these foundations do not have to be elaborated, though that task forms an essential step in building a constructive ethic. Our own Western tradition has been so deeply informed by these themes that we can say that our own exposition is making explicit the general structure of that moral tradition. The key terms in that tradition are "freedom," "equality," "power," and "love";[8] they form the ingredients of our historical expressions of justice. That structure is common to the biblical and Western tradition and, by implication, to all of human experience, although this is a comprehensive hypothesis rather than an established generalization. The differences within this tradition lie primarily in the configuration of these elements and consequently the meanings that are given to "freedom" and "power." Furthermore, various cultural traditions differ in the emphasis which they place upon the individual, personal

[8] These terms are ambiguous, as Richard McKeon has made clear in his works on the philosophic tradition, but each interpretation, ordering, and grounding of the meanings of the terms in some comprehensive notion of justice has attempted to give historical shape to man's social and cultural world. See Richard McKeon, *Freedom and History* (New York: Noonday Press, Inc., 1952), and a variety of articles on terms such as "equality," "responsibility," and "property."

community, and more objective structures of political order. Here again, the centrality of the biblical tradition in Western history and in the selection which guides our analysis places the "We-relation" (personal communal relationships) in a pivotal place for understanding personal and social fulfillment. The power of this tradition, however, is also subject to our "lived" experience of sociality; so far as the biblical tradition and its symbols can illumine, sustain, and renew the scope and depth of human community, it continues as the *logos* of that social reality. Hence, appeal to that tradition is no substitute for the grasp of the nature of social reality and the renewed appropriation of the tradition in the new context of its revelatory power. We point to the tradition here rather by way of acknowledging the root notions from which we draw. Our principal task remains the clarification of the truth in our experience to which that tradition points and which it seeks to renew. A serious hermeneutic task remains to be done with this tradition, but the key to that task (for social ethics at least) is found in the structure of sociality with which we are concerned. Consequently, we are at work here on the constructive task of discerning what is given in experience as the truth of man's being with his neighbor; the appreciation and new appropriation of the tradition which shapes this understanding and renews this human community are serious tasks in ethical hermeneutics which remain for the future.[9]

Three essential tendencies were isolated in the triadic structure of the "We-relation": (1) gesture as the concern for response, (2) interpretative response as openness to otherness, and (3) empathic understanding as passion for unity. These tendencies were isolated on a relatively high

[9] Extensive work has been done by biblical scholars on these themes. However, the development in this text of the "We-relation" has not been evaluated in the context of that tradition, and it is to this specific task that we refer. This would mean an attempt to appropriate that tradition anew—and especially the understanding of the relationship between the old and new covenants.

level, since communication presupposes the potentially meaningful gesture and the centered self of a social world. Three basic elements are represented in this triadic structure: dynamic, form, and unification. However, on the high level of the triadic structure, all three elements appear in each essential tendency but with a different dominance. Thus, the notion of gesture involves the elements of dynamic, form, and unification. Gesture is the power of invocation—calling to attention (dynamic); gesture involves a distance from the other, a standing over against the other which unites a self-surpassing freedom with the power of the gesture. However, gesture is an expression of meaning—a giving of form to a feeling, desire, wish—a meaning-intention (form). Moreover, gesture is an expression of dependence upon the other—need for response and relationship (unification). If one starts with the gesture—and there is good reason to do so in view of the creative breakthrough which language represents—then the *dynamic* element of power and freedom is the ascendant element in the gesture.

The *form* aspect is ascendant in the interpretative response, although, again, on this level all three elements are present in a somewhat different configuration. The *dynamic* aspect is present in the openness to the other's gesture, in the giving of attention to the other. This dimension of freedom as distance from the other in openness to the other reflects, as was indicated in Chapter 4, a fundamental sociality that comes to consciousness in communication. However, the *form* element gains dominance in the mediation of the other's meaning by the respondent and to the gesturer through the interpreted response. Thus, the expression of form as gesture becomes intelligible form through the interpretative response; in elaboration of the interpreted response in language, the expression of form becomes the medium of sharing in a common world and a common culture. The element of *unification* is, as already suggested, the pregiven sociality which comes to expression in gesture and response. However, unification of the meaning-intention of the gesture and consciousness of that meaning come about through interpretation—the exteriority of expression and the interiority of understanding come together in interpretation; in this act, the pregiven sociality becomes a social world as symbolized process.

In contrast to the dominance of form in the interpretative response, *unification* is dominant in the empathic appropriation of the interpreted response by the gesturer. The taking of the stance of the other involves a unification of the gesturer with the meaning of his gesture through his unity with the respondent's appropriation. This reciprocity of perspectives, mediated by the other ("We-relation") and given continuity in symbol, creates a social world; it represents the coming to consciousness of sociality in the unification of the self with its gestures as self-consciousness. However, the *dynamic* element is again prominent in the act of seeing oneself through the meaning of one's gesture to the other—the self-transcending distance from oneself that is mediated by the other's interpretation. Moreover, the *form* element reappears in the empathic reciprocity, since the self as structured identity emerges from this response and in time from the appropriation of social responses to its meaning for the world. The dominance of unification in this third tendency toward unity and integrity reappears in the process as self-consciousness—the unification of the self as openness and freedom with its own form or identity which is mediated by society and language, becoming for oneself what one is for others and thus gaining the further freedom of reshaping what one is for others in terms of the meaning of one's existence for oneself.

Throughout this schematization of the essential tendencies of man in his sociality—the "We-relation"—we would lift up the principle of unification as the pregiven structure of man's being and the lure which moves him to ever richer objectifications and ever deeper reunions. The centrality of the principle of harmony or love, in the most comprehensive meaning of that term, can now be located in the nuclear structure of man's being: his expression of freedom as distance and openness; his form-appropriating and form-giving power; the mediation of his pregiven sociality in a shared world of consciousness through the empathic sharing of forms and their expression in a shared language of gestures, signs, rituals, and higher-order symbols.[10] In this sense, man is the symbolic being who is shaped by symbol and, in turn, reshapes symbols and thus remakes his world. The power of symbol rests, however, on the power of sociality, which it expresses, extends, and serves to renew. Participating in symbols, sharing a world through them, means participating in the relational character of man's being which has been expressed, enriched, and empowered through these symbols. The power of symbol to overcome alienation and to support man's actualization of his potentialities derives thus from the participation of symbols, to varying degrees, in the pregiven sociality of being.

Our task, however, is not to explore the realm of symbol but, rather, to make explicit the norms of sociality which are implicit in this essential structure of sociality. When we say "essential structure," we mean this much as Paul Tillich meant it when he said that this is *the structure through which experience is possible*. It is not an *a priori* structure which is given to direct intuition but is one which is disclosed in experience as its most general character.[11] Furthermore, the historical character of man's existence implies that such structures may change over time, though certainly very slowly; even then, comparable structures would emerge in

[10]The notion of sign and higher-order symbol used here accords with the position taken by Alfred Schutz in his essay "Symbol, Reality and Society," in *Collected Papers*, Vol. 1. The principal reservation pertains to his discussion of the hermeneutics of higher-order symbols. For this set of problems, the work of Paul Ricoeur has proved the most promising to the author.

[11] Paul Tillich, *Systematic Theology* (Chicago: University of Chicago Press, 1951), Vol. 1, esp. p. 166.

such other epochs to make experience possible. The complexity of essential structure is such that one could identify other components, but this simplest structure is sufficient for the explication of the basic norms of sociality.[12] Consequently, we can limit ourselves to this elemental structure and explore its normative aspects.

The normative aspect becomes somewhat clearer if we consider man's alienation from the essential structure of which we have been speaking. Throughout the analysis of the social world, man has been discussed as embodied consciousness. His alienation from himself and from others derives from his power to transcend himself and his situation, to gain distance from the other; however, it is both his freedom and the anxiety of that freedom which introduce the estrangement and bad faith.[13] Three dimensions of this alienation can be associated with the essential tendencies of sociality which we have recognized. The dynamic of the gesture involves concern for response—calling the other's attention—and also anxiety over the response to the other. This dependence upon the other, even if it is the other to whom one belongs, expresses its anxiety as the attempt to control and above all to dominate the other. Hence, power as domination rather than invocation discloses man's estrangement from his essential unity with the other.

The form-giving power of the interpretative response also participates in the anxiety of man's freedom. If the dynamic

[12] Paul Tillich developed three polarities of ontological elements: individualization and participation, dynamics and form, freedom and destiny. The limitation to dynamics, form, and unification expresses the author's concern with a particular problem, although individualization and participation as well as freedom and destiny seem to be on a higher level of complexity which reflects this basic triad. The author is much indebted to Widick Schroeder for general discussions of these problems, though the author takes full responsibility for this line of development.

[13] The priority of unification is nowhere more evident than in the notion of fault, negation, estrangement, and alienation. Jean Nabert in this connection will refer to the sense of total condemnation of and the nostalgia for an absolute communication—an inexhaustible love; hence, the profundity of the negation arises from the depth of the unity within which it arises. See Nabert, *op. cit.* esp. p. 45.

aspect of estrangement is domination, the form aspect is objectification—reducing the other to a thing. The interpretative response discloses the structure of reason through which men participate in universals and share a common world; it also discloses the power of those common symbols through which men are called to equal sharing in a world. However, those symbols may in anxiety become the means of inequality, of exclusion and objectification. The unpredictable character of social existence and the anxiety of our dependence upon others thus find false resolution (false because it restricts the being of the estranged); this false relationship appears in the limiting, rigidifying, and controlling of our world. Thus, our categories become stereotypes, and the equality of a common world becomes the inequality of a narrowed and alienated world. Form mediates equal access to a common world; the same form may become the vehicle of restricting freedom and excluding men from the world to which they belong.

We have, in the foregoing analysis, placed unification at the center of the understanding of man's existence; we can anticipate, therefore, that this tendency will be the crucial mode of estrangement. The anxiety of man's dependence upon others appears also in his empathic taking of the stance of the other, in the creation of a reciprocity of perspectives. The unity of love is a unity of differences—particular beings in relationships which actualize their potentialities; the form of that actualization is openness appropriate to the being and mutuality of fulfillments. Thus, the unification of love fosters creativity and renewal on ever more inclusive levels of human community and appreciative awareness.[14] However, the anxiety of dependence can lead to an empathic identification in which selfhood is dissolved; thus, it can generate

[14] The term "appreciative awareness," drawn from Bernard Meland, touches the contemplative aspect of personal enjoyment and fulfillment which can easily be scanted by our preoccupation here with personal community and ethical norms. We introduce it to point to the comprehensive character of love as unity of being with being in mutual enrichment.

pathological dependence; this is alienation as loss of selfhood. Inversely, the unification of self and other in love under conditions of estrangement may become exploitation of the other's dependence. In either case, the equal power of free beings in relationship dissolves: one either assimilates the power of being of the other or surrenders to the other's power of being. The true meaning of inequality is complementary fulfillment according to the principle of love; in estrangement, it becomes exploitation. Since man is social by nature—a relational being—exploiter and exploited suffer from this degradation of human complementarity; collective domination dissolves particular right, whereas exploitation exaggerates particular interest.

This somewhat schematic account of the structures of alienation presupposes an understanding of man's freedom within the unity of a social world. Alienation discloses the anxiety of finite freedom. When we view the essential structures of sociality in terms of their negation—the world of estrangement—the normative configuration begins to take clearer shape. Reconciliation discloses the power of love to unite without violating particular being and freedom. On the dynamic side, the alienated expression of power has its counterpart in a normative structure of equal freedom. There are many ways to state this dimension in our Western tradition; here it depends upon the principle of love and mutuality as the normative expression of man's relational being; love implies the mutuality of free initiation and free response. Whatever restrictions may be put upon the power of initiation in the context of other interests (reflexively equal freedom is a mutually limiting principle within society), the essential norm on the dynamic level is equal power of consent and initiation.[15]

[15] The development of this normative pattern, although it arose from different interests and along a different path, has disclosed marked congruity on the social level with H. Richard Niebuhr's later work. A reconsideration of his remarkable essay "The Center of Value" has been very helpful. See H. Richard Niebuhr, *Radical Monotheism and Western Culture*, pp. 100–113.

The unification through form heals the sphere of shared culture and law. From the cultural side, the deformation appears as objectively imposed inequalities in the common world to which all belong. On the law or institutional side, this deformation appears as the objectification of man and his transformation into a thing. The subjective side of this essential structure is man's right to belong, to be treated as equal before the law, and to be recognized in the culture and its social formations with the dignity of a person. Hence, the equal freedom of consent on the dynamic side has its counterpart in equal dignity of personal being through participation in forms.

Estrangement appears in the dimension of form primarily as exploitation, especially within the secondary structures of man's social world. The other side of this distortion of human reciprocity, as we noted, is the assimilation of particular being to the mass in collectivization. Form (expressing unity) manifests itself as justice in the social world, overcoming the exploitative structures of exclusion and denial of access by allocating values and resources on a principle of equal access and reciprocity. Thus, the justice which affirms equal freedom as right to consent and interest also manifests itself as equality under law and actualizes these dimensions of justice by maintaining a balance in the claims and counterclaims of men for access to the world.

Chart 5 attempts to schematize the essential structure of sociality, its estrangement under the anxiety of existence, and the normative structuring of that sociality as it has emerged in the Western tradition. One can allow a great deal of variation in the relative weighting of these normative structures, so long as one grants the presence of the elements and their general ordering. This structure has been built on the nuclear structure of sociality, although its reference has been throughout to the derived structures of social and political organization. We shall state the articulation of this essential structure on these organizational levels in the final section of this chapter, where we undertake to order the

**Chart 5** STRUCTURES OF SOCIAL ALIENATION AND JUSTICE

| Essential structures of sociality (Relational being) | Alienation from essential structures (Anxiety of existence) | Norms of sociality * (Love as justice) |
|---|---|---|
| 1. Dynamic: (Unity) Self as will Self-transcendence (Power) | 1. Estranged freedom: Domination | 1. Justice as equal freedom: Consent in decisions (Mutual Limitation) |
| 2. Unification: (Form) Pregiven cultural values (Order) | 2. Deformed community: Exclusion and objectification by given order or partial order | 2. Justice as equal right to participate in culture and society (Participation) |
| 3. Form: (Unity) Conditions of embodiment and functional interdependence (Law) | 3. Alienated reciprocity: Exploitation Collectivism | 3. Justice as equal access to conditions of life and opportunity (Complementarity) |

various models of scientific analysis. We use the nuclear structure of sociality to establish the norms; secondary structures are meant to broaden the scope of human interdependence and enrich the reciprocities of social life; the risk of such extension is the enhancement of estrangements and the ramification of the destructiveness of social power. The criterion of secondary structures is their adequacy for preserving human community against its own alienations and for raising man's social existence to more inclusive levels

* These are hypothetical imperatives drawn from Western tradition. They could be grounded as norms of communication.

of community. This is the broad problem of the relationship of love to justice which needs more precise explication than is possible here. Nevertheless, the *telos* of the derived structures is located in human mutuality and reciprocity, so that love furnishes the criterion of adequacy for any state of justice; on this ground, the essential structure of sociality furnishes the normative elements for more complex organizations. However, the mutual openness, interpretive response, and empathic sharing which disclose love in the "We-relation" become justice in secondary structures.

Chart 5 fails to do justice to the work of love in preserving and extending the sway of justice in human community. The "We-relation" is the *telos* of extended social structures; it is also the continuing source of their vitality and humanness. Personal growth and communal integrity require continual nurture in the families, friendships, work groups, associations, and recreational groups within the society. Even this support to the human dimension, which needs to be sustained by secondary structures, cannot overcome the powers of alienation and estrangement which grow within complex societies. Here we recognize the role of faith communities, free inquiry in schools, and open debate in bringing judgment and perspective on the community. The power of love in nuclear structures can be overwhelmed by destructive forces without the cultivation of these disciplines of private and public freedom. Mass propaganda in technological societies clearly poses a serious threat to such "prophetic" elements within the society.

The creative power of the "We-structures" in the society poses the question of the *true form* of personal community and the relation of this true expression to secondary structures of law and justice. "We-relations" vary in degrees of intimacy and openness. However, the understanding of love in the biblical tradition of Judaism and Christianity has been a shaping power in our evaluation of this "We-structure." Openness, mutuality, and reciprocity formulate the justice of the "We-relation," whereas our biblical tradition—directed to the overcoming of alienation—points to the creative character of love as reconciling acceptance, sharing the destiny of the excluded, and sacrificing one's claims on the world for the community to which we belong. This redemptive power is the source of reconciliation and renewal by which all "We-relations" are nurtured; it is intensely disclosed as the *logos* of relational being in the "disclosure events" which are central to the great religious and cultural traditions, though with varying degrees of intensity and fullness. In this sense, the task of special communities of faith is to evoke, nurture, and extend the reconciling power of man's relational being—not calling men to another history or another existence but deepening their humanness in their historical situation.

This would seem to be an optimistic picture of human hope, resting as it does on the nuclear structure of sociality and looking to the reconciling power of love amid the destructive forces of history. In fact, the press toward a biblical tradition rather than a straightforward humanism derives from the profundity of man's existential estrangement and the ambiguity of the basic structures as they become manifest in history. The biblical tradition evokes a trust in the goodness of the power in which human community is rooted. This is a faith commitment which forms the internal reality of our biblical memory. The hope implicit in this exposition of man's relational being derives from that confidence; it is expressed, however, with full recognition of the ambiguity surrounding man's historical situation. Men and women of the highest integrity have appraised the basic structures of sociality in our time and concluded that the potentialities of humanity are so great and the destructiveness so overwhelming that the whole enterprise is absurd. This very ambiguity of our historical enterprise and man's power to evaluate it push toward a commitment—a coming to terms with the human project in an ultimate sense.

We have to leave the exposition of ethical problems and possibilities of a high-technology society to another occasion. This hermeneutic task requires the concrete explication of these essential structures and their deformation within the organization of our own society. We mention this problem again only to indicate that the essential structure gives no determination of the precise weighting of particular values in the relational complexes of a concrete problem; incompatibilities of value occur at every juncture and call for decisions. Here one would draw upon a particular understanding of the Western tradition or specific disclosures of the "human" ordering of these elements. We have already suggested that the biblical tradition, as we are interpreting it here, furnishes such a hermeneutic symbol in the notion of love. Within this notion, the disclosure of old and new covenants can be drawn upon for particular themes. From this configuration, the man standing within this tradition gains a paradigmatic structure with which he may appraise the claims and counterclaims of justice in the contemporary world. The significance of that biblical tradition, from this perspective, is not that it provides the essential structure but, rather, that it illumines the meaning of this structure which is given in experience—pointing to its source and ultimate fulfillment. Whether one draws from these depths of our own Western tradition or lifts up dimensions of the philosophic, humanistic, or scientific traditions, some weighting of this essential structure becomes necessary in the hermeneutics of our historical situation. In every case, however, the appropriation of one or another tradition involves commitment of existence within that tradition; it also calls for a new appropriation of that tradition within the historical situation; this is truly a hermeneutic task in which both the tradition and the contemporary situation are reshaped and renewed. The power of one or another of these traditions is evident in its illumination of our historical situation and in its power to renew humanity.

## SCIENTIFIC MODELS AND SOCIAL ORDER

Although a substantive analysis of the relationship between love and justice carries us beyond the limits of this introduction, some ordering of the scientific styles on a normative basis can be developed from the basic structure of Chart 6. Our concern here is with the styles of scientific analysis; subsequently we define the structure to which their analyses are appropriate. We are concerned, moreover, with the derived or typified structures of the social world, since objective models attempt to give some determination of the organization of these structures. For the sake of simplicity, we can distinguish three broad levels of unification in the society in which different dimensions of man's sociality become objectified: the political, the social, and the economic. In each of these structures, the expression of alienation and the task of justice take a somewhat different form. The ordering of these values in Chart 6 provides a rough schematization of the appropriate models for analysis and the limits of these models in dealing with the human project. We recognize, of course, that the hermeneutics of concrete historical problems involves far more complexity than the present analysis; this type of ordering provides a basic starting point for more concrete analyses.

The economic organization includes man's embodied participation in all the natural structures; thus, it involves his dependence upon nature and reciprocity with his fellowmen. These are the least variable levels of human existence in the sense that they are the most routinized and subject to law. Man's embodiment is a basic structure of orderliness in his existence. The ordering of mutual support and reciprocity approaches equality and balance in this sphere. Mechanistic notions of balance and equivalence, along with the objectified formulation of laws of exchange, are especially appropriate to this level of activities. The behavioristic models of

**Chart 6** SOCIAL MODELS AND SECONDARY STRUCTURES OF SOCIAL ORGANIZATION ACCORDING TO APPROPRIATE NORMS OF JUSTICE IN THE SOCIAL WORLD

| Scientific models | Corresponding social structures | Appropriate norm of justice | Character of alienation |
|---|---|---|---|
| Intentionalist (Reciprocity) | Unifying values of common culture | (Unification) Harmony of creative freedom | Assimilation |
| Voluntarist (Domination of Master-Slave) | Political structures | (Dynamics) Equal freedom as power and consent | Domination |
| Functionalist (Organic Equilibrium) | Social system and institutions | (Unification) Equal participation in processes | Exclusion |
| Behaviorist (Mechanistic Balance) | Processes of exchange (Economic) | (Form) Equal access and reward for effort | Exploitation |

lawful order of exchange between systems serve well for this level of routinization and can give some degree of determination to the identity of the society. When societal existence is most orderly, its identity is most determinate. The dynamic role of the self can be held constant for certain purposes on this economic level; consequently, society can be treated, to all intents and purposes, on a physicalist model without undue distortion. The successful development of economic models of this type can be understood as an expression of this lawful character of allocations and exchanges in man's interdependent activities. This is particularly true where the economic activities of the society are differentiated from other structures, such as kinship relationships; to this extent, the objective systematization of economy makes the behaviorist model more appropriate; routinization is characteristic on this level.

Several crucial issues arise in the ethical evaluation of economic or behavioristic models for processes of interdependence. The inequality of power and the development of exploitative structures which control exchange lead to injustices which violate human interdependence. No objective model of exchange can do more than acknowledge this kind of friction; in principle, such models treat all units alike and opt for a minimization of constraints in the exchanges. However, the interdependence of life in society is such that these restrictions and exploitations ramify throughout the culture and develop more radical inequalities on higher levels. Consequently, the economic can be viewed as the most abstract and the most conditional to the fuller development of the society but also as subject to the claims of justice from higher levels of the social organization. Hence, the behavioristic model can yield very useful accounts of the reciprocities in an idealized sense; however, the evaluation of imbalances or collective control requires some principle of justice, *i.e.*, on this level, an interpretation of equality of access and the limitation of particular interests. To this extent, the economic or behaviorist models require the most thoroughgoing translation to the appropriate levels and problems of the society, since they consider the functioning of the system but not the just allocation of values. The damage done to persons and society by the imposition of economic models on social morals in Western society during the past century is sufficient warning of the inadequacy of these models for direct application to social policy. From this perspective, it is evident that such models introduce greater and greater distortion as they are extended to higher levels of social and political organization. Nevertheless, the basic value of equality of access and balance of exchange formulates a fundamental value of social justice; so far as the norm of equal access to resources, opportunities, and the conditions of life can be systematized in a society, the ground has been laid for a more just order.

Social organization comprehends the structures of participation in the shared meanings and values of the society through social groupings, distributed honors, and shared values. Various social forms participate in this process, from the parent-child relationships through which socialization occurs to the associational ties of communities and the stratification systems of the society. The core of this organization is the common culture upon which the reciprocity of perspectives rests; sharing in this common world provides a universe of discourse and communication. This value-consensus is the principle on which organic models of society are built; thus, the various processes within the society are understood functionally as contributing to the maintenance and development of the value-consensus. The appropriateness of such functional theories is evident, since social organization institutionalizes the common culture; to this extent, a structural-functional model can approximate the interdependence of personal gratifications, shared goals, and common expectations. The principle of equilibrium in these models is an expression of justice as a kind of balance; it formulates love as participation in a common set of values and norms. The functional model puts a maximal premium on justice as an allocation of gratifications on the basis of disciplined contributions to the societal enterprise; it translates the value-consenus to a system of sanctions and then builds the pattern of motives and rewards.

The problem of this model for ethical evaluation, especially when it is carried beyond the level of social organization to political analysis, is that it states the problem of unification of the society on too low a level, trusting the process to overcome the alienations and estrangements which make every embodiment of a common culture an embodiment of inequalities; in this sense, functional models overestimate the justice of social institutions. The givenness of social identity in the value-consensus leads the functionalist to pass over the domination, discrimination, and exploitation which hamper the just distribution of common goods and values; the functional model has no real alternative to the status quo. In this sense, both behaviorists and functionalists underplay human freedom; they gloss over the struggle for power and the incompatibility of values of society. In essence, they distrust reason in society and overestimate the objectivity of their models. The focus of both of these models on systematic interdependence leads them to *assume the existence of the balance* which their abstract models presuppose. The fact that social process does at times approximate such balance is some warrant for the utility of these models—*provided that they are used with reservation on the scope of their applicability*. The fact that fundamental conflicts of interest and value occur in society leads the ethicist to evaluate these models in relation to problems of justice and the hope for human community. Since the functionalists gloss over conflicts of interest, we would anticipate that their major difficulties would arise in extending their analyses to the political level.

Political organization mobilizes the interests and vitalities of the society in an order by which the balance of conflicting interests can be maintained and more general interests realized. In terms of Chart 6, this is the dynamic level of power and equal freedom; so far as it is organized, political structure includes the lower levels; it preserves and develops the rights to participation in common values; it sustains claims to equal access and reciprocity in sharing the conditions of existence. The political organization balances freedom as interest; in the democratic tradition, it preserves freedom as consent in decisions which affect one's interests. There are, of course, various traditions within which organizations of power have occurred; but in the democratic tradition of the West, the principle of equal freedom has become crucial to the political process.

The voluntaristic model is most appropriate to deal with interest and power; it is essentially a political model of social process. The voluntarist takes account of the incompatibility of interests and values in society; he recognizes the inequality of access to various opportunities and the tendency of every group and structure to dominate and exploit; he understands the inequalities implicit in every value-consensus; he knows that a value-consensus can legitimize exclusion and discrimination. Hence, the voluntaristic model is appropriate for the understanding of social identity as a struggle for justice; in many ways, it is a useful model for ethical analysis.[16] The fault of the voluntarist, as we have seen, is that he generalizes his model to other levels of social process, either transforming the meaning of history to the struggle of exploiters and exploited or projecting on the historical stage a tragic process of domination and struggle. These deficiencies for ethical analysis are limitations rather than radical objections to the model, since any serious grappling with human history indicates the cogency of this understanding of power.

An intentional analysis on the level of everyday takes unification as harmony for an overarching principle, at least in the way that this inquiry has considered it.[17] To this extent, the other models provide limited and yet significant ways of dealing with certain aspects of the everyday world.

[16] This voluntaristic model was applied with modifications by Reinhold Niebuhr in ethics of social realism; see his *Nature and Destiny of Man* (New York: Charles Scribner's Sons, 1943), esp. Vol. 2, Ch. 9.

[17] Alfred Schutz wedded his intentional sociology to Max Weber's voluntaristic model. This was a source of fundamental ambiguity and limitation in his generalization of the intentionality of the everyday world, at least in the opinion of the present writer. Schutz's actual researches moved away from this limitation; in this sense, intentional sociology should be understood as utilizing a variety of models in a critical way and testing their adequacy in the everyday world.

We have already noted the ways in which more abstract models of the social process develop notions of harmony as balance and equilibrium. The significance of the intentional level of analysis for social ethics is that it provides a more concrete grasp of the many dimensions of social experience and sets restrictions on the imperialism of the various models. An intentional analysis will deal with freedom as power but will also consider transcendence; it will consider equal rights and equal access over the whole range of problems arising from alienation. Its principal contribution to the other models is its emphasis on man's constituting freedom as he struggles with value and meaning. This is the basic difference which sets intentional analysis off from the structural-functional models. Both approaches center, as interpreted here, in the unification of the social process; both start from the value-consensus of the common culture. However, functional analyses tend to play down human creativity and self-transcendence; they take the values of the culture as given and treat the individual units as constituted by the process. As we have seen, this is a useful perspective for certain limited purposes and underlines the pregiven character of social identity. However, the constituting power of personal freedom and the openness of horizons of meaning are too crucial to human society to be assimilated to these functionalist views. Consequently, we have found ourselves throughout this text primarily at odds with the functionalist reductions. Another way of stating this difference would be to say that the functionalist concentrates on the systematic institutionalization of common culture, while taking the values of the culture for granted; by contrast, intentional analysis accepts broad levels of typification in social organization but is concerned with variety and possibility on the personal and cultural level. The main deficiency, therefore, of the intentional analysis may often be its tendency to play down the determinism and uniformity in social identity; on the other hand, alternative models gloss over man's creativity.

## *AN ETHIC OF RESPONSIBILITY*

The perspectives on social process in Chart 6 are abstractions from social process. These perspectives have been isolated from one another in order to identify major aspects of social process. This leaves an additional task for social ethics: the unification of these perspectives. Each of the perspectives—behaviorist, functionalist, voluntarist, or intentionalist—has its own way of unifying other dimensions of social process. The behaviorist treats man's will as *product* of conditioning. The intentionalist understanding approximates the everyday world most fully; consequently, it seeks to comprehend these other dimensions rather than reduce them. Now we need to make explicit the principle of social process within which these other perspectives are united.

We have already considered this problem of unity in relation to the norms of the social world (Chart 5); we treated the norms of justice as manifestations of love in the social world; these norms, as indicated in the third column of Chart 5, disclose dimensions of love; they reflect man's struggle to overcome alienation and realize the interdependence of his being in the world. When we treat love as *the* principle in historical process, we lift up the dimensions of separation and unification; law, order, and power are viewed as dimensions which contribute to or distort the actualization of human freedom and community. Power, order, or law may function, at one time or another, as the decisive source of creativity or destruction. The historical task of social ethics is to discern the interplay of these elements and to assess the relevance of particular norms in actualizing historical possibilities. Consequently, the unification of perspectives by love offers no *a priori* solution to particular historical problems; it merely ranks the values in terms of which such decisions can be made. Ethical reflection is no substitute for historical hermeneutics in social ethics. On the other hand, historical discernment without norms is subject either to the prejudice of merely subjective interest or to taken-for-granted cultural values. We propose an ethical style which we call historical contextualism; it proceeds from the conditions and pregiven structures of an historical world and yet explores new values and possibilities amid competing and complementary interests.

The term "responsibility" fits historical contextualism, so we shall develop our discussion around this term. We are affirming that an ethic of interdependence or love is the fullest expression of an ethic of responsibility. We are also affirming that an ethic of responsibility implies an ethical style somewhat like the historical contextualism which we are developing. There are other understandings of responsibility within other ethical styles; these styles lift up other dimensions of human freedom and power, giving different meanings to the term "responsibility." In order to do justice to these styles and their use of this term, we shall first construct a typology of responsibility and then unify the perspectives under the principle of love which has guided our inquiry.

Responsibility is a concept which relates action to an agent with a causal tie, as Richard McKeon has observed, and applies a judgment of value both to the action and to the agent. It is this reciprocal character of the term "responsibility" which has made it so useful and so ambiguous in ethical discussion. The term actually carries too much weight and accomplishes more than any single term can effect without introducing ambiguity. Nevertheless, it is an extremely useful term and most appropriate to the intentional understanding of ethical action, since it takes account of objective meanings and subjective response or answerability. As H. Richard Niebuhr indicated in *The Responsible Self*, the notion of man as "answerer" discloses the relational character of nature, social process, and history. Man is seen as involved in, responsive to, interpreter of, and accountable for a world.

There are two broad distinctions in our everyday use of the term "responsibility" which emphasize different aspects of the word. One distinction is that between responsibility "to" and responsibility "for." We speak of being responsible *to* some authority—a group, society, cultural value, or ultimate reality. We also speak of being responsible *for* the consequences of our actions. These are different aspects of the notion of responsibility. Another broad distinction is that between an objective and a subjective understanding of the meaning of responsibility, as when someone in a court, jury, community, or journal says, "He is responsible." The person addressed may not *feel* that he is responsible, but the court may consider him to be so (objectively). On the other hand, one may feel responsible for something or someone, and yet the community would not hold one responsible. This subjective dimension of responsibility could be called internal, and it might or might not coincide with the communal or group understanding (external) of one's responsibility. These two pairs of interpretations (accountability to, consequences for; external, internal) yield a fourfold table in which we can typologize the principal meanings of responsibility. Moreover, this fourfold table, which is presented in Chart 7, corresponds to the scientific styles which we have been discussing—behaviorist, functionalist, voluntarist, and intentionalist.

All four dimensions of responsibility in Chart 7 are aspects of a full-blown understanding of responsibility. They are stated here in the historical terms of intentionality, with the diagonal arrow indicating the way in which the pregiven order of cultural and social values forms the background for decisions oriented to the future. In this sense, the retrospective view toward this pregiven order lifts up what we have called societal identity, whereas the prospective view toward fulfillment and historical completion lifts up the societal project.

Each of the values in the different perspectives on responsibility contributes a significant element to decision-making. *The behaviorist stresses form or law,* as we have seen in Chart 6; thus, he treats "being responsible" in terms of the determinate conditions of existence in which an entity functions. The behaviorist sees responsibility, if he uses the term at all (and it really does not mean very much to him), as adjustment to conditioning in which the survival of the entity is at stake. If we interpret this dimension in the larger context of historical process, we recognize that there are conditions of embodiment and survival which impose themselves upon all entities and have to be taken into account in any historical decision. The limitation of this perspective is that it reduces man's historical action to conditioned response, thus obscuring the dimensions of power, creativity, and concern for emerging values.

*The functionalist stresses the pregiven order* of social and cultural values; in Chapter 5, we have identified this dimension with the typifications and interests which shape societal process; at least this is the direction in which functionalist thought has moved in recent decades with the appearance of structural-functional analysis. The functionalist sees the pregiven order of society as the source of whatever values and possibilities can be actualized, so that responsible action is conformity to those values. The dominant principle in this perspective is adaptation to institutionalized patterns, with corresponding internal gratifications. We have acknowledged that the pregiven typifications of the common culture (societal identity) do form an important dimension of social process and therefore of responsibility. However, the functionalist treats the given order—usually the order corresponding to the interests of his own milieu or society—as the true order and endorses conformity to the *given* rather than to the humanly most *desirable.*

*The voluntarist also stresses accountability to an authority,* but the authority is conceived in an internal sense—responsibility to one's own interests and integrity. Since the voluntarist lifts up the dynamic element of power and will, as we have seen, he stresses self-initiation in his understanding of responsibility and tends to subordinate all other values to the development of one's own power and creativity. We have already seen in Chart 5 that consent and equal freedom are essential norms of social existence, so that the stress on the will of the agent serves to counterbalance the behavioristic stress on determination by external conditioning; the functionalist emphasis on external authority is likewise counterbalanced by creativity. However, the interests of

**Chart 7** THE MEANING OF RESPONSIBILITY IN THE BEHAVIORIST, FUNCTIONALIST, VOLUNTARIST, AND INTENTIONAL PERSPECTIVES*

| | **Accountability "to" authority** | **Accountability "for" consequences** |
|---|---|---|
| (Past) | | |
| | Functionalist<br>(Order) | Behaviorist<br>(Law) |
| External | *Adaptation*<br>Responsibility as conformity to a pregiven order of cultural values | *Survival*<br>Responsibility as adjustment to conditions of existence |
| | Voluntarist<br>(Power) | Intentionalist<br>(Love) |
| Internal | *Integrity*<br>Responsibility as decision from interest and spontaneous drive | *Completion*<br>Responsibility as self-fulfillment in the context of communal fulfillment |
| | | (Future) |

* The author is indebted to Robert Terry for this schematization, presented in an unpublished paper, "Freedom, Responsibility, and Social Science," at the Divinity School, University of Chicago, 1966; the schema combines elements in Richard McKeon's discussion of responsibility (see footnotes to Chapter 8) and in Alfred Schutz's discussion in *Collected Works*, Vol. 2. The author, of course, takes responsibility for the applications made from this schema.

particular agents and groups do not in themselves guarantee the actualization of human community and common interests. Only an invisible harmony could produce unity from discrete interests. Voluntaristic theories of power need to be set in the larger context of historical concern for general as well as particular interests of the society.

*The intentionalist stresses accountability for consequences;* he considers these consequences in terms of self-fulfillment in the context of total fulfillment. Each epoch in historical development poses possibilities of more adequate human interdependence; this richer interdependence may be functional, involving further reciprocities of exchange; it may be social or political; in every case, the mutually limiting, complementary, and completing aspects of actions disclose the freeing and unifying power of love, even as their antitheses disclose man's alienation from himself and others. Love is the comprehensive category of responsibility; it includes sensitivity to conditioning needs, to pregiven cultural values, and to competing interests.

The actual decisions of a society are made from day-to-day by men, women, and children in a multiplicity of roles and situations; whether as parents, teachers, friends, officials, or professionals, men and women struggle with the possibilities in their actual situations. They shape and reshape their projects and actions in response to these possibilities. We shall look more carefully at the integration of social-scientific understanding and social-ethical reflection in these decision-making processes in the next chapter. For the moment, however, we simply recognize this concrete level of decision-making; we acknowledge that intentional analysis of responsibility as fulfillment is also an abstraction from the unity of this concrete process. In our own analysis of intentionality, concern with limiting necessities of the social situation (law as determination), participation in a pregiven institutional order (continuity of typifications), and recognition of the vitalities and interests which have to be balanced in any viable social process (power) enter into the decision-making of the responsible society. When one or another dimension is scanted or bypassed, an inadequate expression of fulfillment occurs and deeper alienations ensue. We make no claim that any particular society or set of decisions contributes inevitably to love and mutual completion. We affirm only that the unifying principle of the social world is love, that is, the independence of all beings and their relational participation in a common world. Consequently, the destructive character of evil issues from the violations of freedom *and* community; to deny the dignity of another is to posit within the public world a counterethic—a denial of one's own humanity and consequently of all humanity. This is not simply a matter of law, given cultural values, or particular interests, though it is all these things; it is a matter of man's essential being. This fundamental principle of love accounts for the lure to community and the pain of broken community in man's experience; it also accounts for man's insatiable thirst for freedom.

Historical contextualism considers the fitness of any set of conditions, any organization of values, and any set of interests for the emerging needs of human community and personal freedom. In this sense, love as concern for particular being and concrete situations overcomes the generality of legalistic ethics and the partiality of an ethic of interests. Furthermore, historical contextualism appreciates the organic continuities and competing vitalities of social process; it respects both the conditioning of the past and the emergent values and possibilities of new historical situations. An *existential contextualism* could develop around a voluntarist theory, where power and the conflict of interests would shape historical decisions. A functionalist view could generate a *cultural contextualism,* in which historical decisions would be understood as adaptive or maladaptive within the pregiven social order. A behaviorist view might develop a *rationalistic contextualism,* in which the generalizability of decisions would provide a check on arbitrariness of consequences. All these elements enter into historical contextualism, but they are controlled by fitness to the claims of the historical situation and the realization of personal freedom, cultural participation, and equal access to the conditions of life. Furthermore, the principle of love as human interdependence places equal access to the conditions of life as prior to any other values in this hierarchy; if survival is contingent upon these conditions, an interdependent human community presupposes access to those conditions. Similarly, equal opportunity to participate in the common culture and society takes priority over particular interests or power; an interdependent community presupposes sharing a common world, language, values, and meanings. Similarly, particular interests are presupposed in shaping an interdependent community of common interests; we affirmed this in the notion of consent in the decisions affecting one's interests; communal completion is inadequate as a substitute for personal fulfillment, for it ceases to be interdependent completion.

Love universalizes the relatednesss of man's being as it is experienced in the "We-relation." Love in the social world expresses itself as freedom and community; we have used this principle to order the scientific perspectives on that world. We have claimed that only a comprehensive principle such as love can account for the richness and creativity which we experience in the social world; moreover, only the violation of love can account for the destructiveness which we experience in this world. The power of love and its lure to completion are the grounds for the historical contextualism which we have been developing. The violation of love in exploitation, objectification, and domination is the antithesis which subverts man's struggle for meaning and fulfillment. In lifting up the principle of love and its subversion in alienation, we could rest on the natural level and simply acknowledge the ambiguity of historical existence—faith versus absurdity. The implicit hypothesis of the present inquiry is that man's social world is more than the playing off of contrary powers in a dialectic of absurdity. Our informing perspective is that love as the power of giving, openness, and reconciliation shapes the natural, social, and cultural world toward enriched interdependence and harmony, luring man to freedom as particular being in an interdependent world.

This is the problem of religion and ethics; it is at the boundary of our introductory concerns. It extends beyond the horizon of this work toward the ultimate grounding of our experience of the social world as freedom, participation, and law. Every social and cultural tradition lives through higher-order symbolic sources which speak to these questions and illumine the claims of man's social world—his guilt, hopes, defeats, and fulfillments. The deciphering of those symbols lies outside the scope of this introductory work. For the present, our case for ordering the scientific perspectives rests upon the intentional understanding of interdependence and love. Our historical contextualism serves, therefore, to identify the relative significance of the values of survival, adaptation, and integrity; it also unifies these values in the historical lure to fulfillment and completion. Whether that lure is more than a temptation, whether the sacrifices of moral commitment are more than masochism, whether the interdependence which underlies our social world promises fulfillment and completion in mankind—these are questions of ultimate meaning which point beyond the relationship of science and ethics toward the substance of the social world itself: the religious reality of mankind.

We have already indicated the principle which we affirm and how it is grounded in experience. The task remains in subsequent inquiry to clarify its source, power, and ultimacy in the experience of the social world. On the formal level of our introductory inquiry, we have been able to handle the problems of a science and an ethic of the social world from the disclosure of the freedom and relatedness of personal being; however, this relatedness points beyond itself toward the question of ultimate meaning, even as every moral claim poses the question of its ultimate grounding. In these depths of man's struggle with faith and despair, historical contextualism opts for man's historicity and freedom, affirming the unity of his personal experience and yet recognizing the partiality and ambiguity of his versions of that comprehensive unity which lures him toward personal and historical completion.

Ordering the scientific models and perspectives is introductory to the much more difficult task of a hermeneutics of the actual struggles in the society. However, this ordering clarifies the appropriateness and limitations of scientific models in terms of a basic order of social values. Concrete analysis would, in principle, proceed from this basic structure. Beyond this formal level, one has to discern the emerging struggles for value and meaning and determine the appropriate configuration of values through which resolution may come. In relativizing the styles that now dominate the social sciences, we suggest their appropriate levels of significance and their limitations. In this sense, we deny the neutrality of the models but affirm their utility when due allowance is made in application to social policy. We have also indicated the crucial place of intentional analysis as the criterion of adequacy of scientific interpretations and as the framework for research in the ethical field. Much is now being done to explore psychological structures with this type of analysis, but too little has been done thus far in social science.[18] A major contribution of social ethics to the substantive development of social science may come in cultivating this style of scientific study; such a development would serve to balance the tendency to use social science

[18] Reference was made earlier to the interesting research of Harold Garfinkel, but the basic style is time-consuming and difficult, so that the lure of massive quantification diverts students from it.

in the objectification of man to a standardized consumer unit.

One further task remains in this formal inquiry into the perspectives of social science and social ethics on the social world. We took our point of departure in the "lived" world of everyday, but we have moved far from this base in considering various scientific models and the evaluative implications of their organization of social reality. The task remains of clarifying the ways in which social science and social ethics can and should contribute to social policy. This question is posed not so much in factual terms. Social science is, in fact, playing a considerable role in shaping social policy. The degree to which various ethical perspectives affect these policy decisions is an interesting and important field for research in social ethics. Not too much is known about this. Our question, however, is somewhat more formal and normative in character. We need to clarify how these disciplines should contribute to the clarification and development of social policy in the society. In concluding this section on "Ethics and Society," we are asking how the practical man of affairs and the informed citizen should see the significance of these disciplines for policy-making activities. We are asking, therefore, about the kinds of collaboration between social science and social ethics which would be appropriate and desirable in shaping public policy for a complex society.

# 8 *the responsible society*

The formal relations of science and ethics to policy are spelled out—including the important role that social science has played in social criticism and the points at which collaboration with social ethics could be fruitful

DURING MOST of human history, men have assumed that events were ordered by cosmological forces beyond human control. In such a cultural world, moral obligation meant conformity to a sacred tradition or obedience to natural laws. The thought that man might shape and reshape his world marks a change in cultural climate which has emerged gradually in the Western world. Although the idea of man the maker has deep roots in Western tradition, its prominence as a social philosophy is much more evident in recent centuries. Clearly, technological mastery has given credibility to this perspective on history. When life is brutish and short, men may dream of remaking history, but they are "sore let and hindered."

Man as maker of history is integral to the notion of a responsible society; in such a society, decisions are made with awareness of the values to be realized and in accountability for the consequences of social policy. The responsible society is the milieu of man the maker of history. The man of history and responsibility is the man who surpasses himself by taking his history upon himself and bearing its burdens.

"Responsibility" is a relatively new term in the ethical vocabulary, appearing in the nineteenth century with a somewhat ambiguous meaning.[1] The term evaluates action and attributes it to an agent; it does so in lieu of cosmic or natural structures of obligation. The historical awareness of the nineteenth century, the scientific and technological revolutions, and the collapse of metaphysical systems had undermined fixed notions of obligation. The term "responsibility" was a way of filling this gap by defining the scope of accountability and obligation in contexts of law and common culture. Responsibility was, in this sense, the ethical corollary of man as maker of history; placed in a world where he had to fashion his future, man identified himself as the one who was answerable for that future. The term was likewise the corollary of a democratic tradition in which men took responsibility for the decisions which affected their interests by participating in the making of those decisions. The idea of the responsible society seeks to articulate these dimensions of man's historical awareness and power.

Our analysis of the human sciences took history as *the* category in which man is to be understood; it also presupposed *the image of man as made by history and as maker of history*. In this perspective, social science enlarges man's social awareness; at the same time, social science may purport to remove man's responsibility by substituting its own determinations. This latter form of imperialism, however, proved self-contradictory. This imperialism in the sciences of man was traced to a misunderstanding of the difference between theoretical models and the processes of "lived" experience. Ethics is as prone to this error as the social sciences, but our inquiry has focused primarily on clarifying the nature and function of the sciences of man. We have thus attempted throughout to sustain the sciences of man

[1] See Richard McKeon, "The Development and Significance of the Concept of Responsibility," *Révue Internationale de Philosophie*, Vol. XI, No. 39, 1957, pp. 3–32. The term "responsible society" became a central theme of World Council of Churches discussions on social order at the Amsterdam Assembly. We pick up that theme here, although it has not been significantly developed in World Council studies.

in their fundamental achievements and to clarify the points at which they have exceeded their own limits. The inquiry has been, therefore, an attempt to explicate the integrity of man as maker of history while giving due recognition to the sense in which he is a product of history. Insofar as history produces man, a science of man is possible; to the extent that man makes history, human science is a broader aspect of man's freedom to surpass his history.

The social sciences celebrated the collapse of traditional cosmologies, but they could not tolerate the historical ambiguity which this collapse brought in its wake; they hastened to replace that metaphysical structure with their positivistic dogmas.[2] The responsible society is neither cosmological in its ordering nor antimetaphysical in its orientation. Man is lured constantly beyond the versions of justice, order, and harmony which he has achieved; he presses constantly toward more ultimate and inclusive horizons of meaning; in coming to terms with his future and the problem of fulfillment or defeat, he wrestles with ultimacy from first to last, and the more so as he becomes immersed in his historicity.[3] This historical sense prevents him, however, from asserting dogmas as science or entertaining absolutes

[2] This problem has been touched upon in Chapter 1.

[3] This is a specification of the meaning of the responsible society which reflects the author's interpretation; a radical existentialism breaks the continuities of history which we recognize; the idealistic tradition achieves continuity in atemporal ideas, as in Ernst Troeltsch's struggle with this problem of history. Existentialists like Jean-Paul Sartre and Maurice Merleau-Ponty seem to have supplemented their break with ultimates by a commitment to quasi-Marxist solutions. We take each of these solutions, including the Marxist dream, to represent a metaphysical quest for the "sense" of the process which gives meaning to particular events and points to an ultimate resolution. Hence, the notion of man as maker of history is not an identification with the sophistic tradition; man is understood here as *essentially religious* and the *public realm* of societal action as embodiment of the quest for ultimate meaning. The secular periods of history—and they are recurrent, as in epochs of the Old Testament—are not beyond religion but struggle with the forms in which the substance of faith has been expressed and shared. Hence, the public realm, or what we rephrase in ethical terms as the "responsible society," is the locus of embodiments of ultimate meaning and the sphere of expression for ultimate concerns. In our era, it can be anticipated that the theological task will work from ethics and history, but it cannot be avoided.

of other varieties. In this sense, the responsibile society is the open society; it lives in accountability to the past, and yet it reshapes the future in the light of its vision of man's social and cultural possibilities.

This analysis relativized scientific determinism by interpreting the sciences of man as reflections on "lived" experience. In a similar way, ethics was set in a historical context as discerning the emerging "sense of history," in John Wild's phrase.[4] The recognition of man's being as *situated* in a historical milieu may lead to skepticism, but it has not been taken in this sense here. This is the relativism of any historical perspective on universal structures. This historical sense imposes limits on the adequacy of scientific and ethical structures; man's immersion in history means that he seeks clarity and simplicity while living with ambiguities. A science or ethic which transgresses that ambiguity ceases to clarify "lived" experience and substitutes its own creation for man's living world. The solution to historical ambiguity is risk, commitment, and answerability. This is what history is about; it is what man is about in making history. When we develop the notion of the responsible society, we are addressing ourselves to this human search for temporal integrity in which the past becomes the material for fashioning a future through human decisions. Social science and social ethics have significant contributions to make to man in his struggle with history; they are, by the same token, constantly tempted to substitute their enterprises for that history.

This inquiry has separated social science and social ethics from each other in order to clarify the distinctive contributions which their reflections contribute to the illumination of "lived" experience. The adequacy of this interpretation of a science and an ethic of the social world is testable only by the justice it has done to the actual work of these disciplines; we believe that the scope and possibilities of both

[4] We are indebted to John Wild for this view of ethics; see the discussion and footnotes of Chapter 7.

disciplines have been delineated. In addition, we sought to test our interpretation by overcoming the ideological controversy within the social sciences; this methodological approach tried to affirm the particular contributions of various perspectives. The phenomenological approach enabled us to locate the various styles, to understand the sources of their ideological points of conflict, and to appreciate their specific contributions. To this extent, the interpretation has met the test of adequacy on the ideological issue; these sciences exist, they have done sound research in limited areas, and they are compatible with one another in a larger context. The stage is now set for the construction of a substantive ethic, but this lies beyond the scope of our introductory work, since it requires an elaboration and foundation of the substance of human fulfillment.[5]

One task remains in order to complete the composition of elements for a social ethic. We need to identify the points of unification of social ethics and social science in relation to "lived" experience.[6] The nexus of these disciplines is located in the decision-making of the society. Even as they take distinctive paths in reflection on the commonsense world, they reunite in clarifying the practical activities of that world. Hence, the unity of these disciplines comes into focus within the practice of the responsible society.

## *THE NEXUS OF SOCIAL SCIENCE AND SOCIAL ETHICS*

Science and ethics intersect in the commonsense world whenever attempts are made to communicate the insights of these disciplines. In this sense, the common culture is

[5] Hendrik Kraemer, on a visit to the United States in the 1950's, pointed to the development of a social ethic as the most pressing need of the modern world; this inquiry confirms and continues that basic insight. This notion of social ethics includes a hermeneutics of the ethical situation, which is in many ways inseparable from the construction of the substantive ethic.

[6] See the final section of Chapter 7 for this discussion.

constantly bombarded by new materials and insig
typifications and evaluations are in constant change,
ever imperceptible the shifts. There are few Copern
revolutions in the common culture; changes come at t
periphery and penetrate slowly to the core. In this sense,
the typifications of everyday life are permeable structures with only relative continuity; poetry, art, humanistic disciplines, and philosophy introduce refinements and new insights within the common culture, and these in turn alter the values which undergird past typifications. The Soviet commissars are right in being uneasy about the poets; they can and do create new images and new possibilities for the culture and ultimately for the society; they are wrong only in believing that they can control this process. These humanistic disciplines cultivate freedom for the society; they introduce reflective distance. In a similar way, social science and social ethics can alter the taken-for-granted understandings of the everyday world. A technological society which esteems innovation can assimilate scientific and technical changes more readily; on the other hand, challenges to the value-consensus are assimilated slowly.[7]

Our discussion of the nexus of social science and social ethics is limited to the level of social policy. These disciplines intersect on many levels of the everyday world through popular writings and public discussion.[8] They inform the practical activities of citizens. They influence decision-makers, legislators, judges, and opinion-makers. The investigation of these practical levels of impact would be necessary

[7] This attitude toward scientific and technological change presupposes, of course, a shift in cultural values through which innovation in these aspects of culture is endorsed.

[8] The sciences of man have cultivated social criticism throughout their development but even more prominently since World War II. Chapter 2 touched upon only a few aspects of this phenomenon. This is a significant avenue to explore in understanding the importance of "scientific" credentials in order to gain a hearing for a social critique. These social scientists have been the true and false prophets of America's recent history; needless to say, they also point to the paucity of social-ethical reflection.

preting a particular social problem; for example, the of the civil-rights movement in the United States in 1950's and 1960's should include some understanding of shifting factual understanding and evaluative interpre- ation in the practical resolution of issues. Scientific and ethical reflections were evidently significant factors in the process, but their degree of significance is far from clear. We shall confine our attention to the level of social policy, although this is an abstract level, since the norms for the relationship of the disciplines should apply to any level of concreteness.

Social policy is an aspect of practice; to this extent, it generalizes society's goals and projects; it gives shape to societal values. The everyday world is a world of coping, doing, mastering, and shaping. Reflection occurs within this world as an enclave of theory in the interest of practice. We develop limited strategies for coping with problems in everyday life, whether these are procedures for walking or more complex strategies of driving and commuting. We do not call these typifications policies, since they are seldom conscious or formalized. Social policy is more conscious and formalized; it is typification of a course of action with evaluation of procedures; it shapes our understanding and expectations; it provides the imperatives of action and the guidelines for decisions. Human projects are vaguely defined; they are empty and can be filled only in the course of action; the trip downtown is in hazy outline and takes shape in the course of execution. Many decisions about means, evaluations of alternative steps, and substituting of other means may intervene in the course of filling out a project. Policy is more precise.

Even when clearer policy is called for, we allow for ambiguity in "playing it by ear." Formal policies are needed on an organizational level to set the ground rules for lower-level decisions; such policies in turn provide clues as to the kinds of decisions which need to be referred to higher authority. On the societal level, legislatures and courts set broad lines of public policy which furnish guidelines; social process operates flexibly within such lines. Social policy usually comes to conscious formulation as difficulties are encountered in the society or significant ideals are to be implemented. Much that could be policy is simply taken for granted within the common culture as "that which is done"; on the other hand, Chicago's Burnham Plan set guidelines for urban development with a concern for participation in the lakefront. In the following discussion, we are concerned primarily with the formal development of policy; this would include policy on a practical level, such as school desegregation, or on a more formal level, *e.g.*, in urban planning.

The norms for the collaboration of social science and social ethics are implicit in their cognitive styles, since these styles define the way in which they modify everyday attitudes.[9] Each discipline can clarify the pregiven structures of the "lived" world only to the degree that its reflections take relevant aspects of that world into account. When social science abstracts from valuative aspects, its picture of the everyday world loses those dimensions of "lived" experience; hence, its contributions have to be transposed to the valuing process of everyday. We have already defined the aspects of "lived" experience which are clarified by various styles of social science and ethics; consequently, the norms for their mutually limiting and reciprocal roles are drawn from the preceding inquiry.

The normative relationship between the disciplines can be tested in contributions to social policy, because these disciplines illumine *practice* from different perspectives; they are theories of practice. Practice is the middle term which integrates their contributions. The priority of practice

[9] The cognitive style of social science is introduced in Chapter 3 and explicitly delineated in Chapter 5; the cognitive style of social ethics is outlined in Chapter 7.

in this inquiry is of a piece with the historical understanding of man and society, since the man of history is the man who is situated and engaged.[10]

Social science, according to the preceding discussion, is reflection on the regularities which are discernible in the world of doing; it is a theory of practice, so far as practice is shaped by past conditioning and typification. *Thus, social science is a theory of the conditioned character of practice.*

Social ethics is also reflection on doing, but it focuses upon the moral qualities of willing, social relationships, social structures, and cultural ideals; it is reflection on value in social process. Whatever the ultimate source of its valuative perspective, social ethics views man and society in their intentionality; it evaluates the adequacy of doing in relation to man's nature and fulfillment. *Thus, social ethics is evaluative interpretation of the intentional character of practice.* Social ethics asks about the "goodness for what and whom" in societal process.

We have already noted the evaluative aspects of scientific theories as they project the course of the social world (Chapter 7); each scientific model imposes some view of meaning on history. We acknowledged this limitation on scientific detachment, and yet we affirmed the relative objectivity of scientific inquiry. The social world is a world of meanings and values; it is a "lived" world of intentionality; hence, reflective theories of those processes imply some notion of the "goodness for what" in social process; the conditioned character of practice can be isolated only analytically from its valuing intentionality, and as scientific models project past conditioning into the future, they disclose their own understanding of *what the process means.* However, the present discussion of the intersection of science and

[10] We have noted throughout that science and ethics are reflective attempts to clarify and illuminate "lived" experience. There are, to be sure, other views of these disciplines, which we have tried to locate in relation to this interpretation. We shall attempt to identify alternative ethical perspectives in this chapter.

ethics relativizes both disciplines to social policy. The discussion in Chapter 7 relativized the scientific styles in terms of the rich dimensions of sociality; it was in this sense that scientific styles were ordered by degrees of abstraction. Social policy relativizes both science and ethics by setting them in the context of practice. Relative to historical process in the responsible society, both social science and social ethics are abstract, detached, and partial. Consequently, these final considerations bring our inquiry full circle; we are back to the concrete unity of internal and external temporal structures and to the historical integrity of past and future within a vivid present. We take our stance in "lived" experience. The insights of science and ethics are transmuted into action within the give-and-take of everyday life; in that context, their contributions to the responsible society become manifest. We confine the discussion to the policy level, however, for the sake of simplicity and economy of space; we presuppose only a continuity between more concrete processes of decision-making and more formalized policy-making.

Three points in the intersection of these disciplines are taken up in this discussion. In terms of social policy, these are crucial points of limitation and completion between the disciplines; moreover, they furnish guidelines for collaborative research. The formulation of these points of intersection is set within the context of a society's struggle for temporal integrity, relating its past and future to the decisions of its present situation. In addition, the ethical dimension of temporal integrity is lifted up in order to identify the nexus of science and ethics. The focuses of intersection are (1) societal identity, (2) cultural integrity, and (3) historical fulfillment. Social science and social ethics make contributions to the responsible society at each of these focuses of temporal integrity. Although the specific content to be clarified in social policy varies in different societies and from epoch to epoch in each society, the formal problems of temporal integrity persist; consequently, this formal discussion should furnish guidelines over a broad range of problems.[11]

## SOCIETAL IDENTITY

An essential ingredient of the responsible society is a consciousness of societal identity. We are familiar with this concept in personal development through the work of the personality sciences. A significant mark of maturity is self-awareness.[12] Such consciousness on the social level means a grasp of the forces at play in the shaping of social relationships; it includes awareness of the values and institutions which condition the decisions and activities of the everyday world. Awareness of the conditioning forces of the past, sensitivity to tradition, and understanding of the regularities which inform our day-to-day activities furnish the reflective distance which makes policy a work of freedom.

The conception of social policy as that which is shaped by human reflection presupposes social consciousness—a distance from the conditioning structures of the pregiven social world. To this extent, the conscious development of social policy presupposes a science of man's social world or its equivalent. When the past ceases to be taken for granted as a sacred past of tradition, man has gained sufficient

[11] This discussion presupposes the development of independent disciplines of social science and social ethics. Comparable functions have been exercised by elites in traditional societies, but the disciplines are usually fused with kinship and cultic roles. Hence, the exercise of these functions becomes differentiated, more formalized, and more visible in complex societies. The political, ethical, and theological critiques of the Old Testament prophets exemplify these functions in a striking way. This, however, is a general problem of comparative anthropology.

[12] At root, we take this to mean a power of self-transcending distance, which depends upon consistency in internal awareness and social responses. The most illuminating discussion of this concept is given by Erik Erikson, *Childhood and Society* (New York: W. W. Norton & Co., Inc., 1950), esp. the discussion of identity versus role-diffusion, p. 228. The stress on "career" in this understanding is taken up under the notion of human fulfillment as an aspect of temporal integrity.

distance from, and consciousness of, that past in order to make it his own and to reshape it to his needs and interests. This is essentially the work of objective reflection; it is theoretical reflection on the conditioned character of practice; we have identified this task with the human sciences. We recognize, of course, that societies have always had some measure of such reflection, but these counterparts to social science were usually ideological in character and directed to evaluative concerns of the society. The most rigorous scientific reflection on the given form of social identity involves evaluative interest, but the application of scientific method allows for much more reliability of observation and comparability of interpretation than is possible in ideological formulation.

Social consciousness is a fundamental ingredient of social responsibility because it explicates the structures of accountability which shape the expectations, sanctions, approvals, punishments, and rewards of everyday existence.[13] Our everyday world is shaped and defined by typifications of role activities and corresponding sanctions; this sedimentation of the past makes our social world predictable and manageable. Chapters 5 and 6 indicated the way in which social science deals with these problems, so that further exposition in this context is unnecessary. Social science enhances man's self-consciousness; it increases society's consciousness of the values by which it is shaped; it clarifies the institutional arrangements by which the everyday world is organized; it illumines the character of man which a particular society engenders; to this extent, it enhances the society's freedom and consciousness of its own identity. Man is ruled by his past until he makes it his own, because

[13] One aspect of responsibility is the external system of sanctions by which interests are limited and men are held accountable for their actions. Social-scientific formulations tend to reduce responsibility to external accountability. The truth in their formulation is to be found in this aspect of social experience.

he repeats that past until he has possessed it in awareness.[14] The profound contribution of therapy to personality is a recovery of the past; the significance of social consciousness in the responsible society is freedom to transcend the past. Social science contributes to the temporal integrity of society primarily by bringing to social consciousness the conditioned, pregiven identity of the society as a structured process.

Social ethics exercises a critical role in relation to the scientific illumination of societal identity. We have already explored this critical function in detail throughout this inquiry; so far as scientific interpretations of society substitute their abstract schematizations for the "lived" processes of society, they limit the scope and richness of societal identity. Moreover, these scientific models, since they are rightly committed to as much determination as they can achieve, often fantasy a degree of determination which pertains only to the puppets in their scientific models. Social ethics, as one of the disciplines of freedom within the society, has a special obligation to criticize such imperialism in the sciences of man. In its preoccupation with precision, the sciences of man readily lose sight of the importance of intentional analyses which unfold some of the richness of human meaning and valuation. From the ethical point of view, this preoccupation with precision limits the value of much scientific work. The charge that social science belabors the obvious has its foundation in this preoccupation with precision. When science loses its subject matter for the sake of an ideology of what science is about, it becomes scientism.

If social ethics has a limiting function in relation to the scientific clarification of societal identity, it is also dependent upon social science or its equivalent for its evaluative interpretation of the state of the society. The identity of the society is more than a mere given for the responsible society; it is also that social world which men have created and for

[14] The completely traditional society (as an ideal type) would be one dominated by the sacred presence of the past.

which they are answerable.[15] Consequently, evaluative interpretation raises the identity of the society to consciousness and appraises its moral accomplishments and failures. This task of evaluative judgment presupposes societal consciousness; in this sense, a science of the social world is a precondition of an ethical appraisal of man's social enterprise. It is no accident that the prophets of the Old Testament were the social critics of their time; their awareness of Israel's calling evoked an evaluation of promises made and broken. Similarly the leading social ethicists of the past have been insightful commentators on the societal identity of their times. A more realistic and insightful appraisal of the processes of justice in the Roman world than that furnished by Augustine in *The City of God* would be hard to find. Social ethics requires knowledge of the culture, its institutionalized norms, and its actual operations; without such knowledge, ethics remains a formal discipline.

In shaping social policy, the responsible society comes to terms with its conditioned structure and with the ethical evaluation of that structure. Social policy is thus an expression of social accountability when it takes upon itself both the determinations of the past and the answerability for this past. An initial step in developing an adequate social policy is an objective appraisal of the conditioned structure of the situation.

We can illustrate the problems arising around social consciousness with the struggle in the United States over racial segregation and discrimination. The Moynihan Report on *The Negro Family* applied an extremely abstract demographic model to the data on Negro family life; it considered the data in correlation with the status of Negroes in occu-

[15] The idea of the responsible society includes a notion of answerability within history both to the past and for the future. To take on one's own history is to assume freely the consequences of past misdeeds as well as the benefits of past achievements. The story of Germany since World War II is a dramatic example of a society trying to become answerable for its past. The civil-rights movement in the United States since World War II has had a similar character in relation to slavery and Jim Crow.

pation, education, and social organization.[16] The conclusions were devastating; the Negro family had suffered radically in the course of slavery and subsequent discrimination; the status of Negroes was low on other indices. The obvious conclusion was that the target for reform must be the Negro family. Thus abstract correlations were taken to be causal relations; many problems of social change and adjustment were obscured; national policy was turned toward creating a middle-class Negro family rather than extending employment opportunity. Social-ethical critiques as well as scientific clarifications followed the publication of this report, and serious misdirection of public policy was avoided. Similar errors have been made before, but the Negro issue is so controversial that this misplaced determinism could not stand very long. However, Moynihan was not ill-intentioned in this study, and the basic concern of his inquiry was legitimate; a suitable policy for racial integration requires an appraisal of institutionalized racialism and an evaluation of the inequities of this system. Moynihan's ethical concern for adequate social policy was sound; his confidence in abstract models was excessive.

Ethical evaluation of societal identity comes into proper perspective when it is seen in relation to social policy. The answerability of contemporary society for a history of slavery and racialism comes fully to consciousness when the identity of the segregated society is disclosed. Policy-makers cannot resign in despair before this tragic past; they cannot shrug off that past as someone else's doing; the temporal integrity of a society imposes accountability of subsequent generations for the work of their ancestors; the work of policy is to redeem that past by accepting and transforming it. We cannot live from the gifts of these predecessors without bearing the burdens of their moral faults. Their faults are our own, and amends have to be made when this identity comes to consciousness. This also means acknowledging

[16] See the references to the discussion of this problem in the footnotes to Chapter 7.

those distortions which may simply have to be suffered.[17] The policy-maker threads his way between the excessive determinism to which science is prone and the overzealous judgments to which ethicists are inclined; he seeks to cope with the conditioned past and its faults in awareness of the need for new understanding and more equitable policy.

The unification of the society with its past in social consciousness depends upon rigorous objective reflection. It requires an open society and freedom of inquiry. Social science can contribute this objectivity in developing policy; consequently, social ethics is most dependent upon scientific investigation for this social consciousness. Social science has done a great deal in this field of policy. The failure of social ethics to contribute significantly to an understanding of societal identity can be attributed largely to its isolation from the human sciences.[18] The present inquiry begins a rapprochement, but much of the work in this field needs to be developed around specific problems. The emergence of the responsible society depends to a considerable extent upon the development of collaborative work between social science and social ethics so that appraisal of societal identity can be integrated with evaluative interpretations. In the development of the responsible society, this is the problem of answerability for the achievements and faults of the society's past.

## *CULTURAL INTEGRITY*

Closely related to the problem of social identity, but representing a somewhat different dimension of social unification, is the problem of moral integrity. Social consciousness may

[17] One thinks of the division of Germany after World War II. This was a consequence of the Nazi debacle. It represented a tragic consequence which may simply have to be accepted and borne.

[18] The notable exception was the work of Reinhold Niebuhr in politics, and even here it was independent political observation that marked his work. In terms of the ordering of sciences in Chapter 7, the political sphere is the most dynamic and hence the most appropriate field of social ethics for nonsystematic interpretation.

stop at the point of appraisal of actualities of the past. On the level of policy, this is the question of recovering the past in order to shape the future. However, there is an additional dimension to the moral appraisal of social identity; this is the problem of consistency between ideal and actuality, intention and fulfillment. It is the problem of cultural integrity. Social ethics limits the work of social science in recovering the identity of the society, but social science and social ethics are complementary disciplines in appraising the cultural integrity of the society.

Integrity of ideal and practice is an essential ingredient of the responsible society; it is answerability to the ideals which shape the society and obligation to embody them in practice. This is not the question of the adequacy of the ideals; it is a question of the embodiment and universality of those ideals; freedom as a cultural ideal belongs to all the participants of the society and to other nations. A peace-loving people who are guided by an ideal of negotiation and agreement can hardly wage war indiscriminately and extol the peaceful character of their internal life. The press toward universality extends beyond cultural and national boundaries. This, then, is the problem of responsibility for values shared in a common culture and expressed in the institutions of the society.

Social science and social ethics contribute in complementary ways to social policy in developing this cultural evaluation. This is essentially a social-ethical task, since it is an *evaluation* of the adequacy of a social embodiment of ideals. However, it is also an *objective* appraisal on the basis of antecedent actualizations, so there is no reason in principle why the evaluative work should be exercised by ethics rather than by social science. In fact, the overlap of these disciplines comes fully to light as they intersect around this problem in social policy. Such immanent moral reflection on the consistency of ideal and practice requires a grasp of social processes and institutions; it likewise demands a selective concern with the actualization of particular ideals.

The complementary character of these disciplines in this aspect of policy-making can be seen clearly in such works as *An American Dilemma* by Gunnar Myrdal and *The Other America* by Michael Harrington.[19] Both these works use scientific materials to test participation in shared values as an expression of ideals within the society. Myrdal's famous study looked at the Constitutional ideals of liberty and equal opportunity so far as they were extended to members of the Negro community. Hence, the scientific account of the American identity was set in relationship to selected ideals of the American ethos. The inconsistency between ideal and practice was set in relief by the intersection of scientific account and ethical concern. Michael Harrington accomplished a similar task with respect to the ideal of equal opportunity and the actualities of America's culture of poverty; the vicious circle of poverty imposed limitations on access to the opportunities which might be proffered in the society, thus defeating the moral ideal through the restrictions in the social structure.

This complementary work of science and ethics is an essential ingredient of responsibility, since it brings professed intention directly into relationship with accomplished actualities. The imperative is the rational and moral thrust to consistency, to bring social expression into line with cultural identity; however, it is an evaluative thrust to embody the good rather than the evil of the society, thus it reflects the essentially moral quality of man and society. Hence, the imperative of cultural integrity discloses the internal press of the society toward sharing of values.

Much of social policy is built upon mythology of social ideals rather than actualities of societal practice. This is particularly true in complex societies of large organizational

[19]These studies have already been noted; in addition, studies in correctional work, prejudice, housing, and other aspects of social participation carry on a constant appraisal of American ideals of freedom and equality.

structures, because the values and norms of these structures become insulated from public consciousness. For example, the arbitrary practices of the educational and welfare bureaucracies in the United States are only gradually becoming evident through the protests of community organizations in the slum areas of the cities. These bureaucracies develop administrative rulings which affect multitudes, and yet their activities are subject to no higher scrutiny. Societal ideals may be actualized and extended in some of these structures; they may likewise be radically subverted by organizations which were intended to enhance human freedom and dignity.

An immanent moral critique within a society always verges on muckraking, but it expresses the moral responsibility of the human sciences when it is exercised with objectivity and discretion. The task of social science, or the ethicist acting as social scientist in this function, is to go beyond ideology to societal self-consciousness and moral sensitivity; *the step beyond ideology to meaning* can be accomplished by bringing social actualities into juxtaposition with cultural ideals. The discussion of value-implications in Chapter 7 becomes critically important in this context, since various styles of social science have specific value-implications when they are brought into the context of the everyday world.

The immanent moral critique is a complicated process, since it brings together the theoretical grasp of the sciences, the axiological orientation of the culture to certain moral and social values, and the practical course of the everyday world in its orientation to the future. The complexity of the temporal structures involved can be systematized in the following way: a model of the society as *intending an ideal* is placed in the *past* and viewed as simultaneous with the actualization of processes in the *past* which were inconsistent with the ideal; these two retrospective views are set before the society in its practical orientation to the future as a human possibility, thus bringing the future of the society under the judgment of its own ideal; if the project is continued as a simple continuity from the past, it subverts in social organization the intention which it professes; the society comes under an immanent judgment of bad faith. The retrospective character of this judgment of consistency makes it accessible to the observational methods of the scientific discipline; it is prospective, thus moral reflection, in the sense of challenging the society with inconsistency in perpetuating into the future its past organization of the social world.

This immanent critique of society implies an ethical evaluation by social science or social ethics, since a selection from the cultural ideal and consequently a selection of materials in the constitution of the social identity are made in terms of an ethical interest or problem; to this extent, any science which engages in such a critique has taken the interests of the everyday world and social policy as its point of reference, thus taking the ethical concern as central rather than locating its center of interest in the development of the discipline. This is a justifiable task within the sciences, however, since the judgments to be made are retrospective in character on the basis of pregiven values and moral commitments.

A complex, high-technology society has greater opportunities to achieve cultural integrity because its sciences of man make appraisals of integrity more accessible to policy-makers. On the other hand, such complex societies insulate their communities, organizations, and major structures from one another to such an extent that the moral integrity of the society becomes a major problem. One of the major contributions of social ethics to the responsible society is to appraise the adequacy with which institutional practices embody societal ideals. Social scientists may well exercise their ethical responsibilities in this sphere of problems, even as social ethicists may cultivate their scientific skills for clarification of these problems. The ideal situation would be the development of centers in which scientists and ethicists could collaborate on these tasks.

### *HISTORICAL FULFILLMENT*

The prospective character of social policy calls for an evaluation of the ideals of the culture in the light of man's moral possibilities. The temporal integrity of the society involves answerability to its past, obligation to embody its ideals, and commitment to an enlarged humanity. In this third dimension of historical integrity, the ethical mode of reflection makes its essential contribution, though here again science and ethics are related, now as complementary.

The responsible society rests upon man's creative role in shaping his future and bearing the consequences for his social policies. This obligation toward the values to be actualized and accountability for the embodiment of these values place an increasing burden on policy-makers; the transition from the sacred or traditional society to historical responsibility in technological society has imposed increasing anxiety about the future. The most dramatic manifestation of such accountability, though far from the only one, is the terrifying threat of nuclear warfare with which modern man negotiates his daily measure of peace. We could say the same of his population problems and his struggle to create a habitable world within metropolises.

The development of adequate policies to deal with the future requires the clarification of emergent values and the critique of accepted ideals of the culture. The United States has witnessed a dramatic example of this revision of policies as it moved from a rural culture of individualistic enterprises to a societal state of bureaucratic organizations. The continuing appeal of rural values in political rhetoric suggests how shocking this transition has been, even though it has been accomplished over a period of almost a century. In a rapidly changing society, new values and the means for their actualization are the constant concern of the policy-makers. There are, to be sure, certain core values which persist, but they are reinterpreted in the course of such fundamental social changes. Here again, a dramatic instance has been the weakening of states' rights in the United States for the sake of more universal standards in education, employment, human rights, and social opportunities.

The peculiar task of social ethics comes to light as we consider the prospective character of social policy. We can perhaps see this even more clearly by comparing this aspect of ethical reflection with its function in social consciousness and cultural integrity. Social ethics is *empirical ethics* in the appraisal of the identity of the society; this is the truth of the empirical tradition in ethics which looked upon responsibility as a matter of accountability to the system of rewards and punishments operating in the society. The values and ideals of the common culture are embodied in the structures of accountability within the society; objective reflection on the operation of these values leads to an understanding of man as conditioned by rewards and punishments. In the field of social consciousness, as we have seen, the task of ethics is to recognize these structures of accountability without letting them obscure the constitutive role of man's struggle for meaning and value. An understanding of ethics which obscures this societal dimension is inadequate to the ethical task in the responsible society; in the ethical tradition, rationalistic ethics scants these conditioning structures of accountability.

Evaluation of cultural integrity in the society is the work of *rational ethics;* this is the truth of the rationalistic tradition in ethics. The universality of moral ideals is inherent in the strain toward consistency and noncontradiction. It is this rational strain in cultural critique which has shaped and reshaped the extension of human rights in the Western tradition. Social ethics, or social science in its ethical concern, contributes to this generalization of social ideals as it reflects on the consistency of ideal and practice in the society. Empirical ethics obscures this rational dimension of man's cultural responsibility.

However, the unity of ethics, empirical and rational, emerges in the formation of social policy as a human project; here the inherited structures of accountability (empirical) and the given ideals (rational) are unified in new historical creations which transmute both ideal and practice. This task discloses man's creative and destructive possibilities; consequently, it illumines his struggle to achieve meaning in history. This is the role of social ethics; it is ethics as evaluative hermeneutics, including but surpassing merely empirical or rational propositions. In shaping history, the policy-maker is not content with empirical appraisals of societal identity; moreover, he has to move beyond problems of cultural consistency, particularly in periods of rapid change. The policy-maker has responsibility for discerning the shape of an emerging history as a moral and human possibility. He has to engage in evaluative interpretation of the emerging sense of the historical situation. He has to grasp the judgment of history on inadequate cultural ideals. He has to assume the risk of commitment to moral possibilities which have not yet been tried in the crucible of history.

History as task and possibility becomes the unifying principle of the responsible society. In making history more human and overcoming internal conflicts of interest and value, policy-makers are lured to commitments which extend beyond any security which past or present experience can offer. This is the essence of the public realm and the responsible society: it is commitment to a horizon of meaning which unites past conditions and present needs in a policy which can enrich man's personal, social, and cultural possibilities. To be sure, much of policy in the day-to-day life of society contributes only a fragment here and a piece there to this historical enterprise. However, major decisions disclose awareness and ethical evaluation of the prospective movement of the society. In these major decisions, it is evident that the scientist can furnish much in the way of awareness and the ethicist much in the way of evaluative understanding, but the practical decision-makers of the society finally have to express their good or bad faith in the commitments and decisions which their policies express. The essential role of ethics in such policy is to evaluate existing social ideals and values in terms of man's moral possibilities. To this extent, social ethics can never be simply a selective interpretation and rationalization of the past; its essential work is to discern the emerging possibilities of a human world and a more inclusive human society. Ethics in its essential work is evaluative hermeneutics of history. This is the truth of contextualist ethics. The contextualist tends to discount man's accountability to sedimented structures of reward and punishment; he may also mistake the ideals of the common culture for his own insights; nevertheless, he affirms the risks, commitments, and creativity which mark the truly moral action.

We can illustrate this social-ethical contribution to policy by a story which is told about some clergy leaders who went to President John F. Kennedy to make a report on their concern about the nuclear bomb. They apologized at the start of the conversation by remarking that the President would not be pleased with their report, since they were opposing the use of such weapons. The President answered that he looked for this kind of moral evaluation from them; this, as he saw it, was their responsibility. This is a somewhat extreme example, but it suggests that the ethical evaluation of man's moral possibilities reaches beyond given inhumanities to human possibility; ethical discernment is religious in the profoundest meaning of religion.[20] In this sense, the

[20] We take religion as embracing man's ultimate concern for being. The ethical opens on the future as the risk of overcoming nonbeing in commitment to being, of sacrificing the world which man has for the world to which he belongs. Religion thus gives symbolic form to man's ultimate possibilities and historical limitations. Called to being, he is beset with contingency and ambiguity.

social ethicist is clearly not the policy-maker, though he has a significant task to fulfill in clarifying the implications of alternative policies. The policy-maker—in our example, the President—may have to make many practical compromises, but he needs to make these decisions with an appraisal of moral possibilities and the resources of ethical criticism.

We have already made clear in Chapter 6 that a social ethic requires foundations in an understanding of man and history which make possible some evaluative interpretation of the possibilities of a human society. We acknowledged there, and we can repeat here, the relativity of such human insight into the emerging sense of history. The established ideals of the society and the given structures of accountability are both subject to critique in the light of these emerging possibilities of history. To this extent, the ethicist and the policy-maker stand at the boundary of past and future in discerning the possibility of historical fulfillment. The responsible society comes to its fullest integrity in shaping its future, even as it struggles with its greatest dangers in this creative work. Society surpasses itself again and again in actualizing its humanity within more comprehensive orders of community; by the same token, it risks its own destruction again and again in moving beyond given obligations and structures of accountability to new values and new possibilities of community. Here again, the struggle for historical fulfillment discloses the ultimate hope and the judgment of ultimacy which make a *human* history possible.

We have played down the role of the social sciences in the prospective movement of the society, but scientific understanding plays a significant role in this anticipation of the future. The notion of an ethic of consequences rests upon the possibility that man can grasp empirically the effects of various policies and thus appraise alternative courses of action. This is the application of means-end analysis to the field of ethics. The relative truth in this understanding of ethics derives from the predictability of many aspects of social process. The conditioned regularities in the society are such that courses of action can be anticipated on the level of policy, even though anticipation is only within predetermined conditions. The notion of a responsible society does not depend upon an ethic of consequences; it merely affirms that man assumes the burden of shaping his own history and becomes accountable for the effects of his decisions. However, social science can make an increasing contribution to this prospective work of social policy by projecting conditions from antecedent states of the society as they will appear in the future *without* societal interventions.

Social ethics completes the work of social science in policy by its interpretation of human possibilities in the historical situation; to this extent, social ethics reaches beyond the given society to that society which man is called to fashion. This is the most precarious work of social ethics and involves the constant risk of serious distortion. Social ethics limits social science in the field of social consciousness and complements social science in the appraisal of cultural integrity. Social ethics also completes social science by moving beyond the scientific projection of the future as an extension of the past; ethics points to man's obligation to surpass the given in his quest for fulfillment. At this point, however, the roles of science and ethics are reversed; social science limits social ethics in this aspect of social policy by clarifying the persistent conditions which limit alternative courses of action in the society. Social ethics becomes utopian without this limiting awareness of the sedimentation of values and typical courses of action on the deeper levels of social process. Hence, we see the reciprocity of these disciplines in clarifying the moral possibilities of the responsible society even at the boundary of past and future where man makes his future.

### *THE FUTURE OF THE DISCIPLINES*

Our analysis of the mutual limitation and complementarity of social science and social ethics has indicated broad guidelines for the autonomy and collaboration of these disciplines. It has been a fundamental thesis of this inquiry that the social sciences have increasingly lost touch with the concrete processes of the society and man's history-making through their preoccupation with abstract models. For this reason, we have urged the need for a critique of the social sciences by their partner in the theory of social practice, the discipline of social ethics. A corollary hypothesis of the inquiry has been the claim that social ethics can develop as a significant factor in the shaping of social policy only if it comes to terms with the work of social science and collaborates in the scientific enterprise. As we have considered the points of intersection of these disciplines in social policy, and especially their contributions to social awareness, cultural integrity, and historical fulfillment, the interrelation of the disciplines and their mutual limitations have become more and more evident. Each discipline is impoverished by insulation from the inquiries and findings of the other. In a complex and rapidly changing society, this impoverishment also means significant losses to the field of public policy.

Our understanding of the significance of these disciplines has been markedly advanced by considering them in relation to the concrete processes of the everyday world. Correspondingly, our grasp of their relationships has been strengthened by seeing their contribution to various aspects of social policy. To a large extent, these disciplines emerge in self-conscious form as man becomes more aware of his history-making power and responsibility. They are, to this extent, increasingly important disciplines in the responsible society. The implications are that these disciplines need far more collaborative work than has thus far characterized their development.

We can anticipate that three new expressions of reflection on practice would emerge from such collaboration. The social ethicists would assume much more responsibility for scientific observation and inquiry; their style should include an intentional social science; such inquiry could be exercised through evaluative participation in major structures of the society. In a complex society of large organizations, the educational, welfare, political, industrial, and other structures need internal appraisal and evaluation; such evaluative ethics presupposes a familiarity with these structures which is not even possible for those who exercise considerable responsibility within them. In its collaborative work with the sciences of man, social ethics would thus become far more empirical in its work of evaluative interpretation. It would be more truly an evaluative theory of doing.

A second major shift in the development of the disciplines should come with the establishment of centers for collaborative research. The anxiety of social scientists over their scientific status and the fear of ethicists that they may be entangled in mere facts would have to be overcome before such a step could be made. However, there are signs in both disciplines of a concern about clarifying the history-making work of the society and about contributing to man's historical responsibilities. So far as this concern with the society can take priority, the rigors of scientific work can be protected and the concern for ethical evaluation can assume its proper place. The possibility for centers of collaboration would undoubtedly emerge around common concerns with social policy. According to the interpretation in this inquiry, such collaboration would be quite consistent with scientific concern for reliable observation and objectivity.

Finally, the consultative contributions of social science and social ethics to social policy need to be institutionalized more adequately. To a large extent, the social sciences are being used in social policy in a somewhat *ad hoc* way. We cited the example of the Moynihan Report, but studies of prejudice could also be adduced to confirm this. In general, planning and policy research have oscillated between the extremes of artistic, somewhat utopian work and ecological, manipulative planning. In both cases, the quality of scientific materials entering into policy-making and the degree of ethical sensitivity have been extremely limited. It is premature to talk of contributions to this policy level, however, since the collaborative research of social science and social ethics in terms of policy is the prior step in this development. Nevertheless, the emergence of a policy-studies center in Washington, D.C., suggests that the need for such reflection and research in a complex society is already being felt. With the increasing complexity and broadening possibilities of human fulfillment and human destruction, we can anticipate that social science and social ethics will find more and more collaborative tasks and opportunities. The findings of this inquiry into these disciplines would suggest that such collaboration is an appropriate expression of their reflective contributions to the responsible society.

### *UNITY OF THE DISCIPLINES AS PRACTICE*

We have viewed societal identity, cultural integrity, and historical fulfillment as distinct and relatively independent expressions of the formation of policy in the responsible society. If we refer these modes of responsibility to Chart 7 in Chapter 7, it becomes apparent that historical fulfillment is the decisive perspective for evaluating social policy. The problem of policy is ultimately how the future is grasped and appraised. The essential meaning of responsibility is accountability for human fulfillment in the shaping of the society's future. This is the implication of the priority of the practical which has informed this whole inquiry; reflection arises in the context of man's practical concern with shaping his future and understanding the meaning of his history.

Other perspectives on responsibility in the social sciences would acknowledge the decisive significance of future consequences in formation of policy, but they account for the future in different ways.

The behaviorist or environmentalist understands the future as a product of antecedent sets of forces, so he subsumes historical fulfillment under societal identity. He understands man as a product of social conditioning, so he interprets societal responsibility as the frictionless expression of that conditioning. Since social science cannot avoid some determination of the relationship between past and future, it finds itself immersed in ethical valuations, which we subsume under the notion of historical fulfillment. The behaviorist sees historical fulfillment and cultural integrity as the mere extension of the logic of societal identity.

The functionalist understands historical fulfillment as the actualization of the values which are institutionalized in the social order; hence, he reduces historical fulfillment to the logic of cultural integrity. He plays down man's creativity in the development of social policy, because he views responsibility as conformity to the given order of society. However, this order is not viewed in a static way. Cultural integrity is the unfolding of the logic of values as they move toward consistent expression in the historical embodiments of cultures. This implicit notion of a strain toward consistency is thus the basic understanding of history and responsibility within functional theories. The policy-maker is responsible so far as he participates in this process of generalizing the pregiven social order: he is the expediter of the organic continuity of the social order. Hence, the best policy-maker would be the social scientist who grasps functional theory.

The voluntarist takes the shaping of history as a basic concern, but he looks to the interests of emerging elites or masses as the source of that future. The voluntarist is the realistic politician when it comes to policy: he regards the interests which can be mobilized as decisive for any policy, so he understands responsibility not as accountability to societal fulfillment but treats societal fulfillment as the consequence of the historical expression of interests of dominating groups or factions. The ethical dimension of historical fulfillment is the realization of universal aspects of human interdependence. The voluntarist understands those universal aspects as the rationalizing of the particular interests of dominant groups. When the policy-maker can generalize particular interests into a viable societal identity, he has made a responsible contribution to historical fulfillment.

Hence, each perspective deals with the future in its own way, disclosing its understanding of societal responsibility in the way it accounts for the emergence of the future. Historical contextualism takes historical fulfillment, by which it means man's creativity and accountability for enlarging human interdependence and community, as the essential meaning of responsibility. Consequently, the historical contextualist places societal responsibility properly in the hands of the policy-maker, statesman, citizen, and legislator rather than in the sphere of the scientist or ethicist. The policy-maker gains freedom through the use of science and ethics, since they give him distance and sensitivity. However, the policy-maker has to determine the fitness of one or another perspective for the circumstances in which he finds himself. He has to discern the claims and possibilities of the situation. He may sense that certain limiting structures of societal identity need to be preserved. He may believe that the issue is one of cultural integrity—of actualizing rights which are implicit in the social order. He may sense that the interests of a submerged group need to be recognized and extended. Or he may believe that new values need to be apprehended and embodied in new structures for the society. In each instance, however, he appraises the appropriate expression of responsibility according to his interpretation of the historical situation. He stands at the intersection of past and future, so he stands at the decisive point of responsibility—the place of man's creative accountability for his history.

Responsibility for historical fulfillment is the task and risk of the everyday world. The social scientist loses perspective when he believes that his retrospective reflection is a substitute for the creative decisions of the everyday world or even that it should be. The ethicist is also out of touch when he presumes to substitute his evaluative reflection for historical accountability. The policy-maker has to discern the right and the good within the limiting conditions of the possible, reshaping the pregiven order of society in the light of its hopes for human fulfillment. This is the creative burden of history to which theoretical disciplines are ancillary, even when they are reflections on social practice and morality. The policy-maker and citizen wrestle with horizons of uncertainty and hope, knowing that their decisions for and against man express the good or bad faith of the society. This is the world of practice for which our diagnostic and evaluative reflections can be means of increasing freedom and moral sensitivity. This is the world of policy and practice in which society expresses its ultimate faith and assumes its decisive responsibility. This world of practice is the historical embodiment of the unity of social science and social ethics as societal responsibility.

# selected bibliography

Berger, Bennett. Review of *The New Sociology* and *Sociology on Trial*, *The New York Times Book Review*, September 20, 1964, p. 7.

Berelson, Bernard, Paul Lazarsfeld, and William McPhee. *Voting* (Chicago: University of Chicago Press, 1954).

Bettelheim, Bruno. *The Informed Heart* (New York: The Free Press, 1960).

Black, Max (ed.). *The Social Theories of Talcott Parsons* (Englewood Cliffs, N.J.: Prentice-Hall, 1961).

Boorstin, Daniel. *The Genius of American Politics* (Chicago: University of Chicago Press, Phoenix Books, 1958).

Brown, Robert. *Explanation in Social Science* (Chicago: Aldine Publishing Company, 1963).

Buytendijk, F. J. J. *Phénoménologie de la rencontre* (Paris: Desclée de Bouwer, 1952).

Calvez, Jean-Yves. *La Pensée de Karl Marx* (Paris: Éditions du Seuil, 1950).

Comte, Auguste. *The Positive Philosophy of Auguste Comte*, 3rd ed., translated by Harriet Martineau (London: Kegan Paul, Trench, Trübner, 1893).

Dahrendorf, Ralf. *Class and Class Conflict in Industrial Society* (Stanford, Calif.: Stanford University Press, 1959).

Duncan, Otis Dudley, and Leo F. Schnore. "Cultural, Behavioral and Ecological Perspectives in the Study of Social Organization," *The American Journal of Sociology*, Vol. LXV, No. 2, 1959, pp. 132–146.

———. *The Negro Population in Chicago* (Chicago: University of Chicago Press, 1957).

Durkheim, Émile. *Moral Education* (New York: The Free Press, 1961).

———. *The Elementary Forms of Religious Life* (New York: The Free Press, 1947).

Duverger, Maurice. *An Introduction to the Social Sciences* (New York: F. A. Praeger, 1964).

Erikson, Erik H. *Childhood and Society* (New York: W. W. Norton, 1950).

Farber, Marvin. *The Foundation of Phenomenology* (Cambridge, Mass.: Harvard University Press, 1943).

Freud, Sigmund. *Civilization and Its Discontents* (London: Hogarth Press, 1957).

Friederich, Carl J. "Some Observations on Weber's Analysis of Bureaucracy," in R. R. Merton (ed.), *Reader in Bureaucracy* (New York: The Free Press, 1952), pp. 27–32.

Friedman, Milton. *Capitalism and Freedom* (Chicago: University of Chicago Press, Phoenix Books, 1963).

Garfinkel, Harold. "Common-Sense Knowledge of Social Structures: The Documentary Method of Interpretation," in Jordan Scher (ed.), *Theories of the Mind* (New York: The Free Press, 1962), pp. 689–712.

Geertz, Clifford. "Ideology as a Cultural System," in David Apter (ed.), *Ideology in Discontent* (New York: The Free Press, 1964).

———. "The Growth of Culture and the Evolution of Mind," in Jordan Scher (ed.), *Theories of Mind* (New York: The Free Press, 1962), pp. 713–740.

Gendlin, Eugene T. "Expressive Meanings," in James M. Edie (ed.), *An Invitation to Phenomenology* (Chicago: Quadrangle Books, 1965), pp. 240–251.

Goffman, Erving. *Asylums* (Garden City, N.Y.: Anchor Books, 1961).

———. *Encounters* (Indianapolis, Ind.: Bobbs-Merrill, 1961).

Gusdorf, Georges. *Introduction aux sciences humaines* (Strasbourg, France: Publication de la Faculté, 1960).

———. *L'Expérience humaine du sacrifice.* (Paris: Presses Universitaires, 1948).

Hacker, Andrew. "Sociology and Ideology," in Max Black (ed.), *The Social Theories of Talcott Parsons* (Englewood Cliffs, N.J.: Prentice-Hall, 1961), pp. 289–310.

Hartshorne, Charles. *The Logic of Perfection* (La Salle, Ill.: The Open Court Publishing Company, 1962).

———. *Reality as a Social Process* (New York: The Free Press, 1953).

———. "Husserl and the Social Structure of Immediacy," in Marvin Farber (ed.), *Philosophical Essays in Memory of Edmund Husserl* (Cambridge, Mass.: Harvard University Press, 1948).

Haselden, Kyle. *The Racial Problem in Christian Perspective* (New York: Harper & Row, 1959).

Heid, William H. "Carl Rogers and B. F. Skinner: Ethics and Social Scientific Analysis," May, 1965 (an unpublished paper).

Hofstadter, Richard. *Social Darwinism in American Thought* (Boston: Beacon Press, 1955).

Hollingshead, August, and F. C. Redlich. *Social Class and Mental Illness* (New York: John Wiley, 1958).

Homans, George C. *The Human Group* (New York: Harcourt, Brace, 1950).

Horowitz, Louis (ed.). *The New Sociology* (Fair Lawn, N.J.: Oxford University Press, 1964).

Husserl, Edmund. *Phenomenology and the Crisis of Philosophy,* translated by Quentin Lauer (New York: Harper Torchbooks, 1965).

———. *The Phenomenology of Internal Time-Consciousness,* translated by James S. Churchill (Bloomington, Ind.: Indiana University Press, 1964).

———. *Ideas,* translated by Boyce Gibson (New York: Collier Books, 1962).

———. *Cartesian Meditations,* translated by Dorion Cairns (The Hague: Martinus Nijhoff, 1960).

Huxley, Thomas. *Evolution and Ethics and Other Essays* (New York: Appleton, 1901).

Kaufmann, Felix. *Methodology of the Social Sciences* (Fair Lawn, N.J.: Oxford University Press, 1944).

Konvitz, Milton, and Gail Kennedy (eds.). *The American Pragmatists* (New York: Meridian Books, 1960).

Langer, Susanne. *Philosophy in a New Key* (New York: Mentor Books, 1948).

Lauer, Quentin. "Introduction to Edmund Husserl," in *Phenomenology and the Crisis of Philosophy* (New York: Harper Torchbooks, 1965).

Lévy-Bruhl, Lucien. "Comte et Mill," *Révue Philosophique de la France et L'Étranger*, Vol. XLVI, 1898, pp. 627–644.

Lindzey, Gardner (ed.). *Handbook of Social Psychology* (Reading, Mass.: Addison-Wesley Publishing Company, 1954), Vol. 1.

Martindale, Don (ed.). *Functionalism in the Social Sciences,* Monograph No. 5 (Philadelphia: American Academy of Political and Social Science, 1965).

———. *The Nature and Types of Sociological Theory* (Boston: Houghton Mifflin, 1960).

Mauss, Marcel. *The Gift,* translated by Ian Cunnison (New York: The Free Press, 1954).

May, Rollo, Ernest Angel, and Henri F. Ellenberger (eds.). *Existence* (New York: Basic Books, 1958).

McKeon, Richard. "The Development and Significance of the Concept of Responsibility," *Révue Internationale de Philosophie,* Tome XI, No. 39, 1957, pp. 3–32.
———. *Freedom and History* (New York: Noonday Press, 1952).
Mead, George Herbert. *The Philosophy of the Act* (Chicago: University of Chicago Press, 1938).
Mehl, Roger. *La Rencontre d'autrui* (Neuchâtel: Delachaux et Niestlé, 1955).
Merleau-Ponty, Maurice. *The Primacy of Perception and Other Essays,* edited by James Edie (Evanston, Ill.: Northwestern University Press, 1964).
———. *The Structure of Behavior,* translated by Alden Fisher (Boston: Beacon Press, 1963).
Mill, J. S. *Auguste Comte and Positivism* (London: Trubair, 1866).
Mills, C. Wright. *The Sociological Imagination* (Fair Lawn, N.J.: Oxford University Press, 1959).
———. *The Power Elite* (Fair Lawn, N.J.: Oxford University Press, 1956).
Moynihan, Daniel. *The Negro Family* (Washington, D.C.: U.S. Dept. of Labor, Office of Policy Planning and Research, 1965).
Nabert, Jean. *Éléments pour une éthique* (Paris: Aubier, 1962).
Nagel, Ernest. *The Structure of Science* (New York: Harcourt, Brace, 1961).
Natanson, Maurice. *The Social Dynamics of George Herbert Mead* (Washington, D.C.: Public Affairs Press, 1956).
Niebuhr, H. R. *Radical Monotheism and Western Culture* (New York: Harper & Row, 1960).
———. *The Kingdom of God in America* (New York: Harper Torchbooks, 1959).
Niebuhr, Reinhold. *The Nature and Destiny of Man* (New York: Charles Scribner's Sons, 1943).
Parsons, Talcott. "Christianity and Modern Industrial Society," in Louis Schneider (ed.), *Religion, Culture and Society* (New York: John Wiley, 1964), pp. 273–298.
———. "Evolutionary Universals in Society," *American Sociological Review,* Vol. XXIX, No. 3, June, 1964, pp. 329–357.
———. *Structure and Process in Modern Societies* (New York: The Free Press, 1960).
———. *The Social System* (New York: The Free Press, 1951).
———. *The Structure of Social Action* (New York: The Free Press, 1949).

———, E. A. Shils, K. D. Naegele, and J. R. Pitts (eds.), *Theories of Society*, 2 vols. (New York: The Free Press, 1961).

——— and R. F. Bales. *Family, Socialization and Interaction Process* (New York: The Free Press, 1955).

———, R. F. Bales, and E. A. Shils. *Working Papers in the Theory of Action* (New York: The Free Press, 1953).

——— and E. A. Shils (eds.). *Toward a General Theory of Action* (Cambridge, Mass.: Harvard University Press, 1951).

Payton, Benjamin F. "New Trends in Civil Rights," *Christianity and Crisis*, December 13, 1965.

Peirce, C. S. *The Pragmatic Philosophy of C. S. Peirce*, edited by Manley Thompson (Chicago: University of Chicago Press, Phoenix Books, 1963).

Pfuetze, Paul E. *The Social Self* (New York: Bookman Associates, 1954).

Polanyi, Karl. *The Great Transformation* (Boston: Beacon Press, 1957).

Ricoeur, Paul. *Philosophie de la volonté* (Paris: Aubier, 1949).

Rossi, Peter. *Why Families Move* (New York: The Free Press, 1955).

Scheler, Max. *The Nature of Sympathy* (New Haven, Conn.: Yale University Press, 1954).

Schroeder, Widick. "Talcott Parsons' Ordering of the Sciences: A Résumé and Critique," *Journal for the Scientific Study of Religion*, Vol. IV, No. 2, Spring, 1965, pp. 162–174.

Schutz, Alfred. *Collected Papers*, 2 vols., edited by Arvid Brodersen (The Hague: Martinus Nijhoff, 1962).

———. *Der sinnhafte Aufbau der sozialen Welt*, 2nd ed. (Vienna: Springer-Verlag OHG, 1960).

Shibutani, Tamotsu. *Society and Personality* (Englewood Cliffs, N.J.: Prentice-Hall, 1961).

Shils, Edward. "The Calling of Sociology," in Talcott Parsons, E. A. Shils, K. D. Naegele, and J. R. Pitts (eds.), *Theories of Society* (New York: The Free Press, 1961), Vol. 2, pp. 1405–1450.

Smelser, Neil J. *Theory of Collective Behavior* (New York: The Free Press, 1963).

Spencer, Herbert. *The Data of Ethics* (London: Williams & Norgate, 1907).

Spiegelberg, Herbert. *The Phenomenological Movement*, 2 vols. (The Hague: Martinus Nijhoff, 1960).

Stein, Maurice. *Eclipse of Community* (Princeton, N.J.: Princeton University Press, 1960).

Stein, Maurice, and Arthur Vidick (eds.). *Sociology on Trial* (Englewood Cliffs, N. J.: Prentice-Hall, 1963).

Strauss, Anselm L. *Mirrors and Masks* (New York: The Free Press, 1959).

——— (ed.). *The Social Psychology of George Herbert Mead* (Chicago: University of Chicago Press, Phoenix Books, 1956).

Sullivan, Harry Stack. *The Interpersonal Theory of Psychiatry* (New York: W. W. Norton, 1953).

Sumner, William Graham. "Sociology," in *Selected Essays of William Graham Sumner: Social Darwinism* (Englewood Cliffs, N.J.: Prentice-Hall, 1963), pp. 9–29.

———. *Folkways* (New York: Dover Publications, 1959).

Taylor, Overton H. *A History of Economic Thought* (New York: McGraw-Hill, 1960).

Terry, Robert. "Freedom, Responsibility and Social Science," Divinity School, University of Chicago, 1966 (an unpublished paper).

Tillich, Paul. *Systematic Theology* (Chicago: University of Chicago Press, 1951), Vol. 1.

Voegelin, Eric. *The New Science of Politics* (Chicago: University of Chicago Press, 1952).

Volkart, E. H. (ed.). *Social Behavior and Personality* (New York: Social Science Research Council, 1951).

Wann, T. W. (ed.). *Behaviorism and Phenomenology: Contrasting Bases for Modern Psychology* (Chicago: University of Chicago Press, 1964).

Weber, Max. *The Methodology of the Social Sciences* (New York: The Free Press, 1949).

———. *From Max Weber's Essays in Sociology*, edited by Hans Gerth and C. W. Mills (Fair Lawn, N.J.: Oxford University Press, 1946).

White, Robert W. "Competence and the Psychosexual Stages of Development," in M. R. Jones (ed.), *Nebraska Symposium on Motivation, 1960* (Lincoln, Neb.: University of Nebraska Press, 1961).

White, Winston. *Beyond Conformity* (New York: The Free Press, 1961).

Wild, John. "Authentic Existence: A New Approach to 'Value Theory,'" in James M. Edie (ed.), *An Invitation to Phenomenology* (Chicago: Quadrangle Books, 1965).

———. *Existence and the World of Freedom* (Englewood Cliffs, N.J.: Prentice-Hall, 1963).

———. *The Challenge of Existentialism* (Bloomington, Ind.: Indiana University Press, 1959).

Williams, Robin M., Jr. "The Sociological Theory of Talcott Parsons," in Max Black (ed.), *The Social Theories of Talcott Parsons* (Englewood Cliffs, N.J.: Prentice-Hall, 1961), pp. 11–21.

Winter, Gibson. "Society and Morality in the French Tradition," *Review of Religious Research*, Vol. I, No. 5, 1963.

Woodham-Smith, Cecil B. *The Great Hunger: Ireland 1845–1849* (New York: Harper & Row, 1963).

Zaner, Richard. *The Problem of Embodiment* (The Hague: Martinus Nijhoff, 1964).

# *index*